Becoming Educated

AC / SS
Adolescent Cultures, School & Society

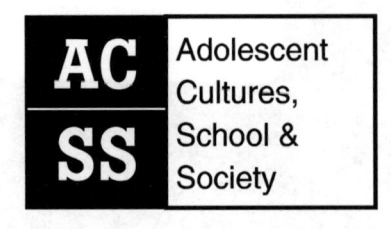

Joseph L. DeVitis & Linda Irwin-DeVitis
GENERAL EDITORS

Vol. 67

The Adolescent Cultures, School & Society series
is part of the Peter Lang Education list.
Every volume is peer reviewed and meets
the highest quality standards for content and production.

PETER LANG
New York • Washington, D.C./Baltimore • Bern
Frankfurt • Berlin • Brussels • Vienna • Oxford

John Smyth and Peter McInerney

Becoming Educated

Young People's Narratives of Disadvantage, Class, Place and Identity

PETER LANG
New York • Washington, D.C./Baltimore • Bern
Frankfurt • Berlin • Brussels • Vienna • Oxford

Library of Congress Cataloging-in-Publication Data
Smyth, John.
Becoming educated: young people's narratives of
disadvantage, class, place, and identity / John Smyth, Peter McInerney.
pages cm. — (Adolescent cultures, school and society; vol. 67)
Includes bibliographical references and index.
1. Educational sociology—Australia.
2. Children with social disabilities—Education—Australia.
3. Social classes—Australia. I. McInerney, Peter. II. Title.
LC191.8.A8S55   306.430994—dc23   2013046519
ISBN 978-1-4331-2212-5 (hardcover)
ISBN 978-1-4331-2211-8 (paperback)
ISBN 978-1-4539-1262-1 (e-book)
ISSN 1091-1464

Bibliographic information published by **Die Deutsche Nationalbibliothek**.
Die Deutsche Nationalbibliothek lists this publication in the "Deutsche
Nationalbibliografie"; detailed bibliographic data is available
on the Internet at http://dnb.d-nb.de/.

The paper in this book meets the guidelines for permanence and durability
of the Committee on Production Guidelines for Book Longevity
of the Council of Library Resources.

© 2014 Peter Lang Publishing, Inc., New York
29 Broadway, 18th floor, New York, NY 10006
www.peterlang.com

All rights reserved.
Reprint or reproduction, even partially, in all forms such as microfilm,
xerography, microfiche, microcard, and offset strictly prohibited.

Printed in the United States of America

Table of Contents

Acknowledgments ix

1. *Setting the stage: exposing the 'grand erasure'* 1
   Becoming infected! 4
   Becoming educated as a construction 7
   Schooling as a cultural production...but of a particular kind! 8
   Developing a 'critical constellation' for the rest of the book 9

2. *Going about our research craft: critical researchers as political authors* 13
   Introduction 13
   Putting the critical back into educational research 15
   Theorizing our research: an evolving criticality 17
   'My place, my school, my world': context matters 20
       The political landscape 21
       The spatial landscape: place(s) young people call home 23
       The educational landscape and profiles of participating schools 25
   An extended case study: space, place and identity 27
       Research design 28
       Research methods 29
       Ethnographic interviews 29
   Critical ethnographic narratives: representational challenges 30
   'It's definitely easier on your nerves going to school here' 32
   Concluding remarks 33

3. *From deficits and deficiencies to strengths and capabilities: puncturing notions of disadvantage* 35
   Introduction 35

Poverty, deprivation and exclusion: the material realities of social and educational disadvantage   37
Deficits, deficiencies and differences: what lies behind the label 'disadvantage'?   41
    Theorizing social reproduction and educational disadvantage   42
    Poverty, disadvantage and education policy in Australia   44
    Schools and the perpetuation of educational disadvantage   48
Becoming educated: young peoples' narratives of disadvantage, opportunities and constraints   50
Concluding comments   61

4. Bringing class out of the closet   63
Introduction   63
Why class is important in 'becoming educated'   65
Stepping up to the 'injuries of class'   70
The making over of a 'residualized' school   73
What is a westie?   79

5. Celebrating space, place and neighborhoods   81
Introduction   81
Contesting the deficit discourse   81
Speaking back to pathological views   85
Bringing young people into the conversation   89
From despair to hope   99
Concluding comments   102

6. Identity and capacity to aspire   105
Introduction and positioning   105
'Poverty of aspiration' or 'poverty of opportunity'?   107
Negotiating a learning identity in hard times   110
'Young people as the new public intellectuals'   113
Aspirations and learning identity for 'ordinary kids'   115
    (a) Access to 'opportunity resources' and local immediacy   118
    (b) Possessing and using navigational maps   119
    (c) Opportunities to 'practice navigational capacity'   121
    (d) Precedent setting and capacity to aspire   123

7. Re-framing what it means to be educated   127
Why are we having 'boring, meaningless shit'?   127
Looking for the 'print of class' in the process of becoming educated   131

Confronting and puncturing the 'hands-on' myth	133
Are these really broken communities?	135
Aspirations or imagined futures: are they the same thing, and does it really matter?	137
Some last words…at least for the moment!	140
References	143
Author Index	159
Subject Index	165

Acknowledgments

If there has been a consistent theme coursing through our research over the past several decades, it would be hard to find one more important than that of listening to the voices of young people. On the topic of *Becoming Educated*, we can't think of a more deserving or appropriate group who should be acknowledged at the outset.

We, therefore, want to start our acknowledgments by thanking the courageous, thoughtful and insightful young people who so generously shared their stories, lives and hopes for the future with us. While some of these stories were often difficult for some young people to tell, they were unequivocal to a person, in wanting their stories to be heard so that other young people like them might be the beneficiaries. Any errors or omissions, are therefore, entirely ours.

This research could not have occurred without the financial generosity of the Australian Research Council (ARC) for a Discovery Grant (DP 110112619) *Young people's narrative of socio-economic disadvantage and educational opportunities in the context of place-based interventions*. We express our appreciation to the ARC for its continued trust in our research.

The Victorian Department of Education and Early Childhood Development (DEECD), as always, were most helpful in allowing us access to schools in which to speak with young people, and in this regard, we particularly want to thank the principals and staff of the schools who were involved in the research. In these busy times, it is so easy for schools to say 'no', but in this case, that was never likely to occur.

The Faculty of Education and Arts, Federation University Australia, Ballarat, continues to provide a small oasis in which this kind of research is possible, and we thank the Dean, Professor John McDonald for his powerful support behind the scenes. We express our appreciation to the Collaborative Research Network, Federation University Australia for assistance towards the publication of this book.

Chris Myers, Joe DeVitis, Linda Irwin-DeVitis, and the staff at Peter Lang Publishing continue to be the best educational publisher we have ever worked with, and we thank them for continuing to provide the space in which this kind of counter-hegemonic work can occur—notwithstanding that Chris tells us he still has to turn a buck! The best way we can pay you back Chris is by doing the best research we can.

None of the incredibly powerful portraits that constitute the heart of this book would have been possible without the truly remarkable skills of *in situ* transcription undertaken by Solveiga—a fieldwork approach to our knowledge not undertaken by anyone we can ascertain. She brought a set of understandings, a sympathy for, and a set of typographical and organizational skills that we consider unsurpassable anywhere. She also spun her magic in bringing this book together in a coherent format, with all of the referencing making sense. We regard it as a privilege to have had access to you for our research.

Finally, John wishes to thank Peter for the amazing work he has brought to a professional partnership that began in 1996, grew and developed through the supervision of his PhD by John, and that culminated in six jointly authored books and countless articles. I could not have imagined a better academic partner and collaborator! This has been without a doubt a truly remarkable partnership, and we all wish Peter well in his retirement and the other pursuits he wishes to pursue. Farewell mate, enjoy, and thanks Jan for allowing me to borrow him!

Ballarat, Australia
2 September, 2013

1. Setting the stage: exposing the 'grand erasure'[1]

Our Australian colleague sociologist Raewyn Connell (2007) has very usefully sparked off a feisty debate in her *Southern Theory: the Global Dynamics of Knowledge in Social Science*. To cut to the chase, the essence of Connell's argument is that the social sciences have become totally captured by models and forms of thinking of the 'metropole', which is to say, the 'rich countries' (predominantly located in the global north), to the detriment and exclusion of other perspectives that are located on the periphery (that is say in the global 'south' or poorer countries) and that have a much more 'indigenous' or 'local' inflection.

Connell (2007) uses the term 'southern theory' for three reasons. First, she says, 'the phrase calls attention to periphery-centre relations in the realm of knowledge' (p. viii) and the largely invisible construal of this relationship. The intent on Connell's part is not to present 'a sharply bounded category of states or societies, but to emphasize relations—authority and exclusion, hegemony, partnership, sponsorship, appropriation—between intellectuals and institutions in the metropole and those in the world periphery' (pp. viii–ix). Second, Connell (2007) is seeking to draw attention to the historical situation whereby 'the [southern] majority of the world does produce theory' (p. ix), but in a context of denial such that while 'data gathering and application happen in the colony…theorizing happens [only] in the metropole' (p. ix)—in other words, the reinforcement of yet another invisibility. Third, for Connell (2007), 'social thought happens in particular places' (p. ix), and while social theorists might like to conceive of themselves as foraying out into places that are 'at the end of the earth', indigenous peoples who inhabit these places do not see their location as in any way remote or exotic, but rather as being 'at the centre' (p. ix). It is literally the case that somebody else's distanciation is another's localization.

We want to take Connell's big sociological idea and use it to trouble the way in which educational knowledge is being constructed (indeed entrenched), for whom, and with what exclusionary effects. In particular we want to use this big idea as a way of viewing the lives and experiences of young people who are in the process of 'becoming educated' and who have become caught up in the workings of capitalism to the point of officially being relegated to and assigned the label of being 'disadvantaged'.

The metaphorical notions of northern and southern theories as expressed by Connell (2006; 2007) are a very useful a point of entry for looking at how young people are crafting educational identities for themselves, but in policy contexts that are oblivious to young people's trajectories and that are also often highly antagonistic to what young people are attempting.

To set the stage a little more, it may be helpful if we first do some rehearsing of Connell's northern and southern theory so that it becomes clearer how we want to deploy this for our current purposes. Connell (2006) claims that mainstream (orthodox 'northern') sociology is trapped within four textual moves or tropes—and we argue that these neatly parallel the way educational policy thinks and positions itself in relation to young people, especially the most marginalized:

(a) the claim of universality;
(b) reading from the center;
(c) gestures of exclusion; and
(d) grand erasure (p. 258)

To briefly address each of these.

The claim of universality is indicative of the dominance of a hegemonic 'one size fits all' homogeneous world view that would have us believe, in effect, that subalterns or subordinates, like young people, are 'all knowable in the same way and from the same point of view…[a] point of view [that] originates in the metropole [and] is not explicitly acknowledged' (p. 258). Furthermore, 'it is only from the metropole that a credible tacit claim of universality can be made' (p. 258). This is a claim that is based on an *inequitable* view of intellectual resources—there are some who have and others who do not, and the latter need to be made beholden to the former.

Reading from the center is a reinforcement of the notion that proclamations and authoritative statements are made by people in high positions to resolve what they portray as some problem or perplexity. What is not brought into question is 'whose problem', 'how it came to be', and 'who the purported answer works for'. What is clearly off the agenda here is that the people deemed to be the 'problem' might know something worthwhile.

Gestures of exclusion carries the notion of subjugation even further by denying the efficacy of interpretations other than those that constitute an endorsement of the metropole or the center. The way this works, according to Connell (2006) is:

> Theorizing addressed to problems arising in the culture of the metropole generally proceeds by quoting and debating other texts from the metropole. The theorists reading list is always an interesting document. Who is not on the reading list is as interesting as who is. (p. 260)

Put most succinctly, 'Theorists from the colonized world are very rarely cited in the metropolitan texts…' (p. 260). Giving this an educational inflection, educational policy makers only cite the works of school effectiveness scholars who claim to have recipes or quick fix solutions, and never invoke or acknowledge the more complex explanations of socially critical educational scholars, except in negative or pejorative terms.

To cap off this abbreviated summary of Connell, this *grand erasure* has to be hidden, occluded and obfuscated behind explanations and justifications so as to appear rational—like, education must be made accountable. Invoking Foucault (1977), Connell puts it that the deployment of 'punitive practices' needs to be 'reticent' in the sense that punishments are administered in ways in which the body is 'no longer touched' (p. 261)—for example, in education through the use of seemingly detached performative and accountability measures. In other words, the struggles and resistances by the subjugated need to be erased and hidden from view so that the colonization is allowed to go on 'unnoticed' (p. 261). To put this educationally, student under-performance has to be portrayed fundamentally as being due to personal inadequacies on the part of young people and the failings and poor lifestyle choices of their families, neighborhoods and communities which are in need of restoration and re-vitalization. In colonial terms, it is as if the educational lives of young people constitutes some kind of 'featureless, cleared space' (p. 262) upon which new developments have to be etched—the metaphorical equivalent of 'terra nullius' (p. 262) in which everything can legitimately be claimed in the name of imperialism. What goes unchallenged under this set of arrangements is any questioning of the dominant prevailing orthodoxy and any questioning of who has the legitimacy 'to occupy the land' (p. 262)—which is to ask the question educationally speaking, where is student voice? The salient point to come from Connell (2006) on this, lies not in any futile attempt to try and emulate 'monological' northern theory in looking for 'one truth', but rather in how to engage young people from within the reality of a 'more inclusive sociology' around their lives that comprises 'a conversation among many voices' around forms of 'indigenous knowledges' (p. 262).

It is our opening contention in this book that the prevailing 'asymmetric' and coercive view of educational knowledge formation and its various complicit educational policy ensembles warehoused from within the international predator organizations of the World Bank, the International Monetary Fund (IMF), the World Trade Organization (WTO) and the Organization for Economic Co-operation and Development (OECD) (see Smyth & Shacklock, 1998 for elaboration), remain trapped within a self-fulfilling logic of an outdated, and delusional 'time warp' (Connell, 2006, p. 257). In this book we are seeking to go considerably beyond the current seriously discredited imperialist/colonialist views in which education is still primarily conceived as a means of taming unruly young people into the service of capitalism. The reality we want to explore instead is one in which young people, to invoke Giddens (1984), are 'knowledgeable agents' (p. 26) in the active process of pursuing their own educational identity formation—something we take up in some detail in this book.

These are ideas that have a good deal of currency, as Gale (2012) put it, where there is 'little regard for what students bring to [schooling], to the learning environment and experience, and [where there is] little regard for what they are potentially able to contribute' (p. 240). The more democratic alternative is to 'structure the student learning experience in ways that open it up and make it possible for students to contribute from who they are and what they know' (Gale, 2012, p. 253) in the process of what we are calling here 'becoming educated'.

To keep the geographical spatial metaphor going a little longer, we want to engage in what Kirk (2007) calls some 'northern exposure'—although we intend deploying that term in a somewhat different sense to Kirk, who uses it to refer to the de-industrialization and 'wholesale erosion' (p. 2) of large swathes of what was formerly the industrial base of northern Britain. For us, the 'northern exposure' is a useful heuristic with which to begin to unmask what Connell refers to as the privileged theory that underpins current sociological, and we would argue, educational theory that is being warehoused in the privileged northern social and economic agencies and institutions.

Becoming infected!

Sahlberg (2011) in analyzing the very different educational trajectory taken by Finland in the past several decades, has labeled the pathway taken by Anglo countries like the UK, USA, Australia, New Zealand, Canada and some Scandinavian countries as GERM—his acronym for the Global Educational Reform Movement. He argues that this 'new educational orthodoxy' has largely been promulgated and promoted 'through the strategies and interests of

Setting the stage: exposing the grand erasure

international development agencies, bilateral donors, and private consultants' (p. 99). Sahlberg's (2011) point is that the neoliberal market-driven ideas that constitute GERM are considerably out of kilter with the educational philosophies of 'high performing and equitable educational systems' like Finland, Korea and Japan (p. 98). He identifies five 'globally common features':

1. 'Standardization' (p. 100) of education in which performance outcomes are set and enforced through external testing and evaluation.
2. 'Increased focus on core subjects' (p. 100) in the curriculum such as literacy and numeracy at the expense of electives like social studies, the arts and music that have been diminished or pushed into the background.
3. 'Prescribed curriculum' (p. 101) as a means of discouraging pedagogical creativity and experimentation and instead concentrating on preparing students for tests.
4. Adoption of 'models from the corporate world' (p. 101) as the primary logic for school management in which schools are regarded as being equivalent to cost centers in the corporate world.
5. 'High stakes testing' (p. 101) that involves closely tying school performance on measured tests to rewards and punishments such as merit pay for teachers, and naming and shaming schools that under-perform.

In respect of these matters there is a good deal of rhetorical concern being expressed especially in those Anglo countries that have most enthusiastically embraced the neoliberal market-driven paradigm, about how to bridge the so-called yawning educational achievement gap. The fact that the problem is being positioned in terms of the metaphor of a derelict 'bridge' in need of propping up, is indicative of an approach that emphasises paste-ups and facelifts rather than fundamental changes or outright rejection. In other words, the countries that have been the most strident advocates of the ensemble of policies around de-regulation, privatization and markets, are the same countries that across a range of educational and other social indicators are consistently showing growing inequalities, employing a paradigm that is demonstrably unable to make any inroads into the problem. At the same time, there is a deeply entrenched unwillingness to countenance any other possibilities—to the point of an obdurate insistence on the necessity of even more of the same medicine, albeit in even larger doses, in spite of the evidence! The prevailing belief is that we only need to do some tweaking or tinkering with the current policy trajectory, and all will turn out fine in the end.

What is perplexing about this is that the muscular policy rhetoric does not square with reality. The overwhelming evidence is that countries that have bought most heavily into the neoliberal GERM are also the ones that by their own metric-driven benchmarking comparisons, are the same countries that are demonstrably underperforming educationally. To take but one example. In the recently released TIMSS (Trends in International Mathematics and Science Study) and PIRLS (Progress in International Reading Literacy Study) directed by the IEA (International Association for the Evaluation of Educational Achievement) (Thomson, et al., 2012), Australia was significantly out-performed internationally at the primary school level in reading, mathematics and science by countries like Finland, Russia, Hong Kong, Singapore and South Korea. To not put too fine a point on it, the media described it as 'Australia's disaster in education' (Topsfield, 2012, 12 December) with Australia ranking 27th out of the 45 participating counties. This occurred in a context in which Prime Minister Gillard has said:

> By 2025 Australia should be ranked as a top 5 country in the world in reading, science and mathematics—and for providing our children with a high-quality and high-equity education system. (Massola, 2012, 3 September)

As Geoff Masters, the head of the agency responsible for educational testing in Australia put it, 'Australia's performance has largely stagnated over the past 16 years' (Topsfield, 2012, 12 December). There is a serious mismatch here between the espoused policy rhetoric and a policy ensemble designed to punish and reward teachers, students and schools, and the existential reality of what is happening educationally inside young lives that deserves closer scrutiny and from a very different vantage point.

As we will explain in more detail in Chapter 2 when we discuss the nature of our research craft, whether or not young people are ultimately successful in 'becoming educated', depends on a complex amalgam of a large number of factors—some in-school, but many of them originating at some considerable distance from what transpires in schools and classrooms. In short, we want to concern ourselves with 'social context'—something that puts us at considerable variance with current policy zealots who 'place the onus of educational inequality on the choices and behaviors of individuals; parents, teachers, and even students…' (Anderson & Scott, 2012, p. 674). As Angus (1993) put it when speaking of the current policy direction:

> Family background, social class, and any notion of context, are typically regarded as 'noise'—as 'outside' background factors which must be controlled for and then stripped away…[so we] can concentrate on the important domain of school factors. (p. 341)

Becoming educated as a construction

Rather than accepting context as 'a nuisance' and as something that has to be 'controlled for' (Anderson & Scott, 2012, p. 675), cleansed or deleted, in this book we take the view that context is the very essence of what has to be unraveled and understood for meaning in what Levinson, Foley and Holland (1996) refer to in the title of their book as *The Cultural Production of the Educated Person*. To have a concern with the social context of education is, therefore, to be concerned with the purposes of schooling and the relationship between school and society, how schooling works to advantage some young people while disadvantaging others, and how matters of ethnicity, race, class and gender intersect with schooling and broad social policy (Smrekar & Bentley, 2011, p. 1).

We find the notion of 'cultural production' to be a helpful axiom with which to frame our exploration of how young people become educated. We take the concept of cultural production to mean thinking about social constructions in ways that go beyond deterministic and reproductive views. As Weis, in the foreword to Levinson et al. (1996) put it, structural analysts see the world through immutable social structures that in the past have 'focused on the ways in which schools distribute messages to students depending on social class location [but which have] ignored the fact that students do not necessarily passively absorb these messages, but, rather interact with them in highly creative ways' (p. xi).

Others, who place an emphasis exclusively on 'culture' have an equally limited view that is circumscribed by the immediacy of local issues and that can end up ignoring the fact that 'such production takes place inside sites that are already differentiated' (p. xi) in a number of ways. For Weis, the considerable merit of a cultural production approach is that it 'enables us to use the insights of structuralists as well as culturalists as we probe how it is that groups construct identities inside specified sites' (p. xi). To illustrate the point, Weis (1996) alludes to the pioneering cultural work of Willis (1977) in *Learning to Labour* which 'took seriously…[how] culture…[was] produced "on the ground", so to speak' (p. xi). The drawback of Willis' cultural study of the lives of the 'lads' who were the informants in his study, was that not sufficient attention was paid to how the 'lads' took school knowledge and used it within the culture they were producing for themselves drawing from many other aspects of their lives.

Where this places us theoretically speaking is seeing cultural production as being 'lodged in that space between structure and agency' (Weis, 1996, p. xi) in a 'dialectical interaction' (p. xi) between the two such that the 'messages [are] distributed through structure' in ways that 'are dialectically related to the production of culture' (pp. xi–xii).

It may be helpful here in setting the stage for the rest of the book, if we rehearse in a little more detail Levinson et al.'s. (1996) argument around 'the cultural production of the educated person' (p. 1). As we have already indicated so far in this opening overview, young people and schooling are solidly located within the 'space between the local and the national' (p. 1). On the one hand, they are using the venue of schooling to advance their own project of identity formation, while at the same time being swept up in the larger project of becoming educated so as to advance national economic imperatives associated with credentialism and skills formation. The way Levinson et al. (1996) put it is that school knowledge 'while offering certain freedoms and opportunities, at the same time further draw students into dominant projects of nationalism and capitalist labor formation, or bind them even more tightly to systems of class, gender, and race inequality' (p. 1). The political processes that ensue between students and the education systems within which they are embedded, mean that 'local educational practices and ideologies may be pitted against those of national priority' (p. 1)—for example, testing, standards, international league tables, measurement of educational outcomes, and credentialing that legitimates educational skills formation. The consequence, when partisan politics is injected into and 'engulf[s] the curriculum', is that students become 'the voiceless objects of educational reform…[and respond in ways considered] recalcitrant' (p. 1).

Like Levinson et al. (1996) we are deploying the concept of the '"educated person" as an analytic construct' (p. 21), but in a context in what it means to be educated is continually being 'challenged and even transformed in the practices of everyday life' (p. 21). In other words, while schools can create spaces for social relations, they can also be sites in which some young people 'may produce practices and identities *against* the schooling enterprise' (p. 21 emphases in original), as is the case when they become 'early school leavers' (see Smyth & Hattam, 2004). To put this another way, 'students bring their own "indigenous" practices and sensibilities into the school, and draw on these to contest the institution's attempt to transform them into obedient, subordinate…citizens' (p. 29). When this occurs we begin to see much more clearly 'the power which school relations have to define identity and aspiration', and 'in the students' creative action, we also see the limits to such power' (p. 28).

Schooling as a cultural production…but of a particular kind!

Mills and Gale (2010) make a point that is especially salient to the young lives we want to explore in more detail in the remainder of this book, when they say:

> At first glance, it may appear as if everyone is free to play the game of schooling on an equal footing…Everyone plays, but differential structures ensure that it is not a level playing field. (Back cover)

Setting the stage: exposing the grand erasure 9

As they go on to discuss in detail in their book, the rules are created and enforced by those in dominant or authoritative positions of power, while others are relegated to the margins 'playing the game from the back of the field'—Mills and Gale's shorthand for the 'cultural aspects of doing schooling in a disadvantaged community' (p. 1). What this means is that some groups (those in areas of high unemployment and who are forced to rely on welfare support), are severely handicapped from the start.

Every time we have in Australia, and we suspect elsewhere in other neo-liberal western countries, the outbreak of yet another set of international benchmark rankings that tell us the bleeding obvious—namely, that there is a huge and growing chasm between the educational 'haves' and 'have nots' in our respective countries—we get a lot of chest-beating about what needs to be done, that eventually dies away until the release of the next equally dismal set of data. In the ensuing clamor for school reform that invariably accompanies these unhelpful international comparisons—see for example the 'Bell Tolls for Classroom Reform' (Ferrari, 2012(a), 12 December, pp. 1 & 4), what continually gets lost in the conservative din to raise standards and punish teachers through simplistic quick fix solutions (see Ferrari, 2012(b), 12 December, pp. 1 & 4, 'Improve the Teachers, Help the Kids'), is any sense that young people themselves might have something worthwhile to say. Their voices get to be completely silenced in any of these calls for reform that impacts profoundly on their lives and futures.

This brings us to the point of entering back into conversation with the inherent sources of inequality identified by Connell (2007) around the argument as to how the monopoly of the dominant 'northern' ideological positions, operate to silence or expunge 'southern', subaltern, marginalized or indigenous voices, theories and perspectives, and the task of *Confronting Equality* (Connell, 2011). While the challenges are not inconsiderable and daunting, according to Connell (2011) we ought not to ignore the 'vigorous and exciting debate [already underway] about how to create a world...that mobilizes the social experience and intellectual resources of the South...' (p. 3). While being mindful that 'there is often an awkward gap between significant questions and the means for answering them' (p. 3), we ought not to deny either that 'the best theoretical ideas bubble up in the midst of empirical research or practical problems and start talking to the facts straight away' (p. 3).

Developing a 'critical constellation' for the rest of the book

We think that the notion of 'a constellation of orienting concepts' (Smyth & Hattam, 2004) is the most apt way of describing how we intend unbundling the process of how young people go about 'becoming educated'. In using the metaphor of a constellation we are borrowing from Walter Benjamin (Gilloch, 2002) for whom a constellation was a kind of 'mosaic' of finely crafted, carefully positioned fragments' (p. 70) that were always open to 'unexpected contingent ruptures' (Bernstein, 1992, p. 8) and undoing, and being re-worked into new and 'enduring connection[s]' (p. 70). Martin Jay (1984) nicely captured Benjamin's notion of a constellation as being a 'juxtaposed rather than an integrated cluster of changing elements that resist reduction to a common denominator, essential core, or generative first principle' (pp. 14–15).

In Chapter 2, *Going about our research craft*, we explain the rationale behind our use of the 'extended case method' and how it enabled us to map the sense in which the young informants in the study were exemplars of 'living the global' in the way they experienced their lives. We explain how notions of 'placemaking' were central to our thinking in the way young people made sense of global processes within local forms of accommodation and resistance. We also lay out in some detail the context in which the study was undertaken, the informants, the schools, localities and what claims to knowledge we felt comfortable to be able to make. As in any study that purports to be a 'critical ethnography', we remained continually prepared 'to be surprised' in our quest for 'an insistence on the significance [of the emergence of meaning] from below' (Gille, 2001, p. 321).

Chapter 3, *puncturing notions of disadvantage* starts from the position that labels like 'disadvantage' and 'poverty' conceal more than they reveal, and in this chapter we peel back the layers to show the shortcomings of omnibus categories like these. We discuss how there is a materiality about disadvantage and poverty that cannot be denied, but we go beyond the renditions portrayed in official statistics and measurements to look at what is missing. We regard these as 'constructed' categories, having limited policy utility for 'targeting' populations so labeled, but what they fail to present is the fact that people do not exist as 'disadvantaged' per se—they are made that way by the workings of capitalism.

In Chapter 4, our framing agenda is one of *Bringing class out of the closet*. From our affluent and comfortable vantage points, we have come to collectively accept and endorse the view that social mobility is largely the result of meritocratic effort, and with a few exceptions, those who fail to succeed do so because of a lack of application of individual effort or because of lifestyle choices, and this is what makes them failures in the educational marketplace. What we challenge in this chapter is the shibboleth that 'class is dead', that we are all inherently equal, and that education is a social escalator available to all. What we discuss here is the patently unequal starting points for many young people, the fact that opportunities are far from equally distributed, and that amelioratives and compensatory approaches are doomed to fail because they are in a state of denial that something is fundamentally wrong with the inequitable way western societies are structured.

Our starting point in Chapter 5, entitled *Celebrating space, place and neighborhoods*, is with the growing policy infatuation in a number of countries with area-based or place-based interventions as the way to both 'red-line' the problem areas and then target them with 'solutions' to supposedly 'fix' the problem. What we reveal in this chapter is a quite different inflection on space, place and neighborhoods, but from the vantage point of young people. We are not interested in the 'ghetto' or 'warehousing' effect of poverty and disadvantage (urban, regional and rural) in official policy approaches. Rather than pursuing an endless constellation of 'risk factors' with which to pillory and blame individuals, what we portray instead are what Nobel Prize winning economist Amartya Sen (1992) labels 'sets of resources' which young people draw upon in making educational decisions. In concert with Lupton (2010), we explore notions of space and place 'in more social, historical, relative, contingent, and dynamic ways to examine the educational experiences of disadvantaged young people' (p. 121).

In Chapter 6, which is structured around *Identity and capacity to aspire*, we tackle what is arguably the most complex contemporary issue in education—how young people shape a desire to become an 'educated person' (Levinson, et al., 1996) and how they create learning identities for themselves in difficult times. We draw on a range of sources, but our starting point is Brown's (1987) conceptualization of 'ordinary kids'—which is to say, those who come from non-affluent backgrounds and who are considered to be no different in their fundamental orientations to life and what they want from it, than their more successful and 'advantaged' peers. We invoke Appadurai's (2004) notion of 'navigational capacity' to examine how these particular young people form pathways for themselves towards their futures, often without the 'scripts' available to them in terms of family exemplars available to those who are more advantaged.

While there can never be any meaningful conclusion to a 'becoming' issue like the one we are exploring in this book, in the final seventh chapter, which we call *Re-framing what it means to be educated*, we draw together the arguments of the preceding chapters and present a careful summation of what has been gleaned from the ethnographic themes and slices in our fieldwork. We end on an optimistic note, largely informed by the courageous stories told to us by these young people, but we make it clear that we are extremely mindful of the obstacles and impediments still to be confronted.

Note

1. Connell, 2006, p. 261.

2. Going about our research craft: critical researchers as political authors

Introduction

> 'I am definitely staying here when I leave school. I am not interested in going somewhere else. It's very close to my family and everything I need is here. I think there will be employment opportunities' (Sally, year 11 student).

> 'Leaving this community isn't going to be a big issue for me. I really couldn't give a rat's arse about this place. It's not a place I'd like to raise kids or do anything here' (Brett, year 11 student).

> 'I don't like this city very much but at the moment I don't have a choice. I can't live anywhere else' (Jasmine, year 11 student).

In this chapter we discuss the theoretical foundations, methodological directions and representational features of a critical ethnographic approach to the research which underpins this study. In particular, we outline the major elements of an extended case study incorporating young peoples' narratives of disadvantage, class, place and identity in regional Australia. As illustrated above, young people's conflicting narratives of place and identity make for fascinating reading, yet all too often what they have to say about their life circumstances, experiences and aspirations is relegated to the margins of policy texts. In foregrounding their perspectives, we affirm that 'young people are experts in their own lives' (Mason & Danby, 2011, p.185) and possess unique knowledge and insights that cannot be obtained from adult informants and second-hand accounts. Mason and Danby (2011) in their appropriately titled paper 'Children as Experts in Their Own Lives' make the point that:

> [a] research agenda that recognizes children and young people as competent interpreters of their everyday worlds opens up new research spaces for understanding their constructions of their social worlds. (p. 186)

Opening up these research spaces is crucial if we are to gain 'insider perspectives' of the impact of new technologies, economic and social changes, and education policies on the lives of the most marginalized young people. Van Galen (2004) claims that working class and poor people in the United States have generally been excluded from debates about what is in their best interest when it comes to the provision of education. We believe this holds true for Australia too where deficit and risk views of low-income students, their families and communities are most prevalent. Typically, responsibility for school failure, diminished employment prospects and financial hardship experienced by young people is seen to reside in a combination of cultural, family and individual deficiencies (te Riele, 2006; Valencia, 2010). However, what we have learnt over several decades of research in schools and communities categorized as 'disadvantaged' is that some of the most compelling insights into education come from young people who have been deemed failures by schools and society.

In previous publications (Smyth, Down & McInerney, 2010; Smyth & McInerney, 2012), we described a quantum shift in thinking about young people when we conceive of them as knowledgeable and active agents capable of speaking back to institutions and authorities, rather than forcing them to remain silent witnesses to what happens in schools. We also acknowledge that the agency they possess operates within structural constraints and opportunities arising from, amongst other things, the political economy and the classed, racialized and the gendered nature of society. As critical researchers we have an obligation to faithfully represent what young participants have to say about the issues under study, but we also believe we have an ethical responsibility to take account of the wider context and the processes which shape their attitudes, beliefs and experiences. Undeniably, there are methodological and ethical tensions involved in bringing empirical research into conversation with a socially critical critique. Decisions about the selection of research sites and participants, the frames of reference of the investigation, the choice of research methods and the textual representation of participants' ideas are all inherently political. Whatever steps we take to redress these tensions we cannot escape the conclusion that we are 'political authors' (Moss, 2004, p. 365) with a point of view and not merely disinterested observers in the research process.

The chapter proceeds along the following lines. First, we make a case for inserting the critical into educational research and discuss the elements of the socially critical approach to the issues under study. Second, we lay out in some detail the context in which the study was undertaken and reveal something of the lives of our participants, the schools, and neighborhoods. Third, we explain the rationale behind our use of the 'extended case method' and how it enabled us to map how the young people in the study were exemplars of 'living the global' in the way they experienced their lives. We explain how notions of 'placemaking' were central to our thinking in the way young people made sense of global processes within local forms of accommodation and resistance. Fourth, we discuss the power of narrative research and the textual strategies used to represent young people's perspectives and ideas. Regardless of the level of methodological elegance in having undertaken a 'critical ethnography', we remained forthrightly committed, as we have said, to being prepared 'to be surprised' and 'an insistence on the significance [of the emergence of meaning] from below' (Gille, 2001, p. 321).

Putting the critical back into educational research

As critical researchers we occupy a methodological and epistemological terrain that has been caught up in the paradigm wars / dialogs of the 1980s (Denzin, 2008; Lincoln, 2010) and, more recently the resurgence of scientific-based research (SBR) sponsored and championed by the neoliberal state. According to Denzin (2008), the institutional structures supporting this return to positivist research in the USA 'converged when neo-liberalism, post-positivism, and the audit-accountability culture took aim on education and schooling' (p. 316). We can see the impact of this phenomenon in Australia where so much of the education reform agenda has been based on a narrow indicator of improving schools by raising student achievement in NAPLAN (National Assessment Program—Literacy and Numeracy) tests. In the USA in particular, we now have a gold standard of educational research with well-defined causal models based on randomized controlled experiments that allow for replication and generalization (Denzin, Lincoln & Giardina, 2006; Ceglowski, Bacigalupa & Peck, 2011). Denzin (2008) suggests the watchwords of this discourse are 'audits, efficiency, high stakes assessment, test-based accountability, SBR' (p. 316). We would add that a preoccupation with school effectiveness and 'what works' in practice now drives policy-making in this field.

This new model of positivist research, which has gained much credence in the wake of the No Child Left Behind legislation in the USA, derides critical and qualitative research methods. Kincheloe and Tobin (2009) go a step further in contending that North American's have witnessed 'a long brewing regressive rejection of progressive values and are [now] operating in the midst of a neo-conservative, militaristic, socio-political fog' (p. 514). They go on to state:

> What we often refer to as Western reason has not served us well in relation to a variety of issues including our geo-political strategies, environmental policies, economic frameworks that transform human beings from interconnected

> community members to "fiscal entities", and test-driven educational reforms that standardize pedagogy and curriculum in ways that deprofessionalize teaching and exclude diverse knowledges that might challenge the status quo. We have often argued that the epistemology that supports such a dehumanizing and oppressive form of reason is a contemporary form of positivism. (p. 514)

The arguments here run much deeper than concerns about education research but they do point to the insidious ways in which schools are caught up in the corporate world of market-driven approaches to education policy and SBR. The acronym FIDUROD has been coined by Kincheloe (2010) to denote the basic features of a contemporary positivist epistemology that shapes western knowledge. In summary, it is:

- *Formal*—produced by rigid adherence to a particular research methodology that never changes…
- *Intractable* –grounded in the assumption that the world is basically an inert, static entity.
- *Decontextualized*—constructed by researchers who have removed a phenomenon from the diverse contexts of which it is part and grant it meaning.
- *Universalistic*—what inquirers discover when strictly following the correct epistemology and the research methods it supports applies to all domains of the world and the universe.
- *Reductionist*—focusing on those factors that lend themselves most easily to measurement…
- *One Dimensional*—shaped by the belief that there is one true reality that can be discovered and completely described by following correct research methods (p. 22–23).

What counts as 'legitimate' educational research in the USA (and to an increasing extent in Australia) now rests squarely on FIDUROD principles that are largely dismissive of the role of context as an essential component in causal explanation of educational inequalities (Anderson & Scott, 2012). Gordon, Smyth and Diehl (2008) argue that the evidence-based approach, a dominant feature of the Bush administration, is fundamentally flawed: it is in fact 'a gross oversimplification and misrepresentation of educational research and authentic educational reform' (p. 1). They claim that 'reliance on randomized experimental trials about what allegedly works in education tells us nothing about how or why those treatments work' (p. 21). Moreover:

> …when we refuse to listen to or take heed of the views of insiders, practitioners and students, then what we have is a knowledge base that is little better than educational superstition. (p. 22)

As they point out 'such official zealotry and naivety based on such huge leaps of faith is truly alarming' (p. 22). In light of these developments, we believe there is an urgent need to put the critical back into education research (Apple, 2010, p. 152), to make explicit the connections between macro and micro social and economic structures, to identify and contest existing social and educational inequalities, and to advocate on behalf of the least advantaged.

We agree with Apple (2012) that 'education must be seen as a political act' (p. 152) and that:

> ...understanding education requires that we situate it in the unequal relations of power in the larger society and in the realities of dominance and subordination—and the conflicts—that are generated by these relations. (p. 152)

These issues have been largely neglected in the school reform movement. Over the years a great deal of faith has been placed in curricula, administrative and funding reforms to improve student achievement and generate educational opportunities for the most disadvantaged young people. However, as Anyon (2005) has documented in her United States studies, the systemic and deeply entrenched problems of urban schooling—and we would suggest regional and remote schooling in Australia—cannot be solved without associated reform of public policies in the realms of housing, wages, health and social welfare. As she points out, 'individual and neighborhood poverty builds walls around schools and classrooms that education policy does not penetrate or scale' (p. 70). What is required is a 'new education policy paradigm' (Anyon, 2005) that acknowledges the interconnectedness of schools and communities and the need to build a more economically equitable society as the basis for school improvement. This calls for a radical research agenda.

Theorizing our research: an evolving criticality

In aligning ourselves with a critical research tradition, we affirm the explanatory powers and emancipatory potential of research which has its roots in criticalist theories of social inquiry. Drawing on Kincheloe's (2010) notion of 'an evolving criticality' (p. viii), we acknowledge that these theories now encompass diverse schools of thought, including Marxist and neo-Marxist critiques, cultural studies, Freirean scholarship, critical race theory, postcolonialist approaches, feminist theories, and post-structuralist and postmodernist insights (Apple, 2010). In spite of differing emphases, these critical perspectives are all concerned with issues of power and oppression and all seek radical transformation of society.

It is not our intent to provide a historical overview of the development of critical social theory, however, we do want to emphasize some of its defining features. Critical theory, as it was originally conceived by the Frankfurt Institute of Social Research in the 1930s, was a supra-disciplinary project which sought to construct a systematic, comprehensive social theory with which to analyze the major social, economic and political problems of the day, most notably the Great Depression, the rise of fascism, the two world wars and the growth of capitalism (Kellner, 1989). Beyond a critique of domination and oppression, members of the Institute saw in critical theory 'a discourse of possibility' for the reconstruction of a more democratic and equitable social order (Kincheloe & McLaren, 1994, p. 139). Thus, from the outset, the Institute was engaged with the practical problems of humanity and was motivated by the possibility of social research contributing to the struggle for a more just world.

From an epistemological perspective, Horkheimer (1972) and his colleagues denounced traditional approaches for their positivist assumptions about the 'objectivity' of knowledge and the search for invariant laws to explain physical and human behavior (Morrow & Brown, 1994). Rejecting the efficacy of value-free, disinterested enquiry, critical scholars drew upon the phenomenological research traditions of anthropology, sociology and social psychology, but went beyond interpretivism to a critical examination of asymmetric power relations that distort human actions and limit the freedom of individuals and groups. In another break with tradition, critical theorists 'rejected the radical distinction between theory and practice as two separate poles of a dualism' (Leonardo, 2004, p. 11). Rather than promoting theory for its own sake they 'encouraged the production of theory as part of an overall search for transformative knowledge' (p. 11). Freire (1996) describes this integration of theory and practice as 'praxis'—reflection and action on the world in order to change it. Kincheloe and McLaren (1994) convey the political and transformative nature of critical research as follows:

> Whereas traditional researchers cling to the guard rail of neutrality, critical researchers frequently announce their partisanship in the struggle for a better world. Traditional researchers see their task as the description, interpretation or reanimation of a slice of reality whereas critical researchers often regard their work as a first step toward forms of political action that can redress the injustices found in the field site or constructed in the very act of research itself. (p. 140)

Critical theory has always had its fair share of critics. As Morrow and Brown (1994) point out, it is sometimes accused of being overly theoretical, lacking attention to empirical and historical research and to the practical strategies to achieve the kind of transformation envisaged in its social critique. We believe that this is a legitimate criticism of some educational research which seems much more intent on exposing weakness and deficiencies in schools and educational institutions rather than illuminating policies and practices that make a difference for young people (Mehan, 2008; 2012). Bringing critical theory to the ground is crucial. According to Kress (2011), one of the pressing challenges for critical researchers is to connect a grand vision of liberation, perhaps better described as 'practices of freedom' (Foucault, 1988), to the micro level of interactions in classrooms, schools and communities and the seemingly benign rituals of everyday life. Although oppression may take visible forms it can also operate as 'quiet violence' (Kress, 2011, p. 261) under the cloak of hegemonic discourses in the form of a competitive academic curriculum in schools (McGregor, 2009). What is called for is a personal, practical, critical research agenda that reveals how macro social forces play out in the daily lives of people.

Traditionally, critical theorists have located explanations for social inequalities and injustices within the political economy and the crisis of capitalism. Without dismissing the contemporary relevance of these factors, Kellner (1989) suggests that proponents need to become more attuned to the struggles and truth claims associated with the growth of 'techno-capitalism' and new social phenomena. In his view, a politicized social theory is needed to investigate 'the possibilities of fusing a class and cultural politics with the new social movements' (p. 229). Apple (2010) makes a similar point when he argues that a critical education research agenda needs to give proper consideration to Fraser's (1997) notions of redistributive and recognitive justice.

Notwithstanding these criticisms, we believe that critical theory 'retains its ability to disrupt and challenge the status quo' (Kincheloe & McLaren, 1994, p. 138) whilst offering a politics of hope and possibility for more equitable social relations. Critical theory, as Kellner (1989) points out, has a capacity to incorporate the ideas and constructs of some of the major theorists and critics of modernity in its work without abandoning the political nature of the project and its origins in theories of social and economic reproduction. In reviewing recent school ethnographies in the USA, Foley (2010) points to the creative ways in which the ideas of neo-Weberian, Marxist, feminist and critical race thinkers have been fused to 'create a new cultural production or class culture paradigm of schooling' (p. 215). In an age of global capitalism, characterized by the ascendancy of neoliberalism, the emergence of new social movements, the threat of nuclear war and ecological crises we believe that a revitalized critical theory still provides the basis for a radical critique and transformation of society.

In the context of this study, critical theory allows us to examine notions of space, place and neighborhoods and the geographical, historical and cultural factors which influence young peoples' identities and destinies. According to Wyse, Nikolajeva, Charlton, Cliff Hodges Pointon & Taylor (2012) the important links between place and identity have been somewhat neglected, especially in the field of educational research. A critical perspective encourages us to look beyond the local neighborhood, region and state for global explanations of the systemic nature of oppression, poverty, social exclusion and educational disadvantage. Critical theory provides conceptual tools with which to challenge deeply ingrained, taken-for-granted and typically deficit-ridden assumptions about young people who live and are schooled in so called 'disadvantaged' communities. It invites us to investigate the benefits and limitations of place-based interventions from the vantage point of the least advantaged and least powerful members of a community. Most importantly, research within a criticalist tradition urges us to theorize alternative futures (McCarty, 2012) and to shed the spotlight on institutional practices and policies which provide a sense of hope and direction for young people.

Having outlined the critical sociological framework of our inquiry we now turn our attention to the contextual features of research into socioeconomic disadvantage and learning opportunities in regional Australia.

'My place, my school, my world': context matters

> Adequate causal explanations in the social sciences depend on the in-depth understanding of meanings, contexts, and processes that qualitative research can provide. (Maxwell, 2012, p. 655)

Although a good deal of the school reform literature emphasizes the effectiveness characteristics of schools in shaping student attitudes and dispositions to learning, it is impossible to make sense of young people's experience of education without a knowledge of their neighborhoods, families, popular culture and economic circumstances (Pierides, 2010). One of the features of critical / qualitative research that sets it apart from experimental and statistically grounded studies is the emphasis attached to context as an integral part of the explanatory processes and not just one of the research variables for which adjustments must be made. Context matters but, as Anderson and Scott (2012) point out, narrowing the notion of context to local settings, institutions and practices without making connections between macro and micro economic, social and political structures and forces deprives researchers of alternative and more holistic explanations for social phenomena. Multi-level analyses of the relationship between structure, institutions and culture, is especially relevant today, as Anderson and Scott explain:

> Given the dramatic global shifts in the political economy from Welfare State to Neoliberal State, such an approach is crucial to understanding how the cultural

level and the constitution of subjectivities is shaped by social, economic, and political forces, as well as the ways this shaping is creatively appropriated or resisted. (p. 677)

In the following section, we elaborate on the local, regional and global context of our study with reference to:

- the political landscape and policies impacting on young people.
- the spatial landscape: the geographical, historical and socioeconomic features of the place(s) young people call home and their relationships to other places.
- the educational landscape and profiles of participating schools.

The political landscape

In October 2012 the Australian Council of Social Service (ACOSS, 2012) released a report detailing the extent of poverty in Australia. It revealed that after 20 years of economic growth—largely driven by a mining boom—more than two million Australians, including 575,000 children, live below the internationally accepted poverty line (ACOSS, 2012). Of particular relevance to this study is the finding that the proportion of residents living in poverty is highest in remote, rural and regional Australia, and young people in these locations are at greater risk of social exclusion than those in urban areas (Skattebol, Saunders, Redmond, Bedford & Cass, 2012). Children from low income, sole parent and welfare dependent families in these areas also experience a greater degree of educational disadvantage than their metropolitan counterparts (Argy, 2007; Australian Government [Gonski Report], 2011). This is reflected in lower year 12 completion rates for students in regional Australia (Foundation for Young Australians, 2010, p. 30) and significant under-representation of low socio-economic status (SES) students in higher education institutions—16% nationally, with rates as low as 8% in the Group of Eight—[the oldest and most elite] universities (Bradley, 2008, p. 52).

The political landscape in Australia has shifted markedly over the past two decades largely as a consequence of neoliberal reforms and restructuring of the economy, financial institutions and human services. Those who continue to spruik the merits of Australia as an egalitarian society do so in the face of damning statistics that reveal a growing gap between the haves and have-nots, high levels of welfare dependency in rust-belt communities, and a large proportion of unemployed and underemployed young people (Saunders, 2011). There is a geographical dimension to this picture as the economic fortunes of different regions in Australia diverge (Vinson, 2007). According to Saunders (2011):

> ...the ebb and flow of the economic forces unleashed by globalization has meant that one of the most important determinants of social disadvantage is location.... [In turn] where one lives can have a powerful impact on access to employment, on the ability of a given level of income to support a particular standard of living and on the availability of the effectiveness of services to address disadvantage. (p. 2)

Schooling is one of the most basic of these services and one of the most highly politicized. Over the past four decades a major shift has taken place in educational policy making in most OECD countries, including Australia. To a large extent, education is now regarded as a tool for economic growth and the imperative to reform education systems, schools and higher education institutions is grounded in economic rationalist thinking of neoliberal governments. Many educational institutions have embraced a culture of managerialism with an emphasis on competition, standards, best practice, measurement and accountability (Angus, 2012a). A tendency to narrow the political debate in education around utilitarian goals, rather than a commitment to social justice and the common good, has led to a major push to vocationalize and standardize the curriculum (Down, 2009). The manifest failure of neoliberal education policies to lift school retention rates, reduce educational inequality and improve employment prospects for young people in disadvantaged circumstances is particularly disturbing, but according to Argy (2007), the reasons are not hard to find:

> Governments in Australia spend less on education and active labor market programs such as training than a majority of developed OECD countries and what is spent on education flows proportionally more to the more advantaged students.

In making the case for a needs-based funding model for government and non-government schools, the Gonski Report has drawn attention to an 'unacceptable link between low levels of achievement and educational disadvantage, particularly among students from low socioeconomic and Indigenous backgrounds' (Australian Government [Gonski Report], 2011, p. xiii). There is compelling evidence that students living in remote, regional and outer-metropolitan locations are more disadvantaged than their urban counterparts, largely because of disparities in the provision of education facilities, programs and resources, including information and communication technologies (Argy, 2007). More than one quarter of the long-term unemployed in Australia are in the age group 15 to 24 years (Foundation for Young Australians, 2011, p. 11) and the proportions are appreciably higher outside metropolitan centers.

Under the pretext of skilling the workforce to make Australia more economically competitive, governments have introduced national partnership agreement policies aimed at raising the school retention and attainment levels of young people which are considered comparatively low by some international benchmarks (Department of Education, Employment and Workplace Relations, 2012). A key element in this approach is a 'learn or earn' policy which requires that young people be in full-time schooling, recognized training or full-time employment (or a mix of these) until 17 years of age (te Riele, 2011). The punitive aspects of this policy are particularly harsh. Young people under 17 years of age are ineligible for unemployment benefits, and access to Centrelink benefits is denied to those under 21 if they have not attained a year 12 certificate or equivalent qualification. Those seeking employment are also likely to suffer considerable financial hardship. According to the Australian Council of Social Services (2012), the low level of the Newstart Allowance ($492.60 per fortnight for a single person) means that many young job seekers are thrown into poverty unless they can call on family support.

In summary, the learning identities and aspirations of youth on the margins of Australian society have been adversely affected by economic and political factors that lie outside their control. This is especially true for those living in remote and regional locations where the relentless pursuit of neoliberal policies has damaged local economies and seriously undermined the safety net provision of the welfare state.

The spatial landscape: place(s) young people call home

> There is a sense that knowing one's place has a powerful sociological resonance; stories and narratives mediate the way space is apprehended and comprehended.
> (Gulson & Symes, 2007, p. 2)

How young people view their world is profoundly influenced by the geographical, historical, socioeconomic and cultural attributes of the place(s) they call home. In many respects, 'place' is a lens through which they begin to make sense of themselves and their surroundings. It is where they form relationships and social networks, develop a sense of community and learn to live (or not live) with others (McInerney, Smyth & Down, 2011). Progressive educators, such as Dewey, have long recognized the importance of place in shaping human identities—hence the value attached to developing curricula around the lives, cultures and interests of young people and their communities. However, according to Green and Letts (2007), notions of space and place are among 'the most under-examined concepts in educational theory and practice' (p. 58). Quoting from Usher (2002, p. 41) they claim that the space has traditionally been regarded as:

> neutral, fixed and immobile, unrelated to the social and without impact on the formation of subject identity and biography. (p. 58)

As we have argued previously, we need to rethink our understandings in these matters to give greater prominence to the dynamic, socially constructed and complex nature of notions of place and space. Space, as Thomson (2007) points out, is 'constituted through social relations and is also constitutive of them' (p. 112). She goes on to state:

> Spatial relations are materially embedded and enmeshed in cultural-economic-political practices...[that] are not simply local but [involve] local/global flows, trajectories and networks. (p. 112)

Gulson and Symes (2007) claim that theories of space contribute to a better understanding of 'the competing rationalities underlying educational policy change, social inequality and cultural practices' (p. 2). Space does not 'over-determine the material and social conditions of life' (Thomson, 2007, p. 113) but thinking spatiality helps us to gain a better knowledge of the geography of inequality and the opportunities for change.

Lupton (2003) has contributed to spatial theory in her analysis of neighborhood effects and urban renewal initiatives in the United Kingdom. She identifies three understandings of space and place embodied in the idea of neighborhood. First, 'the concept...incorporates both place and people' (p. 4). Rather than seeing them as fixed entities, independent of the people who live there, we need to view the characteristics of neighborhoods as being shaped by the interactions of people and place. Second, neighborhoods 'are neither bounded entities nor do they have objective characteristics that are experienced in the same way by all their inhabitants' (p. 4). Drawing on Massey's (1994) insights, Lupton suggests that neighborhoods cannot be regarded as containers in which social interactions take place but should be seen as overlapping social networks ranging from the home area, the residential and shopping locality and the wider urban district or region. Third, 'the characteristics [of neighborhoods] are shaped by their relationship to other places as well as by their internal features' (p. 4). In other words, how residents view themselves is influenced by outsider perceptions of their neighborhood. As we shall discuss further in this account, the stigmatization and negative stereotyping of residents in low socioeconomic communities exercises a powerful influence on the educational identity and aspirations of students.

Young people's stories in this study were obtained from ethnographic interviews with secondary school students in Federation City (pseudonym), a large regional center in southeastern Australia. Once dominated by mining, pastoralism and agriculture, the economy of the region now rests on manufacturing and tertiary industries, including retail trade, tourism, health, education and community services. The city has a rich architectural heritage reflected in a fine art gallery, a city hall and other public buildings. It is endowed with extensive parks, gardens, reserves, and sporting facilities and has several university campuses and a large number of private and public schools. Federation City lacks the ethnic diversity of major metropolitan centers, but is highly stratified along socioeconomic lines. Several suburbs have been ranked amongst the most disadvantaged communities in regional Australia (Vinson, 2007) and have been targeted over a number of years through the state government sponsored neighborhood renewal programs. Overall, the local government area has an unemployment rate of 7.3%, compared with state average of 5.8%, and 19% of those aged between 15 and 19 years are not engaged in work or further education (Department of Planning and Community Development, 2011).

Most residents of Federation City live in suburbs and neighborhoods that make up the greater urban area. Historically, many of these settlements evolved from mid-19th century villages and towns some distance from the city center. Now connected to the greater Federation City area, they still retain a strong sense of identity that finds expression in local schools, sporting clubs, corner stores, churches, pubs, and community centers. In some of the most disadvantaged neighborhoods community solidarity and identity has grown out of a shared experience of poverty and social exclusion. A sense of difference has been reinforced by disparaging portrayals of residents' lifestyles by outsiders.

The social dynamics of the region are changing. Over the past decade the population of Federation City has grown substantially as families, attracted by cheaper rental accommodation and lower house prices, have moved from other regional centers and a nearby capital city to the outer suburbs. Some residents commute long distances between work and home. The concept of a neighborhood school is breaking down as parents with the economic capital enroll their children in better resourced middle-class school districts beyond their immediate locality. Many residents have strong connections to neighboring cities and rural districts. Rather than being bound to a particular location, individuals and families enact their lives in multiple spaces and through 'overlapping sets of social networks' (Lupton, 2003, p. 5).

The educational landscape and profiles of participating schools

Constitutionally, the provision of public education in Australia resides with State and Territory legislatures but over the past two decades Federal governments have come to exert a much stronger influence over education policy through an extension of corporate federalism. Funding for education systems is now contingent on their compliance with a range of accountability measures, including a national curriculum and standardized testing regimes. Amongst other measures, education departments have reviewed senior school credentialing arrangements to accommodate vocational education pathways, moved towards an outcomes-based approach to curriculum, especially in the compulsory years of schooling, and funded (in a limited way) alternative school structures and programs for students in the adolescent years of schooling.

Although curriculum reform has been a priority in some states, a good deal of emphasis has been attached to national monitoring and compliance measures to improve attendance and participation. It is somewhat ironic that in the midst of a centrally-driven, anti-democratic agenda there has been a move towards local school management in most Australian states and territories. In the state in which this study was conducted, devolution has led to the creation of a competitive quasi-market mechanism with a limited measure of self-governance, an emphasis on financial delegation, per capita funding of schools, parental choice, and corporate managerialist forms of school leadership.

The participating schools in this study offer a comprehensive education for young people from predominantly working class backgrounds and both have undergone considerable restructuring over the past decade. Although we interviewed a handful of students in the junior secondary years (8–9) the vast majority of participants were engaged in senior school studies leading to certificates in applied learning, vocational education and/ or academic learning. What follows are brief profiles of the schools.

New Vision 7–12 Community College
With a student population of 1000, New Vision Community College has evolved from a technical high school in the 1990s to a 7–12 community school serving the rapidly growing residential / industrial estates on the southern margins of Federation City. The College is to become a core part of a community learning hub which will eventually include the provision of health services, a child care center, an adult learning center, recreational facilities and an auditorium. Students currently have access to an Adolescent Health Clinic and can take advantage of in-school study groups and after-school tutorial classes. Redefining the image and mission of the school in the wake of negative media portrayals and demographic change has become a major priority for the school leadership. The revamped school website outlines a vision of 'a supportive learning and teaching environment where students can take advantage of challenges and engage in active and fulfilling education to achieve excellence'. There has been a major drive (some would say obsession) to transform the culture of the school with a big emphasis on improvement targets, especially those related to academic achievement, student attendance,

punctuality, dress code and behavior. Students, parents and staff are constantly reminded of these targets through posters, newsletters, assemblies and electronic displays. From our conversations, it appears that many students believe the policies have led to a better learning environment for the academically engaged kids because the so-called 'trouble makers' have left or been excluded.

Federation City Senior Secondary School Campus
Located near the city center, the Senior Campus of Federation City Secondary School has an enrolment of 330 students and offers a broad range of academic and vocational subjects in years 11 and 12. The campus was opened in 1996 after a major renovation to heritage buildings including a town library and former high school. Many students enroll in the city campus on completion of junior secondary studies in the East or West campuses of Federation City Secondary School but a sizeable proportion come from nearby towns and suburbs. The senior campus seems to attract more than its fair share of young people from low socioeconomic backgrounds, many of whom have had a very disruptive school history. Two of our participants had attended five schools previously.

City Campus promotes itself as an adult learning environment where students are expected to take a high level of responsibility for their own learning. There is a dress code but no strict uniform requirement. Students are expected to attend classes, meet assessment guidelines and comply with codes of behavior but there appears to be considerable flexibility in the day-to-day operations of the school. Students can integrate a Vocational Education and Training (VET) certificate into their program and/or participate in school-based apprenticeships. Adult mentors support students in their studies and in planning their pathways to future learning and employment. Although most students seem to cherish the greater measure of freedom at City Campus a few expressed reservations about the lack of structure and controls. As one of our informants pointed out, in a place where there are no uniforms and bells 'you have to organize yourself a bit better. It's a bit more grownup'.

Having outlined the contextual elements of the study we now explain how we crafted our account of an extended case study centered on Federation City.

An extended case study: space, place and identity

Initially developed by scholars in the Chicago and Manchester schools of anthropology in the 1950s and 60s, the 'extended case method' attempted to address the limitations of traditional, single-sited ethnographies which were seen to be inherently particular and incapable of generalization. Gluckman (1958), Van Velsen (1967) and other proponents sought to extend the explanatory value of interpretive research through multi-site analyses of the ways in which micro-negotiations of meaning and practices were constrained and/or enhanced by macro cultural, economic and political factors. Burawoy, a student of Van Velsen, defined the extended case method by highlighting its reflexivity and by advocating it as a means to reexamine the relationship between data and theory. In his words:

> The *extended case* method applies reflexive science in order to extract the general from the unique, to move from the 'micro' to the 'macro' and to connect the present to the past in anticipation of the future, all by building on preexisting theory. (Burawoy, 1998, p. 5)

Burawoy and his colleagues put a new inflection on the extended case study method through his use of the label 'global ethnography' (Burawoy, et al., 2000)—a notion which presents the local and the global as mutually constitutive in shaping social relations. It is particularly appropriate to this study because our young participants are 'living the global' (Eade, 1997) as they forge educational and economic identities in neighborhoods adversely impacted by global flows and processes not of their making. For example, a fundamental shift in the global economy has led to a decline in the manufacturing base in Australia and most Western countries as corporations move offshore to take advantage of low cost labor. It is crucial that we understand how the wider forces of globalization, both educational and in terms of labor market opportunities, operate to change the nature of local social relations. Global ethnography shifts the unit of analysis from a single site, to a focus on the way in which 'global forces, connections and imaginations' (Burawoy, et al., 2000, p. 28) impact social life through particular place-making projects. Importantly, this methodology shows how globalization can be studied 'from below' through participating in the lives of those who experience it.

Research design

Drawing on Schneekloth and Shibley's (1995) concept of 'critical placemaking' the research was guided by the following questions:

- What is the significance of place and locale in the educational lives of young people in contexts regarded as disadvantaged, and how does location affect the value they attach to education?
- What factors inhibit/enhance the geography of educational opportunities for young people in communities of disadvantage?
- How do young people's interpretations of educational possibilities around locality and neighborhood interact with or contradict place-based interventions (e.g. extended learning hubs—an integrated form of service delivery from a single site) aimed at ameliorating disadvantage?

Ethics approval for the research was obtained from the state education system and the affiliated university and 60 volunteer participants, ranging in age from 14 to 17 years, were recruited from New Vision 7–12 Community College and Federation City Senior School Campus. Students attending these co-educational public schools came predominantly from working-class suburbs and outlying districts of Federation City.

Research methods

Conducted between April 2011 and March 2012, the research involved a range of critical ethnographic methods including *in situ* observations, embedded interviews, purposeful conversations, document and artifact collection and analysis, and portraits of participants and school sites. Prior to the first round of interviews we organized two bus tours of the city and surrounds with a small group of about a dozen participants, some of whom were provided with digital cameras and invited to capture images of their neighborhoods. Though a small part of the research, the tour was very successful in getting young people to start to open up a part of the world to which they were prepared to give us access. We gained a feeling for the places they like to hang-out, such as the yabbie [small fresh water crayfish] pond, and the darker recesses of neighborhoods—the dangerous places to be avoided.

Ethnographic interviews

The major component of the extended case study involved two intensive rounds of semi-structured interviews with young people. In total, 56 individual interviews and six group interviews, each lasting from 30 to 45 minutes, were carried out in the two sites. Of the 60 students interviewed, 14 attended Federation City Campus and 46 were from New Vision Community College—a much larger school with a student cohort spanning years 8 to 12. (Refer to Appendix A at the end of this chapter for a detailed summary.) With the cooperation of school principals and teachers, interviews were arranged in scheduled school periods and took place in the privacy of meeting rooms and office spaces. Voluntary informed consent was gained from the participants who were given information about the scope and purposes of the research in a plain language statement. Written and oral assurances were given about the confidentiality of conversations and their right to withdraw at any time. Written informed consent was obtained from parents of students under 18 years of age. Throughout this book we have honored the ethical undertaking given of preserving anonymity by assigning pseudonyms to all participants, places and schools involved in the research.

Broadly speaking, the interviews sought to explore the notion of 'becoming educated' in a context of regional disadvantage, and involved discussions with young people about what they thought about their educational future, whether higher education was an option, how important getting a job was to them, the extent of family support and social networks, the degree of attachment they had to their neighborhood and the educational opportunities and constraints they envisioned. Our discussions were guided but not constrained by the following questions:

- How important is education to you?
- How do you think about your educational future?
- Is going to university an option for you?
- How important is 'getting a job' to you?
- Does living here have an effect on where you think you will be in say five years' time?
- Does living here 'hem you in' or make you feel constrained in any ways?
- In what ways do family, friends and social networks affect the way you think about your future?
- Do you ever look beyond this neighborhood in thinking about your educational future and job prospects?
- What's good about living here, and how does that help you?
- What's not so good?
- Are things improving or changing in this neighborhood? Does this affect you?
- Do you feel attached to this neighborhood? Do you think you will stay or leave? Will you come back? Why?
- Do you think much about yourself beyond being connected to this neighborhood?

With the consent of participants, interviews were audio-recorded and together with fieldnotes were used to prepare transcripts of our conversations. These were later crafted into narrative portraits, a process we describe in some detail below.

Critical ethnographic narratives: representational challenges

One of the main aims of this book is to provide the reader with narrative accounts of young people's lives, especially their experiences of education in a context of regional disadvantage. We have therefore devoted a great deal of space to their stories elicited during conversations and interviews in the two research sites. Narrative research is a well established tradition in the disciplines of anthropology, sociology, and more recently in education—see for example Bickerstaff (2010), Kim and Latta (2010), Moss (2004), Moen (2006), Prosser

(2007)—but as we have noted previously, ethnographic narratives are viewed with considerable skepticism by those in the positivist camp. However, as Brodkey (1987) reminds us, ethnography inevitably deals with lived experience and the stories people tell about themselves and one another are 'practices and artifacts of culture' (p. 46). We do not stake a claim to objectivity nor do we necessarily accept that what people have to say about their lives represents truth in an absolute sense. Rather, as Brodkey (1987) explains, we study stories:

> ...not because they are true or even because they are false, but for the same reason that people tell and listen to them, in order to learn about the terms on which others make sense of their lives: what they take into account and what they do not; what they consider worth contemplating and what they do not; what they are not willing to raise and discuss as problematic and unresolved in life. (p. 47)

As authors we too have a voice. Narratives, as Brodkey points out, do not explain themselves and consequently an interpretive or an analytical ethnography must involve another retelling of the story from the perspective of the author(s). Whilst we have sought to honor the voices of participants in the text, our analysis draws on critical social theory in making more explicit the links between young people's lives and the political, social and economic systems which help shape their experiences. From a socially critical perspective, schools and other social institutions may be viewed as sites with transformative potential but they are also sites of cultural hegemony. One of our main tasks as 'political authors' is to interrupt the deficit discourses and contest those social practices which oppress particular categories of young people.

There are representational and ethical issues involved in combining narrative and critical approaches in our writing (Clandinin & Rosiek, 2007; Prosser, 2007). Brodkey (1987) suggests that authors need to address two fundamental questions in writing ethnographic narratives, namely 'what to tell and how to tell it' (p. 39). As we have described previously, decisions about these matters are inherently political because they involve choices about content, whose perspective is to be included or excluded, and textual conventions. There are potential dangers in this kind of writing. One of these, identified by Krumer-Nevo and Sidi (2012), involves the risk of Othering, 'that is, the risk of portraying the other essentially different, and translating this difference to inferiority' (p. 299). They suggest three modes of writing that have the potential to ameliorate this tendency:

> ...narrative, which enables the retrieval of subjectivity;...dialog, which reveals the personal history of the research participant and her interpretation regarding it; and...reflexivity, which transforms the text by adding the author's own feelings, experiences, and history as a vehicle to understand the research participant. (p. 299)

For our part, we have sought to address the first of these textual issues through narrative portraits of our young participants: a practice that owes much to the writings of Lawrence-Lightfoot and Davis (1997) and explained in some detail in Smyth and McInerney (2013a). Developed from interview transcripts, these closely edited narratives were condensed to a page or two in length and, as far as possible, the words of participants were preserved intact while holding on to the key ideas being presented. As illustrated in the following example, narrative portraits are accompanied by a heading that tries to capture a key insight into the participant's story and brief commentary and analysis.

'It's definitely easier on your nerves going to school here'

Having being schooled in the United States for nearly ten years, seventeen-year-old Adrianna brings a unique perspective to the notion of 'becoming educated'. In the following portrait she relates a little of the family circumstances leading to her move to Australia and describes the differences in schooling in upstate New York and what she has experienced so far in Federation City.

> I started off in United States and the schooling there was okay. Some of the things they taught I didn't agree with but I went along with them. My mum met her now husband on-line and we arrived in Federation City about 8 months ago. He is now my step dad and I am hoping to change my surname to his name when I get older. I enrolled at the Treetops campus halfway through 10th grade. I had already finished that grade when we came into Australia in July so it was pretty easy. I was flying through it but it was difficult learning all the slang and stuff. They wouldn't let me into year 11 because they wanted to make sure I could do it. The culture of the school here is rather different to the one I went to in upstate New York. There were 1500 kids there so it was very crowded and there was a lot of fighting. You get more of a say here. They picked your classes for you in New York, but here I picked my own classes. I don't know much about teaching in Australia but all they did in New York was just talk about all the wars. At the end of every year we had about 2 weeks of standardized testing as well as the normal exams. It was very stressful having to do three hours of testing every day for about two weeks. It's a lot less stressful here. In New York I had to wait about two or three hours before I actually started my test. I think one of my friends had a panic attack because she was overwhelmed. Kids are a little different in New York. They are harder workers. It seems that kids in Federation City don't have as much motivation. They don't have anything they want to work for.
>
> I'm hoping to become a hairdresser when I leave school. I am taking the VET class for hairdressing and so far it is easy. It's not a Technical and Further Education (TAFE) course. I just am doing the taster part of it at the moment but it could lead to an apprenticeship or TAFE course. In the first two classes we have been over all the issues that hairdressers have with their health

and that's put me off a bit. I've not had a work placement with hairdressing yet but we are supposed to do it. I'm also doing health and human development, literacy and numeracy, English. I'm not planning to go to university at this point. I wanted to be a fashion designer but mum has told me that it might be hard to get into that field here so I changed my mind. I always want to go back to the States to see my friends but here is okay. There are no burglaries and no violence. [In New York] there was a girl in my class who had a mum that was an officer and we did have a couple of bomb attacks. It was horrible. It's definitely easier on your nerves going to school here. Where we lived in New York was in the sticks. So we are working to make our home in Australia and are trying to get health care and stuff organized. We have to wait two years before we are considered citizens. Before my step-father collapsed he was doing water delivery. His heart skipped a beat and he dropped and my mum freaked out. He and my mum are planning to go to the states in early May but I don't think he can walk through the security with a pacemaker. (Portrait developed from a transcript of an interview on the 29th of February 2012.)

As a relative newcomer to Australia, Adrianna offers an outside's perspective on schooling and place-related identities. She suggests that students in her Australian school seem to be more relaxed about their education because they are not subjected to the constant pressure of examinations and standardized tests that seem to stifle learning and cause so much grief and anxiety for young people in the United States. We often read about the damaging impact of high stakes testing from teachers and academics but here we have a first-hand account from someone who has actually experienced them. Adrianna reports favorably on several aspects of schooling at Federation City Campus: first, she can choose the subjects that she wants to do and is not bound by rigid curriculum requirements; second, there is much less violence in the school and community. At this stage university is not an option for Adrianna as she makes plans for a career as a hairdresser. Whilst she says she misses her friends in the United States she seems committed to making a new life with her family in Australia.

Together with extended quotes from transcripts, we believe that portrayals of this kind make for engaging reading and add to the authenticity of research because they present a young person's versions of events and their lifeworlds. In addition to narrative portraits developed from interviews with individuals we have also crafted portraits from two-way interviews and multivocal dialogues.

Concluding remarks

In this chapter we have outlined the philosophical, methodological and representational features of a critical ethnographic approach to research focused on young people's educational identities. We position ourselves as 'political authors' engaged in the tasks of: (a) exposing unfair structures and practices that perpetuate inequalities and diminish educational, employment and life chances for young people; and (b) revealing the ways in which schools, neighborhoods and place-based interventions can enhance the learning identities and aspirations of the most marginalized students. We have explained the rationale behind our use of the 'extended case method' and how it enabled us to map how the young informants in the study were exemplars of 'living the global' in the way they experienced their lives. Finally, we have discussed how we attempted to resolve the representational tensions arising from the critical narrative research.

Appendix A: Becoming Educated: summary of Interviews 2011–2012

	New Vision 7–12 Community College	Federation City Senior Secondary School Campus	Total
Male participants	22	6	28
Female participants	24	8	32
No. of participants	46	14	60
Individual interviews	42	14	56
Pairs	6	0	6
Total interviews	48	14	62
Age 12	1	0	1
Age 13	0	0	0
Age 14	3	0	3
Age 15	18	0	18
Age 16	17	11	28
Age 17	7	3	10
Year 7	1	0	1
Year 8	3	0	3
Year 9	0	0	0
Year 10	23	0	23
Year 11	16	13	29
Year 12	3	1	4

Each interview approximately 30 minutes duration: 32 hours overall

3. From deficits and deficiencies to strengths and capabilities: puncturing notions of disadvantage

Introduction

> Hopefully I'm going to [university] next year. If I get a high enough score I would like to do physiotherapy and there will be more options...Mum and dad left school early. They expected me to drop out in the first couple of years of secondary school and get an apprenticeship. When I said I just wanted to finish school their jaws just dropped. I will be the first one in my extended family to finish school (Derek, aged 17 years, New Vision Community College, 2011).

Australia Day is commemorated as a national holiday on the 26th of January—a date which marks the anniversary of the arrival of the first fleet of convict ships from Great Britain and the raising of the Union Jack at Sydney Cove in 1788. According to patriotic sentiment, the official purpose of the day is for all Australians to come together to celebrate what is great about their nation and being an Australian citizen. It's an occasion to fly the flag, participate in civic and community events or simply have a barbecue with family and friends. Not all Australians share this sense of pride and rejoicing. For many Aboriginal people, January 26th is a day of mourning marking as it does the beginnings of a colonial era which resulted in the dispossession of their lands and the destruction of families and cultural traditions. One of the most disturbing aspects of the day is the uncritical celebration of Australia's culture, values and traditions to the exclusion of thoughtful reflection and debate on what might be done to make Australia a more socially just nation. There is a good deal to admire about Australia but it is far from being the egalitarian society portrayed in the popular literature. The much vaunted concept of a 'fair go for all' must seem quite foreign to those in regional and urban communities where entrenched patterns of social and educational disadvantage prevail (Price-Robertson, 2011; Vinson, 2007).

A 'discourse of disadvantage' (Gale & Densmore, 2000, p. 114) is a central theme in education policy. Indeed a good deal of the present rationale for changes to school funding arrangements is premised on the need to improve education access and equity for so-called 'disadvantaged' students (Australian Government [Gonski Report], 2011). However, labels like 'disadvantage' and 'poverty' are not helpful because of what they hide. In this chapter we seek to unmask and unveil these categories which have become so firmly embedded in discourses about social policy and practice. We acknowledge that disadvantage and poverty exist in peoples' lives and to that extent cannot be denied, but we go beyond the superficial labels to look at what is missing. We regard these as 'constructed' rather than natural categories, and as having limited policy utility in 'targeting' populations for 'remediation'. What they fail to show is the fact that people do not exist as 'disadvantaged' per se: they are *made* that way by the inequitable outcomes of global capitalism and neoliberal policies which have largely abandoned welfare state principles in favor of a highly individualistic and market-driven approach to social policy. These categories not only laminate over the political, economic and cultural determinants of deprivation and social exclusion but they run the risk of portraying young people from low socioeconomic backgrounds in disrespectful, demeaning and patronizing ways.

As illustrated in the opening quote to this chapter, the stories we present in this book contradict many of the stereotypical portrayals and pathological views of young people and their families living in communities categorized as 'disadvantaged'. Derek who comes from a low socioeconomic background is imbued with a sense of agency and determination to further his education that surprises even his parents. He defies the deficit-ridden views of young people encased in Ruby Payne's (2002; 2005) culture of poverty (Gorski, 2008). Puncturing contemporary notions of disadvantage allows us to see how the identities of young people, like Derek, are constructed with and against neoliberal policies that have enshrined principles of parental choice, economic gain and individual reward over and above a commitment to the common good. It enables us to see how schools function in ways that sustain the reproduction of educational inequalities but also how they can work in cooperation with local communities to expand young people's horizons, nurture in them a sense of optimism and assist them to pursue worthwhile educational pathways. It moves us beyond a discourse of deficits and deficiencies to one which affirms the strengths and capabilities of young people who experience systemic disadvantage.

The chapter begins with a brief overview of the socio-spatial features and extent of social and educational disadvantage with particular reference to Federation City. We then proceed to a historical analysis of the ways in which the notion of 'disadvantage' has been framed in education policy and institutionalized in schools. Here we expose the deficit thinking, negative stereotyping and stigmatization of people in low socioeconomic communities and show how a discourse of disadvantage has supplanted traditional constructs of inequality and discrimination as explanations for poor living standards and diminished educational opportunities (Coram, 2008). We then turn our attention to student narratives of disadvantage and the educational opportunities and constraints arising from their schools, families, social networks and neighborhoods. Our account draws extensively on portraits developed from interviews with six young people in New Vision Community College and the Senior School Campus of Federation City High School.

Poverty, deprivation and exclusion: the material realities of social and educational disadvantage

> The world in which we live is both remarkably comfortable and thoroughly miserable. (Sen, 2001, p. 1)

Although state and federal governments talk in glowing terms of their commitments to inclusivity, equality of opportunity, and entitlements for all, glaring inequalities persist across schools and education systems in Australia. Large numbers of young people are not only being pushed out of education due to economic and cultural processes of advantaging and disadvantaging (Teese & Polesel, 2003) but they are being shut out of the labor market as well because of profound shifts in the global economy (Aronowitz & DiFazio, 2010). According to the Australian Productivity Commission (2010), between 30–40% of young people are making the active choice not to complete secondary education. The figures are more pronounced in low socioeconomic communities, especially regional and rural Australia where upwards of 50% of students fail to complete 12 years of schooling. Factors contributing to educational disadvantage in these locations include the cost and the availability of transport, levels of family support from private and government agencies, and limited subject choices and access to specialized courses in schools (Considine & Zappala, 2002, p. 134).

Despite the nation's strong economic growth by OECD standards, high rates of youth unemployment, welfare dependency and social exclusion are the norm in many parts of Australia. Over the past two decades major structural changes have taken place in the Australian economy, foremost amongst these being the decline of manufacturing industries (notably, iron and steel fabrication, textile, clothing, motor vehicles, electrical goods) as tariff protection barriers have been removed and domestic industries opened up to global competition. A resources boom, largely fueled by China's demand for Australian iron and coal, has led some commentators to claim that Australia now has a 'two speed economy' with significant regional variation in employment demand and weekly earnings for workers. According to Saunders (2011), geographical fragmentation of the economy is a direct consequence of the ebb and flow of the economic forces unleashed by global capitalism. As a consequence, 'one of the most important determinants of social disadvantage is location' (p. 2). Where one lives can have a powerful impact on access to employment and, importantly:

> ...on the ability of a given level of income to support a particular standard of living and on the availability and effectiveness of services to address disadvantage. (Saunders, 2011, p. 2)

Vinson's (2004) study of the distribution of social disadvantage in Victoria and New South Wales provides ample evidence of the spatial patterns of inequality in rural, regional and metropolitan locales and highlights the crucial role of limited schooling in triggering and sustaining concentrated local disadvantage. If anything, the extent of disadvantage in many parts of regional Australia has worsened since the global financial crisis of 2007–2008.

As we have outlined in Chapter 2, Federation City has many economic, cultural and social assets that enhance its regional vitality but several suburbs—including those that many of our young informants call home—have been rated amongst the most disadvantaged in Australia (Vinson, 2004). In a submission to a state parliamentary inquiry into rural and regional disadvantage (Bodenham & Appleton, 2010), the city's municipal council expressed deep concerns about the negative impact of these 'pockets of poverty' on the economic and social wellbeing of the city as a whole. Key factors of disadvantage identified in the submission included long-term unemployment, low income, early school leaving, limited computer and internet access, physical and mental disabilities, and prison incarceration. To back up its evidence of deprivation, the Council stated that seven percent of adults surveyed in the city in 2007 reported that they ran out of food in the last 12 months and could not afford to buy more. In recent years the demand on local welfare services has increased dramatically as reported in the local newspaper:

> As [Federation City] shivers through one of the coldest winters in decades, struggling families are giving up basic necessities like toothpaste, toothbrushes and shampoo just to scrape enough money together to pay for power and gas bills. Others are going to bed early rather than leaving their heating on during the

night, [Federation City] welfare agencies have said. Hundreds of [Federation City] families – many for the first time – are seeking assistance from major welfare organisations in the city, including Anglicare, The Salvation Army, UnitingCare and St Vincent de Paul (Quinlan, 2011).

Educational disadvantage goes hand-in-hand with economic and social deprivation. In previous studies of school retention and student engagement (Smyth, Angus, Down & McInerney, 2008; Smyth & McInerney, 2012) we documented young people's accounts of the barriers to school participation and achievement arising from poverty, family trauma, and personal hardship in the communities that are part of this study. We drew attention to the social stigma of young parenthood and the enormous barriers confronting pregnant and parenting teenagers as they try to sustain an education and cope with family responsibilities. We highlighted the plight of homeless youth trying to sustain a connection with schooling and revealed the destructive impact of racism on the education of young indigenous students. We explained how educational disadvantage is reinforced through a 'digital divide' in the realms of information and communication technologies (Angus, Snyder & Sutherland-Smith, 2003).

The senior school students in this study did not use words like 'poverty' and 'disadvantage' to describe their circumstances, but they did give graphic accounts of the ways in which their lives and schooling had been affected by family trauma, economic hardship and debilitating medical conditions. Many had little continuity in their schooling, often as a result of transitory lifestyles but also because, in many instances, they did not fit into traditional school settings. Jasmine's story is not uncommon:

> I've been to tons of schools. I've been to four schools before coming to Federation City. From the middle of year 9 I attended the West campus of the Federation Secondary College and then I came to the City Campus this year. I moved about a lot in my life. I lived in South Australia, from the ages of two to four and then returned to this state. I grew up with my sister's dad but then we moved and they broke up. I go to Bay City [pseudonym] all the time because my boyfriend lives there (Jasmine, year 11, Federation City Senior Campus, 2012).

We will have more to say about the spatial dimensions of poverty and disadvantage in the following chapters, but it was most apparent from our interviews that young people in New Vision Community College had a strong sense of the social class location and how this was being played out in school. In particular, students from the most economically depressed neighborhoods were often stigmatized as lazy, unmotivated individuals who made life difficult for others. According to sixteen-year-old Sally, a lot of these students were dropping out of school because they didn't care or were just looking for the easy way out. 'They are the trouble makers who are just not interested in school', she stated. Under a new school management regime with strict attendance and behavioral expectations, students from the poorest neighborhoods were often extirpated from school. Joseph described what happened in these words:

> The kids who don't conform to the policies will be straightened out or we don't see them again. I think a fairly small number would have left with the excuse of getting a job. If the teachers really don't want them they will be eased out. I don't know what's happened to those students who've been expelled (Joseph, year 11, New Vision Community College, 2012).

Not all students were comfortable with the 'ideology of accountability and top-down managerialism' (Angus, 2012b, p. 245) that seems to drive these practices. Sixteen-year-old Brett recognized the unfairness of arbitrary regulations on students living in the most adverse economic and social conditions.

> The kids who have family problems at home won't be able to meet the attendance figure. Life is really difficult for some kids. I know a lot of parents who charge their kids rent to stay in their house. Some kids come from welfare or the parents could be pricks (Brett, year 11, New Vision Community College, 2012).

Brett rubs shoulders with kids in poverty. He know that many families in his neighborhood lack the financial resources to meet the basic educational needs of their children let alone fund after-hours enrichment programs or provide access to internet and communication technologies. These students depend on public transport which can be infrequent and unreliable and many have to supplement family income through part-time casual employment. Brett's empathetic attitude towards the least advantaged and his understanding of the complexities of young people's lives stands in sharp contrast to the authoritarian and uncompassionate ways in which some schools and education systems are disposed to address the issues of student engagement.

Poverty and disadvantage are undeniable realities for many young people in Federation City but the current public mood is largely unforgiving of policies that purport to redistribute wealth more fairly. According to Greig, Lewins and White (2003) there has been 'a powerful backlash against the struggles for equality that shaped Australians and their lives since World War 11' (p. 13). Australia has some of the lowest unemployment benefits amongst the industrialized nations and the situation for young people has worsened with a reduction in Newstart Allowance to a mere $245 a week. Many recipients depend for their survival on the support of families, friends and charities. Currently about 16% of tertiary students come from low socioeconomic backgrounds, however the Federal Government's proposal to raise the figure to a modest 20% by 2020 by offering universities additional funding for every disadvantaged student they enroll has been disparaged by right wing critics. Under the newspaper headline *Universities should not pander to disadvantaged students*, Donnelly (2009) accused the then Education Minister, Julia Gillard, of social engineering and engaging in Fabian style politics. He wrote:

> Discriminating against academically successful students because of where they live or where they went to school is not only unfair; the policy also sends the message that merit, hard work and ability are secondary to membership of a so-called victim group.

So, in a curious twist of logic the privileged have now become the disadvantaged—supposedly the victims of unfair policies that discriminate in favor of the poor. Such callous indifference to the plight of the genuinely disadvantaged is not confined to Australia. Commenting on the situation in the United States, Rose (2005) remarks:

> [t]he level of competition, the state of the economy, the anxiety about social position, the successful shaping of opinion by the political right—all this has contributed to a resolute ideology of individual advancement and a suspicion… toward policies that support equity and a common educational good. (p. 252)

In the wake of a conservative restoration of political values in the United States, Giroux (2012a) writes of a growing culture of humiliation and cruelty whereby those who dare to speak out against the prevailing culture of materialism and self-interest or express support for programs to alleviate poverty risk public denigration.

Why has there been such a shift in public attitudes towards the poor and marginalized? What does it mean to be categorized as disadvantaged? In the next section of this chapter we examine the ways in which notions of poverty and disadvantage have been portrayed in policy discourses and how this has impacted on the lives and educational chances of young people in Federation City.

Deficits, deficiencies and differences: what lies behind the label 'disadvantage'?

The word 'disadvantage' is of Middle English origin and comes from the Old French word 'desavantage'—des- (expressing reversal) and avantage (to advantage another). When used as a noun it denotes unfavorable circumstances or conditions that reduce the chances of success or effectiveness for individuals or groups and when used as a verb it refers to actions or situations where people are put in an unfavorable position to someone or something else. The adjective, 'disadvantaged', commonly refers to those 'socially or economically deprived or discriminated against' (Collins Australian Concise Dictionary, 2001).

Words are not innocent conventions. Although dictionary definitions offer useful insights into the etymological roots of words they fail to reveal the ways in which they are appropriated and misappropriated to serve ideological interests. The term 'disadvantage', for example, hints at deficits and shortcomings of individuals or groups who are often unfavorably compared to those in the mainstream of society. To be described as 'disadvantaged' is to be classed as someone with traits and characteristics that deviate from the norm—someone in need of remediation. In neoliberal times, the term 'disadvantage' has become a convenient label for free-market advocates as they seek to attribute economic hardship and poverty to individual, family and neighborhood failings rather than any faults within the capitalist system.

In exploring contemporary discourses of educational disadvantage we shall confine our discussion to three inter-related themes:

- theoretical perspectives informing notions of social reproduction and educational disadvantage
- education policy responses to poverty and educational disadvantage
- school policies and practices that engage with issues of educational disadvantage.

Theorizing social reproduction and educational disadvantage

In contradiction to much of the school effectiveness research which bleaches context from its analysis, we believe that external social and economic constraints help to explain the differential achievement of students (Mills & Gale, 2011, p. 241). In what follows we rehearse prominent theoretical arguments to account for the social reproduction of disadvantage in education.

Traditional explanations for the persistent failure of particular groups of students tend to focus on attributes relating to the home backgrounds of young people. Supposedly, children from low socioeconomic families struggle at school because they are 'deprived, lacking in motivation, stimulation, proper values and discipline for success in school, and later, the job market' (Gale & Densmore, 2000, p. 14). Valencia (2010) claims that this constitutes a deficit thinking model based on the belief that the students who fail at school do so because of some innate deficits or deficiencies 'manifested in limited intellectual abilities, linguistic shortcomings, lack of motivation to learn, and immoral behavior' (p. 7). Some theorists attribute these to genetic differences, others to culture and class or family socialization. Although the deficit thinking model has been thoroughly discredited by many behavioral and social scientists, it is experiencing a resurgence of popularity in the United States and elsewhere as evidenced in the widespread adoption of Ruby Payne's (2005) professional development program, *A Framework for Understanding Poverty*.

More radical explanations of educational disadvantage have drawn on the New Sociology of Education theories of social reproduction to show how 'schools help transmit the status and class positions of the wider society' (McLaren, 1989, p. 194). According to Bowles and Gintis (1976), the roots of educational inequality lie in the capitalist economy. They argue that there is a relatively simple correspondence between schooling, class, family and social inequalities such that children from high socioeconomic status families typically achieve high status jobs and those from low socioeconomic backgrounds acquire a correspondingly low socioeconomic standing. However, as McLaren (1989) explains reproduction of disadvantage involves more than economic and class position: social, cultural and linguistic factors are also important in shaping people's identities.

Responding to this criticism, French sociologist Pierre Bourdieu, argues that, above and beyond economic factors, 'cultural habits and...dispositions inherited from' the family is fundamentally important to school success (Bourdieu & Passeron, 1979). In essence, students from the dominant or privileged culture inherit different cultural capital than do economically disadvantaged students and, as McLaren (1989, p. 198) maintains, 'schools generally value and reward those who exhibit that dominant cultural capital' whilst simultaneously devaluing the cultural capital of students in subordinate class positions. British sociologist Basil Bernstein (1996) also showed how pedagogy and curriculum are critical elements in the process of devaluing and excluding people in disadvantaged positions. He claimed that 'what teachers teach, how they teach it, and the way that student learning is evaluated convey powerful messages to students about what society considers to be important and valid knowledge' (Smyth, Angus, Down & McInerney, 2008, p. 64). School knowledge, according to Giroux (1988) is 'a privileged discourse that is constructed through a selective process of emphases and exclusions' (p. xxx). He goes on to state:

> Methods of instruction, choice of curriculum content, and the institutional norms of schooling that make up 'school culture' not only confirm and privilege young people from dominant classes but simultaneously 'disconfirm the histories, experiences and dreams of subordinate groups'. (p. xxxi)

Typically this functions through the hidden curriculum which Giroux describes as 'those unstated norms, values, and beliefs that are transmitted to students through the underlying structure of a given class' (Giroux, 1988, p. 51).

Reproduction theorists have contributed to a broader understanding of the political nature of schooling and its relation to dominant society. Importantly, they have shown that the fundamental causes of educational disadvantage lie within unjust social structures and practices rather than faults or weaknesses in individuals. However, according to Aronowitz and Giroux (1987), they have tended to:

> ...overemphasize the idea of domination in their analysis and have failed to provide any major insights into how teachers, students and other human agents come together in a specific historical and social context in order to both make and reproduce the conditions of their existence'. (p. 72)

Drawing on resistance theories, writers such as McLaren, Giroux, Aronowitz and Willis have pointed to 'the partial autonomy of school culture and the contradictions that lie within the reproductive process of schooling' (McLaren, 1989, p. 195). In contrast to reproduction theories which are chiefly concerned with power and how mechanisms by which the dominant culture ensures the consent and defeat of subordinate groups, 'theories of resistance restore a degree of agency and innovation to the cultures of these groups' (Aronowitz & Giroux, 1987, p. 72). Of course such agency always operates within the constraints of a capitalist economy, the apparatus of the state and sociocultural forces but it does provide educators with a sense of hope and possibility that they can make a positive difference to young peoples' lives.

Having outlined a range of theoretical perspectives on social reproduction and educational disadvantage we now turn our attention to ways in which these discourses shape education policy and practice in Australian schools.

Poverty, disadvantage and educational policy in Australia

Questions about the relationship between poverty, disadvantage and schooling did not feature prominently in educational policy documents until the consolidation of the welfare state in the 1960s (Taylor, Rizvi, Lingard & Henry, 1997). Until this time, Australian governments tended to assume that access to universal schooling would ensure equality of opportunity for all students. However, studies by Roper (1970) and Henderson, Harcourt and Harper (1970) confirmed that mass schooling had not broken down the reproductive cycle of poverty and privilege which had continued to deny equality of outcomes in education. Critics began to challenge the principle of meritocracy upon which a good deal of education planning was based. They argued that school structures, a hegemonic curriculum and competitive examination system tended to privilege the knowledge and values of middle-class students whilst excluding working-class students and those from minority cultures, particularly Aboriginal students (Connell, 1998; Taylor, et al., 1997). The vision of education as a right for all could not be realized in a system where young people from low socioeconomic and non-English speaking backgrounds were routinely streamed and sorted into lowly ranked ability groups.

Addressing the issue of educational disadvantage became a major goal of a reformist Labor Government led by Prime Minster Whitlam from 1972 to 1975. Acting on many of the recommendations of the Karmel Report (Interim Committee for the Australian Schools Commission, 1973) the federal government adopted an interventionist approach to schooling chiefly through the agency of the Disadvantaged School Programme (DSP) which allocated funds directly to some 15% of Australian schools categorized as serving 'disadvantaged' (typically low socioeconomic) communities. The principle of equality underpinned the needs-based approach to funding advocated in the Report, the committee reasoning that:

> ...the standard of schooling a child receives should not depend on what his (sic) parents are able or willing to contribute directly to it, or whether he (sic) is enrolled in a government or non-government institution. (p. 11)

The Karmel Report (Interim Committee for the Australian Schools Commission, 1973) broke new ground in articulating a socially democratic approach to education policy making and school reform. Rejecting the notion of individual and/or cultural deficits which tended to underpin rationales for compensatory education programs in the United States and Great Britain, it identified a lack of relational power and inequality of opportunity as prime factors in explaining the underachievement of students from low socioeconomic communities. Although the committee acknowledged that schools alone could not guarantee equality of education outcomes for all social groups they asserted that this should nonetheless be the objective.

Concerned about the inability of centralized bureaucracies to meet the needs of diverse school communities the committee recommended a grassroots approach to the control of schools arguing that responsibility should be devolved as far as possible to the people involved in the actual task of schooling, in consultation with the parents of the pupils whom they teach, and at senior levels, with the students themselves (Interim Committee for the Australian Schools Commission, 1973, p. 10). Importantly, the Report envisaged the school and not the individual disadvantaged student as the unit of action and the locus for change. The committee reasoned:

> The school provides a practical point of attack on the cycle of poverty, for it is a social institution more amenable to change than is the family and an institution where deliberate social intervention is acceptable. (Interim Committee for the Australian Schools Commission, 1973, p. 94)

Despite the innovative features of the DSP the grants made to disadvantaged schools for special programs were relatively small. According to Connell (1998) the per pupil expenditure amounted to no more than four pairs of shoes a year: 'this does not buy an educational revolution' (p. 92). Additionally, Marginson (1997) claims the resources directed to disadvantaged schools:

> ...could scarcely compensate for imbalances in the economic resources located in the home and brought to bear on education, not to mention the inherited cultural capital of the elite families. (p. 62)

In short, while these grants lifted the absolute material standards of government schools they did not improve their relative social role and position in relation to private schools which benefited greatly from the new funding formulae.

Reviewing the performance of the DSP, Connell, White and Johnston (1991) went to some length to reject the commonly accepted view that inequalities in education were a minority problem—if anything, 'the distinctive minority in education was the privileged not the poor' (p. 24) they argued. On the basis of evidence before them they concluded 'there is nothing qualitatively different about the educational problems of the poorest 14% of children' and, in direct contradiction to Ruby Payne's ideas (2002; 2005) claimed:

> [t]here is no reason to think that a strong link between poverty and educational disadvantage is the result of a 'culture of poverty' or anything of that sort. On the contrary, the evidence points to the conclusion that the problem is about the interplay of class relations and the education system as a whole. (Connell, White & Johnston, 1991, p. 24)

The discourse of disadvantage embedded in the report and subsequent school reforms brought unwanted consequences as well as policy attention. Discussing her experience as a principal of a 'rust belt' school in Australia, Thomson (2002) says that being categorized as a disadvantaged school further stigmatized the community with fewer companies willing to invest in the area, teachers choosing to work in less difficult areas, and assumptions made by employers about the suitability of job applicants based on their post codes or schools they attend (p. 99).

The DSP was conceived in an era when Labor governments in Australia were more firmly committed to welfare state principles and a social democratic approach to education policy. However, educational inequality was displaced as a central concern of government policy in Australia from the mid-1980s as the focus shifted from education's role in reducing poverty to its contribution to the production of wealth (Johnston, 1993). This was highlighted in a second major review of education by Karmel (Quality of Education Review Committee, 1985) which emphasized the need for a more skilled, productive and competitive workforce to improve the national economy. A stress on vocationalism and closer links between schooling and industry helped to reinforce this view. Another change involved the broadbanding of equity programs and identification of a range of 'disadvantaged' groups, including; (a) students with disabilities, learning difficulties, behavioral disorders and those at risk of dropping out of school; (b) students from low socioeconomic backgrounds or living in poverty; (c) Aboriginal and Torres Strait Islander students; (d) students from non-English speaking backgrounds; and (e) geographically isolated students. Separate administrative structures and programs were established for each group—'a practice which helped to institutionalize the notions of disadvantaged groups' (McInerney, 2004, p. 89).

As neoliberalism has taken hold in Australia, governments have pursued a model of education based on the so-called logic of the market place and the principle of school choice. However, there is ample evidence to suggest that this principle, together with new funding provisions for private schools has intensified the level of disadvantage in low socioeconomic communities (Angus, 2012b; Bardsley, 2007; Teese, 2011). The notion of 'students at risk' which entered the discourse on disadvantage in the mid-1980s is now firmly entrenched in education policy and practice in Australia, the United States and elsewhere. Writing about the higher education scene in South Africa, Smit (2012, p. 371) claims that the concept 'at-risk has its origins in epidemiology, a medical field where data is used to identify vulnerable sections of the population to target for inoculation against disease. In Smit's opinion, it is based on 'the presumption that it is possible to predict student failure, based on certain characteristics of the student' (p. 371)—for example those in poverty, those with a poor school history, those lacking English language proficiency and those with profound disabilities and health issues.

The medical analogy seems appropriate to the Australian context where problems of illiteracy, disengagement and poor school retention are commonly attributed to individual failings and weaknesses. Young people designated 'at risk' are described in policy documents by indicators such as unstable or severely damaged family relationships, disruptive behavior, a history of institutional care, poor social skills, low self-esteem and so on. All these indicators consign the causes of disadvantage to the individual subjectivities of young people, rather than to economic, political and social inequalities. The net effect of this pathologizing discourse is to shift responsibility for the problem of youth failure away from governments to families and their communities. Correspondingly, the policy solution has been to: compel students to stay on longer at schools and other educational institutions by raising the school leaving age to 16 years (and 17 in some states); mandate a more prescriptive curriculum and modes of assessment; implement standardized testing measures and other accountability measures; and, reinstate the binary between academic and technical education through a greater emphasis on work studies and vocational education pathways for students in disadvantaged communities (McInerney, 2007; Smyth & Fasoli, 2007).

To conclude, over the past two decades there has been a major shift in public policy responses to educational disadvantage as neoliberal governments have largely subordinated social justice principles to the market place. Enhancing individual choice has become the mantra of education policy and as deficit discourses have again taken hold there has been 'a re-casting of group inequality as individual disadvantage' (Coram, 2008, p. 7). How this discourse is played out in schools is the subject of the next section.

Schools and the perpetuation of educational disadvantage

> Children do not choose socio-economic disadvantage, and neither should the education system reinforce that marginalization. (Bardsley, 2007, p. 497)

A dialectical understanding of schooling (McLaren, 1989) enables educators to view schools not just as sites for the reproduction of social and educational disadvantage but as sites of liberation. While it is certainly the case that schools can function in oppressive ways they can also work in humane ways to create opportunities for traditionally marginalized students. In many respects, the policy environment we have described is not conducive to transformative education. Portraying young people as deviants, victims, being 'at-risk', lacking in motivation or having low aspirations reinforces deficit assumptions and schools often contribute to the reproduction of disadvantage through a hegemonic curriculum and discriminatory policies.

A widely shared perception of students in so-called 'disadvantaged schools' is that they lack the academic ability and potential to engage in higher learning (Thomson & Comber, 2003)—that they can only cope with hands-on learning and the so-called 'practical subjects'. Schools in these circumstances are inclined to engage in sorting and streaming practices to identify academic and non-academic students and to implement compensatory programs to cater for students who are falling behind in the education stakes. This can be a recipe for a pedagogy of poverty (Haberman, 1991) as already struggling students are further disadvantaged by being herded into curriculum areas that can only lead them to low-skill, low paid, insecure work (Smyth & McInerney, 2012). In general, a disproportionately higher number of students from disadvantaged schools are engaged in vocational education courses. To some extent this has been driven by lobby groups, such as the Business Council of Australia who have pressured governments and education systems by insisting that schools offer a much more work-oriented curriculum in order to make young people more 'job ready'. However, Polesel (2010) claims that poorer students are being ill-served by VET programs 'both in terms of the labor market value of the qualifications delivered and in terms of actual transitions' (p. 422).

We gained an insight into the sociological aspects of an academic / vocational divide through the stories of our young informants at New Vision Community College. Formerly a technical secondary school with a high proportion of students sitting for applied learning certificates Victorian Certificate of Applied Learning (VCAL), the college was attempting to re-badge itself as a more academically oriented learning center where many more students undertook academic certificate courses Victorian Certificate of Education (VCE) leading to university. The message was not lost on Elisha who recognized the social divide engendered by these curriculum arrangements:

> This school needs to concentrate on VCE [academic learning] more because we are becoming a VCAL school. Some teachers encourage students to do VCAL [vocational learning]—that's only my opinion. And it's the easy option. Most VCE kids are friendly with VCE kids and the VCAL kids hang together. I'm pretty sure that the VCE kids look down on the VCAL students (Elisha, year 12, New Vision Community College, 2011).

Reading between the lines, it seems that students from poorer neighborhoods—those with 'reputations'—were being counseled or directed into vocational education courses. According to sixteen-year-old Riley, family background was a major factor shaping students' educational aspirations and dispositions towards learning. His words convey a sense of the deficit thinking about working class students that serves to perpetuate disadvantage:

> Most of the kids mucking up in primary school end up doing VCAL. The smarter ones do the VCE. The academic culture of the school is going up since [the new principal] kicked in. It's just spiked up. Whether kids do VCAL or not has a lot to do with the family. The VCE families are nice and polite but the VCAL people are rude—but that's stereotyping really (Riley, year 11, New Vision Community College, 2012).

Although schools may promote themselves as inclusive, welcoming institutions, they often function as places of 'socio-spatial exclusion' (Sibley, 1995, p. x) where undesirables or trouble-makers—those who do not fit the image of the conformist, neatly attired middle-class student—are eased out or evicted from school. Inflexible codes of conduct coupled with punitive discipline regimes, such as the 'three strikes and you're out' policy, provide schools with a mechanism for divesting themselves of the most difficult and challenging students. Disadvantage is reinforced in other ways as well. Black (2011) claims that young people from backgrounds of poverty are more likely to be excluded from decision-making opportunities in their own lives. In the context of school they are:

> ...less likely to have access to the learning opportunities that promote participation: they are more likely to receive more passive forms of instruction and to have fewer opportunities to participate actively in their own learning. (p. 466)

To this point we have focused chiefly on the theoretical aspects of social reproduction and schooling together with policies which sustain educational disadvantage. In the remainder of this chapter we draw on young people's narratives as we seek to offer a more contextualized, personalized and grounded account of what it means to be educated in a context of regional disadvantage.

Becoming educated: young peoples' narratives of disadvantage, opportunities and constraints

As we have described in previous studies (Smyth & McInerney, 2012; Smyth & McInerney, 2013b; Smyth, Down & McInerney, 2010), working class students sometimes resist schooling in personally destructive ways but they also reveal themselves as active and informed participants who, when given the opportunity, can contribute much of value about the purposes, merits and shortcomings of schooling. In what follows, we have chosen five portraits to illustrate young people experiences of disadvantage and the educational opportunities and constraints arising from their schools, families and neighborhoods.

#1: Liam's story
What young people have to say about their lives, identities and hopes for the future can be most insightful and, at times, very disturbing. This is particularly true of Liam, a year 11 visually impaired student attending the Federation City Senior School campus. Liam has had to contend with a great deal of family trauma, abuse and fractured relationships throughout his life. When a teacher ushered him into the interview room the emotional scars of a

violent altercation with his step father the previous evening were painfully on show. In the distressing circumstances it was a remarkable effort on his part to front up for the interview and talk so openly about his schooling and life experiences.

> *'This school knows how to help me and I don't think that I'm behind at all'*
>
> I've moved around a lot in my life. Mum and dad were divorced when I was in primary school and I've been to five schools before coming here. My sister and I were bullied a lot in school. When the two of us started to have world war three's I moved back to my dad's place. Then my step dad passed away. My dad got worse and worse in his behavior and so I went back to mum in Federation City. I came to City Campus for a week before school ended last year. I think this is the greatest school I've ever been to. This school knows how to help me and I don't think that I'm behind at all. I have an aide who sits with me in class and helps me with my studies. I have a play station and a TV at home but I need to sit up really close to see things. I was diagnosed with a major sight impediment at three and five and it is getting worse. I have a white cane that helps me find my way around but I'm not really getting any medical help. The ear and eye hospital takes a long time to get into and I'm not sure about getting a guide dog. I am bit of a rock star and if I took him he would go deaf sitting next to the drums.
>
> I'm in a band at the moment and I play guitar and bass. We have a drummer called Jake and we travel to a nearby town for practice. The music teachers here are great, especially the guitar teacher and my drum teacher has also taught me heaps. The campus principal is also a music teacher. He mostly plays wind instruments like the clarinet and he knows how to teach a class. My old teacher was no good. He just gave me theory notes that I couldn't read. The teachers aren't afraid to jump in and have some fun here. Music would be my first choice of a career. I would also like to be a comedian but after that it's a bit hard. I would like to fly a plane but the landing might be a bit bumpy.
>
> I have some big issues at home. My step dad and I got into a bad space last night and he drove me to the point where I threatened to kill him which was not good. When I want to get away from it all I take the train down to the city to go and practice with the band. My grades were not so good last year. I failed music and failed cooking. I couldn't do the theory because I couldn't see it. This year I'm doing maths, English, personal development, and music. It's the best school I've been to and I haven't been bullied or anything yet. I live in a suburb of Federation City and rely on my step father and my mum to support me. My mum has to stay home and look after all the kids. There are seven of us but two of us live with dad. Oh, I forgot to tell you that I had three ex step dads. (Extract from a portrait of Liam developed from a transcript of an interview conducted on March 1st 2012).

The dice is heavily loaded against young people with disabilities. In his 2013 Australia Day address to the nation, Paralympic gold medal winner, Kurt Fearnley, highlighted the extent of disability inequality in Australia in the following words:

> If you have a disability in our country, you're more likely to be unemployed, more likely to be living in poverty and more likely to be less educated than if you didn't have that disability. In comparison to other economically rich nations that are members of the Organisation for Economic Co-operation and Development, the statistics for Australia are damning. In Australia, 45 percent of people with a disability live in, or near, poverty; more than double the OECD average of 22 percent. We rank 21st out of 29 OECD countries in employment participation rates for those with a disability. We rank 27th of the 27 in terms of the correlation between disability and poverty. Our system is broken, it isn't doing enough (Extract from a speech by Kurt Fearnley, 24th January 2013).

The disadvantage experienced by young people with a disability can be a major impediment to schooling and to the realization of a rewarding and fulfilling life. Current statistics indicate that at least 5% of Australian children have a disability of some kind and in the state of Victoria the figure is estimated at 67,000 (Imber, 2010). Mainstreaming of students with disabilities within the education system has increased substantially over the past two decades and students, such as Liam, who meet the eligibility criteria can generally receive in-class support. However, school completion rates are 4 times lower for students with a disability and many experience the trauma of bullying at school. Moreover, advocates for students with disabilities claim that support is generally fragmented and piecemeal. In a highly critical report an inclusive education working group (Imber, 2010) stated:

> there is often a sense that the system is more focused on managing the scarcity of resources available to children with a disability than adequately catering for them all. This is unacceptable. (p. 3)

Liam has experienced multiple forms of disadvantage arising from his low socioeconomic background, a fractious family life, disruptive school history and serious medical condition. It is clear that these factors have impaired his academic achievements and severely restricted his educational opportunities although they have not diminished his desire to make something of himself in the field of music or (perhaps most surprising of all) comedy. Liam receives one-on-one support in class from an Integration Aide (teacher assistant) and credits the music teachers in his new school for giving him the opportunities to do something he really loves. He is in a more hospitable and stimulating school environment than he has ever experienced before.

However, his social life and educational opportunities are greatly restricted because he cannot afford the medical care and aids (such as a guide dog) that would increase his mobility and improve his access to education, training and employment. Without family finance to access medical support for his condition, one senses that Liam has a long and hard road to travel to realize his ambitions.

#2 Fatima and Tanya stories

Close friends Fatima and Tanya are in year 10 at New Vision Community College. Tanya has lived in Federation City all her life and feels very much a part of the community. Fatima migrated to Australia from Sudan and after a few years in Melbourne settled in Federation City with her mother and brothers. In the following dialogic portrait, the two girls talk about their family backgrounds, the importance of education in their lives and their aspirations for the future.

> *'Education in my situation it is important because some kids don't even get to go to school where I came from'*

'I am 15 years old and I was born in Sudan', says Fatima. 'I came to Australia when I was 5 or 6 and learned to read and write. We came as immigrants—me, my mum and my brothers. I don't have a dad. I had to go to a primary school and it took me ages to learn English but I got there. I first went to Catholic school in the metropolitan area and then I came here to New Vision Community College. It's a really good school. They help me with my English and I'm really on the top of it now. My older brother goes to a Catholic boys' college in Federation City. He is doing building and construction. I think he's doing okay. My sister is doing year 8'. 'I went to my neighborhood primary school and then to New Vision', explains Tanya. 'I live in this area and I have two sisters and my mum's having a baby'.

We ask Fatima and Tanya if they have thought about future education options and career pathways. 'Right now I am doing a hairdressing course here', explains Fatima. 'I was thinking I would have my own salon and I've been doing hairdressing course here at school as part of the vocational education program. After that I might do it again next year so I can get a part time job. That's what I want to do when I finish school. All my family has to get their hair braided so some of my family could help me do it as well which would make it much easier for me. At school we do a lot of theory but it would be more interesting if we did hands on and excursions. I want to do a real persons hair'.

'When I finish school I want to be a forensic scientist', says Tanya. I don't know why I'm so interested in that but I did psychology and biology and dad's friends with a forensic scientist. I know there's a lot of study ahead of me. I like studying but not school in general. Mum said if I stick to something then I should be successful. Neither of my parents went to university. I was thinking about going to study forensic science at xxx University'.

Both girls say they value the importance of education and they plan to hang-in with their schooling.

> 'Our school does give us opportunities if you put in enough effort and pay attention but sometimes I don't. I just go to another world', Fatima confesses. 'Some of our friends are going to drop out this year', says Tanya. 'They will be stuck at Maccas [McDonalds]'. 'Education in my situation it is important because some kids don't even get to go to school where I came from', says Fatima. 'It was hard because teachers hit you and that' (Dialogic portrait developed from a transcript of an interview with Fatima and Tanya, 23rd of June 2011).

Educational disadvantage encompasses a broad spectrum of socioeconomic, cultural and linguistic factors, as evident in the narratives above. Fatima's refugee background has helped to shape her educational identity in quite profound ways. Since 1996 more than 20,000 Sudanese migrants have settled in Australia under the Federal Government's Humanitarian Programs (Department of Immigration and Citizenship, 2007). Many are victims of a civil war between North and South Sudan and some have been living in refugee camps in surrounding countries prior to arrival in Australia. It is not uncommon for families to have lost fathers and brothers in the conflict leaving mothers as sole carers. Without the support of a father and speaking almost no English on her arrival Fatima made her way through primary school and is now engaged in studies leading to an applied learning certificate. Tanya comes from a working class background and her parents have minimal levels of education. She is more heavily focused on academic subjects leading to higher education studies.

Both girls acknowledge the value of an education but for Fatima it has extra special meaning. Most schools are poorly resourced in Sudan and participation rates for girls are very low—55% for primary schooling and a mere 32% for secondary schooling (Department of Immigration and Citizenship, 2007). Although she confesses to being rather inattentive in class Fatima says that schooling is opening up opportunities for her that did not exist in her birthplace. She appreciates being able to pursue her career interest in hairdressing through the school's vocational education program even though the course lacks a little of the hands-on approach to learning. Tanya aims to be a forensic scientist although at this stage she does not appear to have much idea of what is involved. Fatima on the other hand has a much better grasp of what it takes to become a hairdresser and gets plenty of practice at home braiding hair with family members.

Hanging in with school is not easy for students in financially stretched households. Fatima is very keen to take up part-time work whilst studying and Tanya suggests there is a good deal of peer pressure on her to drop

From deficits and deficiencies to strengths and capabilities

out of school and start earning cash in the part-time casual workforce of the fast-food and retail trades. It is difficult for young people to fully appreciate the long-term benefits of education especially when they lack the financial resources and, in some instances, the family support to continue with their schooling let alone contemplate higher education options. Her situation is not helped either by welfare policies, such as the New Start Allowance, which offer little financial assistance for low socioeconomic students to pursue post-school education and training options. The situation is especially acute for young people in rural and regional communities who have to leave home to access higher education studies in capital cities.

#3 Tony's story

Sixteen-year-old Tony is hooked on computer games and is keen to pursue a career in multi-media and graphic design. Now in year 11 at the City Campus of Federation High, Tony credits his mother for a good deal of his motivation to succeed in his schooling. A low income, single parent and early school leaver she has sacrificed much for her children.

'Mum puts big importance on education'

When I finished primary schooling, I moved with my mother to Federation City to join my sister. She had won a scholarship to a private boarding school but I missed out. I attended the West Campus of Federation High before coming to City Campus in year 11. They have good facilities here and there are a huge number of subjects to choose from. I'm doing visual communication, maths, English, VET, IT, PE and psychology. An average class size is about 15 to 20 students, although my psychology class has about twenty-five. I am interested in computer games, and when I leave school I would like to do something with multi-media and graphics. When I was younger I used to play a lot of games with my parents and I really enjoyed that. I got the chance to do animation clips in my other high school and I have a portfolio of my work. There are quite a few university courses heading towards animation, but not in Federation City, so I'm looking towards studying in a bigger city. The employment opportunities in Australia aren't great, but overseas there is web design and stuff like that.

This school has quite a bit to offer. The teaching methods are different, but when you get used to them it's okay. School's pretty relaxed here—more like a university. There's no uniform and people can come and go. But I prefer to have bells and uniform. Attendance is left up to the student. You start to be more independent and this will help us in future years. Most people prefer it this way, but they don't get as much learning out of it. I suppose that people from traditional schools are used to rules and structures and they might fall back a bit when they get to university. At City Campus you address teachers by their first name. They are not really your teacher but more like your mentor and you get on better with them. We are at the same level and feel more mature and responsible for our actions. We're not being kids anymore. It's a big step up from year 10 to year 11. There was no homework then, but now you get daily homework so we have to learn to study and revise. We are given study periods to do homework in the library and study lounges. But it's more of an individual thing and they are not really supervised. There are no strict rules what you do. If you don't use it wisely then you don't get your study done. You can choose the time and the place you do it. If you don't have a class till 10.30 you don't need to come till then. I usually just come to school and do my homework. You have access to books and resources that you don't have at home. In year 10 we did have a lot of career counseling things, and we have a pathway transitioning from year 11 and 12 to university.

What you do around your home is important to your schooling—like how you manage your leisure time and keep up with homework. I don't have a job because I don't have enough time to work. I have to create time for myself because things are always changing. You have to keep yourself in a good mental state. My mum is our primary carer and she is in the same position as me now because she has a traineeship with the Federation City Base Hospital. It's up to us kids to take care of ourselves so she doesn't get too stressed. Mum puts big importance on education. She dropped out at year 10, so she is trying to make sure that we get the most of it. The sort of things that might get in the way of me realizing my dream of doing what I want in life are the expectations of taking care of myself, managing my finances, and deciding what university to go to (Extract of a portrait prepared from a transcript of an interview with Tony on 29 February 2012).

Previously we have described how schools can contribute to the educational disadvantage experienced by students through practices of exclusion and discrimination but Tony's experience suggests they can also function in more humane and inclusive ways. Although Tony missed out on a scholarship to a local private college, he has confidence in his local public school which he believes has the resources to further his education in multi-media and graphics studies. Tony echoes what many of his peers are saying about advantages of studying in the Senior Campus of Federation City High. First, students are able to choose from a broad range of academic and vocational subjects (some offered off campus) that are relevant to their interests and aspiration. Second, smaller average class sizes allow students to receive more individual class support than usually occurs in secondary schools. Third, students in City Campus are not bound by the rigid dress codes and regulations that prevail in most traditional high schools. In the relaxed, adult-centered learning environment relationships are based more on trust and friendship and less on the institutional norms of traditional high schools which are inclined to foster a 'them' and 'us' mentality when it comes to student / teacher interactions. However, as Tony points out, students have to take responsibility for their actions and some students do not cope well with the greater freedom they enjoy in this setting.

Exercising control over his learning is important to Tony. 'I came here because I wanted to, not because I had to', he says. Angus (2012b) suggests that for many working-class and marginalized students school is 'somewhat like a foreign country in which they, their families and the people they know seem like outsiders who are not valued and respected' (p. 243). Notwithstanding the financial constraints Tony is likely to face in pursuing higher education options, he has a sense of purpose and direction in his schooling which owes a good deal to the culture of the City Campus and school leadership. The conception of educational disadvantage in terms of deficits that are basically beyond the control of the school is contested in this setting.

Tony's narrative challenges common but ill-informed assumptions about working-class parents who are often accused of not caring about school and showing little or no interest in their children's learning. In numerous interviews with young people we were told how much parents and carers wanted their children to succeed at school. At the very least, they want them to complete their formal schooling and gain a certificate of achievement. However, parents and carers like Tony's mother often lack the social, economic and cultural capital of middle-class parents to invest in their education. In these circumstances, the school becomes a major source of cultural capital for young people.

#4 Shirley's story

Sixteen-year-old Shirley lives apart from her parents in a supported housing center for young people run by a welfare agency of the Uniting Church. A strong independent spirit runs through her story. Now in year 10 at New Vision Community College Shirley has her sights firmly set on a university course and a career in events management—something she has wanted to do from her childhood days.

> *'All I know is that I have to get to year 12 and then university'*
>
> To be honest I've started to get sick of school over the last few months. The problem is just that there are students in the class who don't want to be here. They muck around and stop the rest of us learning and it's starting to get to me now. I am planning to do year 12 and then go on to university. I hear that year 11 is a whole heap better than year 10. I'm in the applied learning course this year but I'll be doing academic subjects next year. I was told that VCE was more for year 11 and 12. I don't know why I didn't pick it up but you can also do hospitality in year 11 and 12. My ambition is to have my own business organizing weddings and things. It's something I've wanted to do since grade 6. I didn't know the word for it but I love big fancy dresses and stuff. There's a new course next year at the university in event management. I plan to work for someone to begin with but then I want to start my own business. A lady

was supposed to get back to me about doing some work experience in the field but she never did.

I still see mum and dad regularly but things weren't too good for me there so I moved out. I have my own place in a supported accommodation centre run by UnitingCare. I'm allowed to be there for 2 years. I'll be 18 then and old enough to get my own place. It's so good there. They are amazing people. They teach you about money things and I'm learning cooking. It was very much my decision to get into events organization. My dad wanted me to be a fitness trainer like him but I didn't want to do that. I don't have any interest in sport. But my parents are happy with what I'm doing because they know I'm not going to be on the dole. I do part-time work at a curry house—next to Macca's.

A lot of research about my future pathways I've done myself and school is going to help me get there. All I know is that I have to get to year 12 and then university. That's all I've got my mind on at the moment. I am doing a special course at school where you learn about people with mental illnesses and disabilities. I didn't realize that in so many places there is no wheelchair access and I learnt sign language and that and yeah I found that really interesting. I don't find maths particularly interesting. I can't see where in life you are going to need to do one of those ridiculously long sums. But I do enjoy reading and writing a lot (This portrait was developed from a transcript of an interview with Shirley on the 22nd of August 2011).

Family rifts, separations and divorce can often derail young people's education but Shirley seems to have been able to cope with the breakdown in relationships with her family and sustain a commitment to her schooling. She has lived independently for some time but now gets on better with her parents who are supportive of her plans for the future. What stands out in her narrative is the strong sense of agency she projects in her account of her educational aspirations and career intentions. It was very much her decision to explore the possibilities of a business career in events management and to undertake a course which opened her eyes to the struggles facing people with physical and mental disabilities. It is somewhat surprising that she has been placed in an applied learning course in year 10 even though she will be required to do academic studies in year's 11 and 12 if she is to gain entrance through the normal avenues to university. Her experience illustrates the potentially damaging effect of tracking and streaming practices in the middle years of schooling where students can find themselves inadequately prepared for entry into academic courses in the senior years.

In common with most of the young people we interviewed, Shirley views education as the means to getting a job and securing a good living standard.

Contrary to some of the prevailing myths about students in low socioeconomic communities, finishing up on the dole is not a desirable outcome nor is long-term work in the fast food industry.

#5 Abigail's story

Fifteen-year-old Abigail is studying a combination of year 11 and 12 subjects at New Vision Community College. In the following portrait, she comes across as a highly motivated student with well-formed thoughts about where her schooling may take her and what she needs to do to become a vet.

'I just want to make my parents proud'

I try to do my best in school and aim for the highest I can get. I've been at here since year 7 and since year 8 I've been doing at least one class that is higher than my class level. This year I'm studying 6 subjects—year 12 English and year 11 legal studies, chemistry, maths methods, psychology and English literature. Next year I only have to do 5 subjects. My dad is a stay at home dad and my mum is a medical receptionist. I have two sisters, one in university studying nursing and the other one is year 9. I would like to do vet science at xxx University but if I can't get through with my tertiary admission score I will do a vet nurse course. I've had pets since before I was born—dogs, cats, ferret and fish. I like learning about animals and how to care for them. Last year I did work experience at a veterinary surgery and I really liked it but I can work my way up through being a vet nurse if necessary. I am willing to go to TAFE to get what I want to in the future because sometimes it can't be helped the marks you get. I did year 11 biology while I was in year 10 but this year I had to drop the subject to do chemistry which would be more useful in vet work. The careers lady last year helped my subject selection.

My family is very supportive of my plans. My older sister wanted to be a vet but then she lost interest. I didn't want to copy my sister. My grandparents are in Melbourne and they will give me a place to stay if I get to xxx University. I'm going to their open day later this year. I know I will have to leave Federation City for study but I would like to come back because my parents and friends are all here and if everything goes well I could set up a practice here. School takes me away from the worries at home and I get lost in the work that I do, especially the English. I don't think I'm so good at English but when it's handed back I'm better than I think. With the VCE there's a lot of work but I just do my homework every night after school. There is no time to do family stuff.

I do have quite high expectations. Since primary school I've done well and I don't want to fall behind. When my sister was in year 10 she fell back and my parents were disappointed. I don't want them to be disappointed in me. I do have some friends at school who want to do well. I don't have a part-time job but I do canoeing and that is my thing every Tuesday morning. I just want to make my parents proud. I want to be acknowledged for the stuff I do and that means getting good grades. My parents know I do well but I want to keep the grades up. They tend not to push me because they know that there is a lot of work and it's my drive to do well.

I haven't heard of anyone from New Vision going on to be a vet. Sometimes you do get discouraged because you are at a public school. Kids at private schools get everything handed to them so you do have to work harder here. My grades will be good but I know that private schools are expected to be higher and have more intelligent kids. Some people do have a bad impression of our school but I usually say that it's not like that really. It's not a bad school. You still get the same education as any other school. Some of the private schools manage to cover up the problems that get media coverage in public schools (This portrait was developed from a transcript of an interview with Abigail on the 27th of February 2012).

Abigail appears to be driven by several imperatives, not the least of these is pleasing her parents, doing them proud and not disappointing them as her sister did. But she also demonstrates her own sense of agency and determination—aiming for the highest she can achieve. She has researched her options well but is realistic enough to concede that the Australian Tertiary Admission Rank (ATAR) score needed to gain direct entry to a veterinary course in xxx University may elude her so she has mapped out an alternative pathway through vet nursing. Abigail makes some interesting observations about the negative media images of her school and the advantage students gain in elite, private schools. You have to work harder in a public school, she concedes.

Liam, Fatima, Tanya, Tony, Shirley and Abigail experience varying degrees of 'educational disadvantage' as a consequence of their socioeconomic circumstances, cultural and linguistic backgrounds, and (in the case of Liam) medical condition. They and many of their peers are often consigned to an 'at-risk category' of students by policy makers and educational administrators. However, what they have to say about their lives, interests and aspirations challenges a good deal of the deficit thinking about these young people and their parents. Whilst still in the throes of making decisions about their careers, they aspire to make something worthwhile of their lives. Generally they have faith in their schooling and believe that success in the senior years will lead to worthwhile and engaging pathways in higher education, training and employment. Teese and Polesel (2003) suggest we need to exercise some caution about these possibilities. They argue that although schools may reduce the demoralizing impact of economic and social degradation in local communities, this will not necessarily translate to better academic outcomes for students. Unlike elite private schools:

> ...poor schools have low levels of investment, both public and private. They are exposed on a wide front to economic and social disadvantage. [Yet] they are expected to manage the same curriculum used by elite schools and to compete with each other for globally high success and prestige. (p. 197)

With the best will in the world, poorly funded public schools struggle to provide the services and facilities to ameliorate the extent of educational disadvantage experienced by students, especially those with disabilities and special needs. Under current Federal Government funding arrangements, public schools in the poorest towns and suburbs are often the least well-resourced and the most disadvantaged while the richest private schools receive funds they cannot credibly claim to need (Sydney Morning Herald, 2012, 13 February). The task of achieving greater equality of opportunity for young people in the poorest neighborhoods of Federation City is daunting in the current political environment. Unlike wealthy miners, financiers and business elites, the poor, the marginalized and the educationally disadvantaged do not have lobbyists with huge bank accounts to speak on their behalf.

Concluding comments

In this chapter we have traced the ways in which discourses of disadvantage have influenced education policy and practices in schools and how in turn these have impacted on the learning identities of young people in low income neighborhoods. We have argued that the notion of 'disadvantage', as currently conceived by free marketers, has become a convenient label with which to describe the failings, weaknesses and deficiencies of individuals, families and communities in poor circumstances rather than to acknowledge any systemic problems within society. An alternative view, which we believe is well captured in the student narratives, is to understand the notion of disadvantage as constituting a set of constraints and limitations which necessarily influence, but not wholly determine, the identity formation of young people. The young people we interviewed possessed a high measure of agency, self-belief and determination to succeed in schooling that went a good way to dismantling the deficit constructions embedded in contemporary policy. Puncturing notions of disadvantage allows us to move beyond a preoccupation with deficits and deficiencies to a consideration of the strengths and capabilities of young people who have been placed at risk by the workings of an inequitable economic and social system.

We will revisit these issues again in the next chapter when we bring class out of the closet.

4. Bringing class out of the closet

Introduction

This chapter does not mince words—whether young people succeed or not educationally is very much influenced by their social class location—which is itself a social construction. It is time we stopped backing away from this reality and began to think beyond the fantasy that education is within the reach of all. Doing that requires that we confront and challenge some well-entrenched shibboleths, but as Varenne and McDermott (1999) put it in their book *Successful Failure*, 'It takes hard intellectual work to clear the decks for only a moment' (p. xi).

To set the stage for what is to follow in this chapter we want to acknowledge and build upon Varenne and McDermott's (1999) argument that it is difficult to think and talk about education and schooling 'without necessarily thinking about failure or success as categories for the identification of children' (p. xi). They make their point more directly when they argue that we 'have organized a terrible problem for ourselves' (p. xi) in the way we have made:

> ...individual learning and school performance the institutional site where members of each new generation are measured and then assigned a place in the social structure based on this measurement. (p. xi)

What invariably follows from this kind of positioning is a singular focussing of attention on 'a Johnny who can't read or a Sheila who can' (p. xiii)—something that Varenne and McDermott refuse to do. As they put it:

> Instead of searching for better ways to explain success and failure...[we need an] interpretive scheme by which success and failure are constantly reproduced as analytic and political categories even by those most dedicated to building the intellectual foundations of a better world...[S]chool success and failure are not simple consequences of the way the human world must be. It is a cultural mockup, what we call a cultural fact. The success and failure system, as a cultural fact, is

real in its connections to the political economy, exquisitely detailed in its connections with the everyday behavior of the people who make up the system. (p. xiii)

One of the ways in which we want to interrupt and puncture the fake way of thinking about what is (or is not) an educated person, is to look at the 'cultural mock-up' or the 'cultural fact' (p. xiii) that is called social class and how it does its ugly and deforming work in the way some young people get to be labelled as successful, while others failures. In large measure this comes down to the language we allow to be assigned to individual young people, like:

> ...skill, ability, disability, intelligence, competence, proficiency, achievement, motivation, self-esteem, objective test, grade level, and so on...

all of which amount to having the effect, at least for us, of the metaphorical equivalent of 'screeching fingernails on the theoretical chalkboard' (p. xiii).

In this chapter we are 'stepping out' somewhat by asserting that far from 'class being dead' (Pakulski & Waters, 1996), we ascribe to the view that it is very much alive and kicking and is having real effects on people's lives. In all likelihood, taking this position will bring us into conflict with those who argue that class has been overtaken by an egalitarian sensibility (see Smyth, Hattam & Lawson, 1998, p. 1), or that it has been superseded by the notion of meritocracy. Our broader agenda is, therefore, to advance how we might understand the notion of 'becoming educated' for young people who come from contexts where they have been *put at* a disadvantage, by looking at how class, identity and aspirations intersect within notions of space, place and neighborhoods around schooling. In this, we find it useful to come at class in the way Byrne (2005) approaches it—not by starting from what is contained in existing analyses of class—helpful though they might be in re-igniting the discussion of class—but rather, to start with what is missing from existing approaches. Byrne's (2005) point is that the 'cultural turn to class' (p. 807) that has involved 'individual experience and personal response' (p. 808), represents a major departure from economistic approaches to class that have focused largely on the nature of waged work. By focusing on the 'collective', the 'relational' and the 'contextual', brings into prominence the 'dialectical' and 'collective agentic potential of class' (p. 808)—albeit somewhat difficult to map this onto the lives of the young people who are the subject of our study.

What we want to be able to do in this regard, to paraphrase Byrne (2005), is to yield up something about how young people think, how they feel about work and their impending prospects of finding it, their identities in the places in which they live, how schooling is helpful or not in pursuing their aspirations, and how all of this is shaping their hopes for the future as they engage in the project of what we are calling 'becoming educated'. All of this is by way of saying that the 'generative mechanism' of class is 'expressed contingently in context' (Byrne, 2005, p. 810), notwithstanding that opportunities for young people from differential backgrounds are formed by global forces that have a powerful shaping effect. Invoking Byrne (2005) again, we are interested in the way class operates within the 'dynamic trajectories of ordinary lives' (p. 809) of young people. Byrne (2005) argues that far from being an 'ascribed' or caste-like immutable quality, rather class is something that is 'achieved' and 'ascribed' in the way groups of people live 'a system of inequality that is continually made and re-made' (p. 811). As Lawler (2005) put it, this conceptualization of class as 'dynamic', resides in, and is continually being 're-made in the large- and small-scale process of social life' through 'claims for entitlement (and of non-entitlement), through symbols and representations, and in the emotional and affective dimensions of life' (p. 797). None of this is to deny or in any way downplay the salience of the place of economics, but rather to underscore the need to engage with 'an undeniably necessary conflict among sources of identity' (Byrne, 2005, p. 814). As British Marxist Raymond Williams (1989) put it:

> I believe in the necessary economic struggle of the organized working class. I believe that this is still the most creative activity in our society…as well as the indispensable first means of political struggle…I believe that the systems of meanings and values which a capitalist society has generated has to be defeated in general and in detail by the most sustained kinds of intellectual and educational work. This is a cultural process which I called…'the long revolution'…a genuine struggle which was part of the necessary battles of democracy and of economic victory for the organized working class. People change, it is true, in the struggle and by action. Anything as deep as a dominant structure of feeling is only changed by active new experience. (pp. 75–76)

Why class is important in 'becoming educated'

In the context of how young people go about making something of themselves, or 'becoming educated', it could well be asked, as Zweig (2004) cryptically puts it in the title of his book, *What's Class Got to Do with It?* In the majority of the interviews we conducted with young people in this research, our experience was like that of Reay's (2005) in that 'while never mentioning class' (p. 915), the stories of these young people were heavily infused with desires, hopes, fears, feelings and emotions around 'ambivalence, inferiority and superiority' (p. 911)—all of which to some degree give us insights into how young people were viscerally experiencing their class location.

Given that our research was undertaken in an Australian context, a little background may be helpful especially as it bears on the relationship between social class and education. There is a long-standing mythology in Australia that we are an egalitarian country in which everyone is accorded 'a fair go'—the Australian idiom for equity of treatment and opportunity. Nothing could be further from the truth—at least, depending upon who we listen to. The official version, along with its subtle but invisible caveats, is:

> We're a thriving, prosperous nation with high rates of employment, good health and high educational attainment, but there are people who miss out on the resources and opportunities to fulfil their potential. Around 5% (or 640,000) of working age Australians continue to experience multiple disadvantage, and income inequality has grown steadily since the mid-1990s (Australian Social Inclusion Board, 2012).

As with any such global statements the devil is very much buried in the missing detail. The view from the 'pointy end'—those who are charged with dealing with the realities of inequality and poverty—is that there is a very different story to be told. In its recent report entitled *Poverty in Australia*, the Australian Council of Social Services (2012) reports among other things that:

- 2.265 million Australians (12.8%) are living below the poverty line
- 575,000 children (17.3%) are living below the poverty line
- there are in excess of 100,000 Australians who are homeless
- the level of poverty is highest outside of capital cities at 13.1%

The short story is that while inequality in Australia might not be as high as in the US, the gap has been widening in Australia and is reflected in geographic location. Since the onset of the global financial crisis (GFC), Australia has very much experienced a dual-track economy, with mining states like Western Australia and Queensland experiencing the fastest rates of economic growth and other parts of the country languishing.

Matters of inequality such as these have quite profound implications for education because of the way resources and opportunities link into educational outcomes and achievements. One of the complicating factors in Australia is the extent to which educational policy and reform have been driven by neoliberal ideas of competition and the prevailing belief in political and media circles 'that education is a competitive business and that excellence is derived by pitching schools and students in competition with each other' (Bonnor, 2012, p. 40). As Bonnor (2012) put it, this '…belief that success in schooling comes from competition drives policy and practice within schools as well as between them—regardless of consequences' (p. 40). This competitive emphasis places huge pressure on teachers and schools to perform, in a context where school choice is almost in hyperdrive—approximately 40%

of Australian secondary students attend non-government schools. Added to this, Bonnor (2012) argues, is the well-entrenched view that not only do 'parents believe they can outsource much of their child rearing responsibility to schools', but this occurs in a context where 'the actual contribution of teachers to learning is deliberately over-stated by those who prefer to forget about other impacts on student outcomes' (p. 42).

We can see the full effect of how social class positioning of students, school location and type operates educationally in a country like Australia, once we begin to pick apart the nature of the respective influences. As Bonnor (2012) writes:

> In Australia 55% of student achievement is related to family SES [socioeconomic status] and this is about average for the OECD. But on top of this there is an additional impact of the SES of schools, an impact which is particularly high in Australia; it takes the total SES impact up to 68%. (p. 42)

As a former Australian Federal Minister for Science quipped, in Australia educational success and subsequent life chances can be fairly easily ascertained through the answers to three simple questions: 'Where do you live? What school did you go to? What do your parents do'? (Jones, 2007, p. 15). Yet we still persist in publishing league tables (see Topsfield & Butt, 2012) that purport to show that educational achievement occurs by dint of individual effort, in the absence of any reference to the wider context.

Feeding this from both sides of politics, class denial continues unabated, with former conservative Australian Prime Minister John Howard saying 'Australia should never be a nation defined by class envy, but rather be a nation united by mateship and achievement', with his political rival and leader of the Australian Labor Party, Kim Beazley saying: 'In Australia, while there is always an element of class politics, the reality is that we are a very egalitarian society in spirit. We may not be in outcomes or experience, but in spirit, we all see ourselves as much the same' (Western & Baxter, 2007, p. 216).

Of course, this kind of argument becomes nonsense in a context where over one third of Australian students attend non-government schools that are funded by taxpayers—compared to only 6 percent in the US where they do not receive any government funding (Hirst, 2013). The notion that Australia is a more egalitarian society collapses when such a high proportion of parents believe that they can 'buy a better education for a child and isolate them in a privileged enclosure' (Hirst, 2013). Here is the rub: 'Australia still feels an egalitarian place. We are an informal people who treat each other as equals and we don't worship success as the Americans do' (Hirst, 2013).

There we have it! Beliefs trump the truth every time. It is certainly the case, as Glass (2008) put it, where 'facts are negotiable; beliefs are rock solid'. (p. xii)

In exploring what he posited might be the emergence of a 'new class paradigm'?, Savage (2003) noted a major shift among sociologists who had sustained the debate beyond the 'proclaimed end of class' (p. 535) in the UK. His point is that while class may no longer hold quite the same significance it did in the past as a 'visible marker of social differentiation' due in large measure to 'de-industrialization, the eradication of apprenticeship as a distinctive mode of training, and the declining fortunes of trade unions', these social changes have called forth a 're-working rather than the eradication of class' (p. 536). Where Savage's (2003) analysis is leading us is not in the direction of re-invigorating class as an arena for social conflict, but rather an opening up of the space for the exploration of 'the meaning of class [and] the nature of class consciousness' (p. 536). As he put it:

> Socially recognized class conflict dissipates into individualized identities in which those who live up to middle class norms see themselves as 'normal' people while those who do not see themselves (and are seen by the powerful) as individual failures. (p. 536)

What is occurring in effect is a re-positioning of relations in which 'middle class self-interest is couched as a universal good' to be aspired towards, and the default position is a 'kind of unacknowledged middle-class standpoint' (p. 536)—all of which suggests that 'these kind of class relations demand a new kind of critical social science' (p. 536). Where Savage departs is that he is thinking beyond structural analyses of class in quite a different and refreshing way, as he put it:

> It is now necessary to invoke a much more subtle kind of class analysis, a kind of forensic, detective work, which involves tracing the print of class in areas where it is faintly written. Above all, the innocence, the kind of unacknowledged normality of the middle class needs to be carefully unpicked and exposed. (pp. 536–537)

According to Reay (2005), this shift towards 'a new sociology of class… has begun to carve out a space for affective dimensions in analysis of class' (p. 913). Reay says that in the past this dimension has tended to be relegated to concerns within psychology, and her argument is that 'the psychic economy of class [is] a legitimate concern for sociology', and that what is needed is:

> …more understanding of how social class is actually lived, of how it informs our inner worlds…[and] how it shapes our life chances in the outer world. (p. 913)

What this approach opens up, Reay argues, is discussion about people's desires, anxieties, excitements, discomforts, fears and sense of shame—all of which are shaped in different ways according to identities held and resources available to be drawn upon. The bottom line for Reay (2005) is that all manner of 'psychic damage [is done by] social class inequalities' (p. 917).

This is a most appropriate frame of analysis in an area such as the one we are exploring in this book where we are looking at how young people make sense of the place of schooling in their lives, and what is helping or hindering them in accessing resources with which to pursue life chances and opportunities. What this perspective facilitates is what Reay (2005) identifies as the 'links between individuals' inner emotional worlds and the external social and structural processes' that are implicated in 'the fashioning of the self' (p. 923). Reay (2005, p. 924) invokes Kuhn's (2002) observation that 'Class is something beneath your clothes, under your skin, in your reflexes, in your psyche, at the very core of your being' (p. 117). What Reay is presenting us with, therefore, is a view of class that is 'deeply embedded in everyday interactions, institutional processes, in struggles over identity, validity, self-worth and integrity even when it is not acknowledged' (p. 924).

In his book *The Moral Significance of Class*, Sayer (2005a) confesses that the whole issue of class is an 'unsettling subject' mainly because of the negative feelings it brings forth and the emotional responses that Reay (2005) has alluded to. Sayer (2005a) says that this opens up 'one of the reasons so many societies are "in denial" about class—that many believe that it is inescapable, and that it is the price we have to pay for the alleged benefits of capitalism' (p. 213). This still begs the question 'can anything be done about class inequalities and the forms of misrecognition and discrimination that go with them'? (p. 213). While the bigger question around leveling up resource distribution is somewhat beyond our scope to answer here, the short answer from Sayer (2005a) is that we do not have to accept a fatalistic view (p. 213). In major part, Sayer (2005a) is arguing that 'We will understand class better if we stop reducing people to occupants of positions, or bearers or performers of class, etc., and attend also to their normative dispositions and beliefs, even though these only contingently affect the reproduction of class' (p. 225). He puts his argument most succinctly when he says, 'Although class is structural to capitalism, capitalism can function successfully with a good deal less economic inequality than occurs in societies such as the USA or the UK [and Australia] and with fewer barriers of symbolic domination...' (p. 230).

To draw together the argument we have been making so far as to why class is important in the project of young people 'becoming educated', Reay (2005) captured it neatly when she said:

> Schools are the repositories for all kinds of fantasies, fear, hopes and desires held by individuals and social groups...and consequently schooling is a fertile ground for exploring psycho-social and emotional aspects of classed identities. (p. 914)

When class is not named as such, or when there is a state of denial that it even exists (Lucey & Reay, 2000, p. 139), then what occurs is a kind of shadow boxing as we duck and weave so as to avoid the real issue. Until we acknowledge that class works profoundly on people's emotions and is 'etched into our culture [and]...into our psyches' (Lucey & Reay, 2000, p. 139), then it will be hard to explain how the 'psychic landscape of social class' (Reay, 2005, p. 912) operates on young people's aspirations and capacities to succeed educationally. As Sayer (2005b) expressed it, social class is about 'moral worth' and 'boundary drawing' (p. 947), and when people make evaluations of themselves and have evaluations ascribed to them by others, this has real effects on their subjectivities, their lives, and their lived situations.

Stepping up to the 'injuries of class'

While we certainly do not subscribe to views that would in any way understate the importance of the damage being done in creating 'spoiled identities' (Goffman, 1963) as a result of interfering with human flourishing—neither, do we subscribe to the pessimistic position that would have the situation as being unalterable. Sennett and Cobb (1977) were correct in alerting us to the sinister workings of power and the way it acts to conceal the means by which social relations are distorted and deformed as a result of the disrespectful treatment of some social groups, compared to others. What we take from Sennett and Cobb's analysis of working class experience, is that when people fail to succeed in a patently unfair and inequitably structured world, the tendency is for individuals to respond by wearing an unwarranted level of individual guilt and culpability in not advancing up what is an unequal ladder of opportunity. To illustrate their point, Sennett and Cobb (1977) describe 'how teachers and students deal...with badges of ability' (p. 79) as 'hidden cues' (p. 82) put out by the school and acted upon differentially by students. In referring to a school located in a working class neighborhood, Sennett and Cobb say that 'by the time the children are ten or eleven the split between the many and the few who are expected to "make something" of themselves is out in the open' (p. 82). While 'ordinary' students might 'not consciously

[be] in conflict with the school...something more complex is happening' (p. 82). As they put it:

> These 'ordinary boys' in class act as though they were serving time, as though schoolwork and classes had become something to wait out, a blank space in their lives they hope to survive and then leave. Their feeling, apparently, is that when they get out, get a job and some money, *then* they will be able to begin living. It is not so much that they are bored in school—many...like their classes. It is rather that they have lost any expectation that school will help them, that this experience will change them or help them grow as human beings. (pp. 82–83)

While there is a good deal of literature around the classed response of middle-class parents to schooling (Ball, Maguire & Macrae, 2000; Reay, 1996) and to some extent the part played by teachers as classed actors (see Smyth, 2012a), there has been less exploration of how young people themselves, mostly those who regard themselves as 'ordinary kids' (Brown, 1987), react, respond and mediate the working of class power in their engagement with schooling. Reay's (2005) work is the exception here, in the way she portrays injury and damage as being perpetrated through educational policies of 'increasing surveillance and regulation of...learning' through testing and assessment focused on 'raising the achievement of working class children' (p. 916). Smithers (2000), for example, found students in the UK can expect to confront in excess of '75 tests and exams during their school careers' (Reay, 2005, p. 916)—with many students reportedly being 'frightened...[that] I'll be a nothing' or anxious that 'I might not have a good life in front of me' (Reay, 2005, p. 916) as a result of their test performance. For Reay (2005), this is indicative of a 'psychic economy of class' which is being mediated through 'fear, anxiety and unease', in a context 'where failure looms large and success is elusive' (p. 917). Clearly, injustice is being incubated here even at a relatively early age, with working class students having 'already internalized the judgments of a pernicious, inequitable education system' (p. 917) in which the resources needed to succeed, are inequitably distributed, and the students have learnt who is valued and who is not.

Reay's (2005) analysis is that the 'psychic damage of class inequalities' (p. 917) is done through 'reductionist discourses in which clever becomes correlated with middle class and stupid with working class' (p. 918)—an occlusion that becomes solidified or ossified through petty forms of 'humiliation' and other 'slights of social class' (p. 918), as mentioned by students, for example:

- 'being looked down on' (p. 918) by teachers because they speak or present differently to middle-class students, and therefore, could not possibly have the qualities with which to become educated;

- not being 'treated fairly by the teachers' (p. 918), in the sense that teachers favor and spend more time with smarter and better performing students who are perceived as being brighter and cleverer (and also more middle-class);
- allocating working class students to lower ability groups, even when they are higher achievers, so as to confirm 'commonsense understandings of ability' (p. 918).

As we mentioned earlier in this chapter, class positioning not only works at the level of the individual and the family, but where a school is located powerfully informs presumptions about who goes there, what goes on inside, and what kind of places such schools must be. We know, for example, that schools in poorer areas are not only often less well resourced, but they are also seen as less attractive places for many teachers to work in because of working conditions, perceptions of career trajectories, and the day-to-day difficulties of teaching students from complex backgrounds. At the level of the students in these schools, there is often also another struggle they have to engage in around contesting the notion that they are attending a 'rubbish' school in which it is impossible for them to achieve. As Reay (2005) put it, what these students have to do is develop a sense of 'optimism...hopefulness and ambivalent defensiveness' (p. 920) in speaking back to often unwarranted public prejudices and perceptions about the nature of their school. This is something that came out starkly in one of our research schools (New Vision 7–12 Community College), in which the students found themselves having to be defensive in speaking back to a knifing incident that had been beaten up by the media in order to disparage the school. Reay (2005) refers to this as 'disput[ing] dominant representations' in which the school is presented in a 'powerfully classed' way intended to convey by 'association, invidious and judgmental understanding of children like them' (p. 920).

Not to be under-rated in importance, Reay (2005) argues, are 'the emotional costs of becoming different' (p. 921)—for that is what is often involved when working class kids succeed educationally. The notion of having to become 'different' is a refrain we hear often, both from students of color as well as those from backgrounds different from the middle-class norms of schooling. Some writers refer to it in the radicalized context as 'becoming white' (Fordham & Ogbu, 1986; Ogbu, 2003) while others frame it as 'class suicide' (hooks, 2000). These students express what occurs as like having to expunge or erase something in order to take on a different persona, and it comes at a considerable personal cost around ambivalent feelings of loss associated with deserting their class backgrounds. The way it works, as one of Reay's (2005) informant's put it, is that their difference makes them feel like they 'stick out like a sore thumb' (p. 921). In aspiring to or transiting to further and higher forms of education, for example, there are feelings that they don't belong, that they are out of place, and the consequence can be one of avoidance, because these are places where people like them do not go to. Their middle-class peers by contrast, are able to construct a fairly seamless compelling narrative around their expected educational trajectory with 'an easily discernible plot and a clearly defined beginning and an end, despite episodic uncertainty and stressful periods' (Reay, 2005, p. 922). In other words, middle-class students are able, among other things, to draw upon a discourse of 'entitlement and self-realization' that is relatively free of any 'lurking guilt or shame' (p. 922). While there are undeniable and understandable feelings of euphoria, optimism, 'excitement, satisfaction and pride' (p. 922) among working class students who succeed, this is severely tempered by opposing fears of the unknown or, as one of Reay's informants put it, of not having 'any safety nets any more' and of being scared 'if the worst happens' (p. 922). For Reay, in many respects, these young people have the worst of two worlds—they are 'caught between two opposing shames'—on the one hand 'of over-reaching and failing' and therefore proving that they are not good enough, while at the same time having deep feelings of 'shame and embarrassment' (p. 923) of where they have come from.

The making over of a 'residualized' school

One of the defining imperatives of the neoliberalisation of schooling that has been underway for several decades in most western countries, has been the process of school improvement that has been framed around the metaphor and practices of the market. In the new scheme of schooling, schools are expected to perform according to targets or standards, or they will be put out of business—literally, closed, teachers sacked, the school re-named and opened under new auspices, or sold off to the private sector. This process of brutalization has had quite profound implications for schools serving working class families. One of the ways this is occurring is through what Schostak (2000)[1] refers to as a 'process of purifying' (p. 42)—in essence, a process of re-inventing a school around a different narrative and removing what is considered to be 'superfluous', 'wrong' or 'waste' (p. 42).

During the period of our research interviews (2010–2012), New Vision Community College was undergoing what might euphemistically be labeled a process of 'modernization', but which realistically amounted to a not-so-subtle form of purification. Vestiges of the old school culture were being obliterated and something new inserted in its place. What was considered by some parts of the media and the community, possibly inaccurately and unfairly, to be a secondary school that was not particularly consumer-attractive, was being re-constituted around a corporatized image of a strictly enforced school uniform policy, a muscular behavior management and discipline policy, and a rhetorical insistence on a level of school attendance punishable by the imposition of failing grades for excessive school absences. But as Schostak (2000) notes, any process of imposing categorizations in order to make individuals 'fit in', inevitably produces 'a waste product...[that] has to be dealt with in some way as a rejected aspect of experience that can find no acceptable place within the subjectivity of the individual' (p. 42). Schostak's underlying point is that: 'what is "left out" does not simply go away, but returns as a politics of the "left out", the residual' (p. 42).

Let us carry forward the conversation about the 'makeover' of New Vision Community College that was seeking to re-invent itself, through the lives of some young people who were engaged in making an identity for themselves in and around the kind of classed issues mentioned so far in this chapter.

Young people rarely discuss their class location explicitly but they do talk about their neighborhoods, family backgrounds, friends and school experiences in ways which give some clues as to how they (and others) position themselves in the social hierarchy. Lydia (year 11) comes from a low socioeconomic background and resides in a neighborhood (Litchfield Crescent) that has been variously categorized as dangerous, welfare dependent, and dysfunctional. Whether or not she stays on at school seems to hinge on a battle of wills between Lydia and her mother and the pressure from her friends to leave before completing a secondary school certificate. Breaking free from these binds may be difficult without access to social capital and a very supportive school system. At the moment she is confused about her further education and employment options and has difficulty envisioning a future outside her immediate neighborhood.

> *'All my friends will probably leave school before year 12'*
>
> I'm 15 years of age and I'm in year 10 at New Vision Community College. I play soccer and enjoy photography at school. I like school. Mum wants me to go straight through but I want to leave half way through year 11. I dunno why I want to do that but I want to be a vet. It was childcare once but then I changed it to being a vet. I like animals. I've got birds, two dogs and fish. Mum told me I have to finish year 12 and do 6 years of university to become a vet but I'll try to get some part-time work when I leave school. All my friends will probably leave before year 12 but I might change my mind if they decide to stay on. My dad doesn't know I want to leave. I live in a housing commission area [public housing] but I don't know much about the people in the

neighborhood. I don't really take any notice of what they do. My dad doesn't have a job. He does nothing. Whether I stay in school or not depends on how my grades go. At the moment they're good. I'm doing well. When I finish I'll pretty much stay in this neighborhood. I know this area better than any other place (Interview with Lydia, New Vision Community College, 5th May 2011).

Elisha (year 12) has a passion for horse riding and has her sights set on being an instructor. However, she is astute enough to realize that horse riding won't get her into university. With considerable support and encouragement from her parents she has embarked on an academic certificate course (VCE) which she hopes will lead to tertiary studies in horse management. How working class students envision their future is influenced in no small measure by the schooling they encounter. Elisha points to a social divide between students studying courses leading to university (VCE) and those engaged in applied learning (VCAL) programs. She says that many students are shunted into vocationally oriented studies. We suggest that working class kids are conditioned through discriminatory sorting/streaming practices and hegemonic curriculum to believe that they are non-academic and better suited to hands-on learning. (Note the limited vocational / employment options which Elisha imagines for girls.) Schools engaging in these practices are complicit in the reproduction of social / economic inequality. This is reinforced by widespread public perception that Elisha's school caters for the non-academic students—those from working class backgrounds. Elisha claims that peer pressure is a major reason why some students leave school before completing year 12 but it was quite apparent from our interviews that a considerable number leave because of the institutional pressures brought to bear on them.

'Horse riding won't get me into uni'.

This school needs to concentrate on academic learning more because we are becoming a vocational education school. Some teachers encourage students to do VET subjects—that's only my opinion. And it's the easy option. I'm pretty sure that the academic kids look down on the non-academic students.... I think education is important when you start having your own family. My dad needs some help to do things sometimes. Our parents don't want us to make the same mistakes. I think there is pressure on kids to give up school within the friendship groups. There were four boys in year 11. One dropped out and got an apprenticeship and another one got an apprenticeship and then there were two left and then they both left. It can be different for a girl. It depends on what the girl is looking for—hairdressing, beauty or childcare (Interview with Elisha, New Vision Community College, 6th June 2011).

The importance of social capital comes to the fore in the following portrait. Tapping into her interest in science, Crystal (year 12) appears to have mapped out a path to becoming an educated person. She seems to be less influenced by her peers than some of her classmates and is quite single-minded in her determination to succeed at school. Crystal has a large measure of family support for her aspirations and has access to institutional resources to further her learning. Unlike Lydia, she has an awareness of what she must do at school to gain entry to higher education—in her case a course in forensic science. Crystal raises the issue of social class and the public / private divide in schooling. She acknowledges that rich kids attending elite private schools have an advantage in the education stakes but she is determined to prove that she can succeed against the odds. As with many of her peers, she expresses pride in her school and challenges the negative media representations of New Vision Community College.

> *'My education is really important to me'*
>
> My mum's a psychiatric nurse and my dad's a maintenance guy. I like the fact that mum's got the whole job thing going on. I've looked at both sides of their work, the hands on and the other way of doing things. I'm going to a public school and I want to prove people wrong about their expectations. I am exposed to a lot of different life stories here and not just rich kids. I'm not sure how my mum managed to go to uni but she has done study. It was more hands on in those days. I am pretty focused about my studies and haven't lost sight of where I want to go. I want to be a good role model for my little brother.... There are always obstacles in pursuing what you want to do in education. The kids that don't want to learn in school get the most attention but you have to concentrate on your work and make it all about you.... There are a lot of kids doing applied learning certificates going through this year—about half—which is really good. It used to be a tech school. I feel like I really belong in this school.... The pictures on the front foyer honor boards show how proud we are of our school. I don't think that we have the best reputation out there. People have just closed their eyes. When we had the stabbing here a few years ago the local newspaper said how bad it was. It's tough to break through that reputation. Some kids have been told that they can't do it so they don't try. I help a couple of boys in my year and try to get them motivated. I don't feel at all hopeless because I like to prove people wrong (Interview with Crystal, New Vision Community College, 7th June 2011).

The classed identities of young people manifest themselves through the culture, structures and institutional norms in schools. In the following portrait, Brett (year 11) gives a most insightful account of the impact of a regulatory regime at New Vision Community College instituted by the newly appointed principal who seems determined to re-invent a working class school around middle-class norms and business practices. Unlike some of his peers, Brett can see through the rhetoric of school improvement targets and the push to instill a work place ethos in students. 'I don't see why we have to be run like a business', he says. Whilst Brett admits that the reduction in behavior problems has led to a better learning environment, as the 'hard cases' have moved on, he is concerned that the attendance and dress code regulations take little account of the complexity and dire circumstances of many kids' lives.

Disciplinary technologies in schools reinforce the practices of exclusion writ large on the lives of students from low socioeconomic circumstances. Brett has a sense of justice and shows empathy for the students 'pushed out' or 'eased out' of school as a consequence of the disciplinary powers operating through the institutional structures and processes of school. Perhaps his past history of resistance and school suspension gives him more of an insiders' understanding of their dilemmas.

'I don't see why we have to be run like a business'

I'm 16 years of age and I've been at school here since year 7. I've got 5 brothers and sisters and I'm the third youngest. My mum's a nurse and dad's a supply manager for the railways. I don't mind coming to school. I guess I've just got to keep going with my studies. I hope to finish year 12 and then take a year off and join the navy. My aunty has been in the navy for years now and it sounds pretty good. To get in you have to put your name down and have interviews. There are certain requirements, like good medical stuff and so on. I would like to become an electrical engineer. The navy, they will put you through anything that you want to do. This should set me up for life because if I leave I can go anywhere. Year 12 is a bit more demanding than last year but I'm managing okay. I'm doing VCE chemistry, physics, maths methods, psychology, and VET engineering. My family and friends are totally supportive of my choice of a career. I'm not stressed out at all. I work as a cash-in-hand farm laborer and I also do martial arts. Running around in short shorts with big sweaty men doesn't appeal to me [his reference to Australian Rules football].

I see this school as probably one of the best scholastic schools as public schools go. The teachers are really good but we have strict rules now. One of them is the 95% attendance rate. You can fail your course if you don't meet this. I don't see why we have to be run like a business. If you take a day off school you have to have a doctor's certificate. You don't even have to have that in the work place. Last year was very good and the attendance rate was 80%. The new principal is driving all this change in uniforms and attendance. The shoes we are expected to wear are the most uncomfortable things ever. He's on a bit of a crusade to make this the best public school in Federation City. It seems a bit drastic to me. The kids who have family problems at home won't be able to meet the attendance figure. Life is really difficult for some kids. I know a lot of parents who charge their kids rent to stay in their house. Some kids come from welfare or the parents could be pricks. There have not been many cases where students have spoken out against the new rules. We've discussed it with the teachers but if we had an argument with the principal we'd get suspended. I praise myself for trying to keep calm in this situation. Anger management classes don't work. We don't have a time-out room for kids who misbehave. Usually you get a warning or you get sent out to another class. I know there are four or five stages before suspension. I've only been suspended twice. There's always a few tensions and personal problems with the changes in the school.

I don't like the new principal. He's like a Jack Russell in a suit. He's got a little dog syndrome and makes up for it with a big bark—like my dad. Jack Russells are vicious little buggers and they bark a lot. I like to think I have a different mindset to other students on these things. I reckon you should respect people above you but don't think they are better than you. I guess there are some positives. Under the new regime a lot of behavior issues have been snuffed out because of the rules. A lot of the hard cases have left and it's probably become a better school but I don't like the way he went about it. I have been thinking that the school's more like a penitentiary and I'm thinking about putting a number on my overalls. Some of the teachers agree with my view which is not a good thing seeing that they are working for the bloke. There are other changes too. In every lesson we now have this thing called a 'learning intention'. Teachers discuss what we are going to learn, how we are going to use it and then how we are going to do it. They write it up on the board. We don't have much say about the learning intent. Teachers just write it up from the syllabus that we have to learn each semester. I can see the benefits of that for the exams and you need a bit of interpretation in some classes but a lot of it in mixed methods is irrelevant (Interview with Brett, New Vision Community College, 28th February 2012).

Riley (year 11) wants to pursue a career in psychology and appears to be well aware of the entry requirements and the demanding nature of the studies. In his stereotyping of the social backgrounds and dispositions of students in his school Riley confirms what we already know about the academic / vocational divide operating in his school. He disparages the applied learning certificate students consigning them to a class of 'muck-abouts' who have little interest in schooling. A sense of entitlement and self-realization is discernible in Riley's words. He does not want anything to stand in the way of him achieving his academic goals. Getting rid of the 'trouble makers'—the 'westies' and kids from housing commission estates (something we will turn to shortly)—is a good thing, because it means that he will get a greater share of his teacher's attention.

'The smarter ones do the academic course'

I want my schooling to take me into psychology and at this point I am looking at about 10 more years of study. I need a Master's degree to get into the field and then I need to work under a psychologist, therapist or clinical psychologist. I wanted to be a lawyer for several years but I've given up on that idea. This year I'm studying maths methods, psychology and two courses of English. I am happy how year 11 is working out for me but there is a lot of homework. The moment you get into it everyone is starting to enjoy it. The new principal helps as well. He is strict but he is fair. The people who are mucking around are getting kicked out and it becomes a better environment. They generally don't show up anymore.

> Most of kids mucking up in primary school end up doing applied learning studies. The smarter ones do the academic course. Applied learning people are rude—but that's stereotyping really (Interview with Riley, New Vision Community College, 28th February 2012).

In an interesting commentary on the place of resources in the aspirations of working class students, Abigail (year 11) makes the point that schools like hers are positioned such that they have to out-perform more affluent private schools just to dispel public misperceptions. As a conscientious, highly motivated student, keen to please her parents, Abigail has researched a number of possible vocational options, but she is in no doubt that students like her have to work even harder to prove themselves, and that the private schools have the luxury of being able to hide their problems—meaning that people are prepared to forgive their mishaps, where schools like her's are castigated. She makes this point in regard to the public/private school divide and social class.

'It's not a bad school'

> I haven't heard of anyone from New Vision going on to be a vet. Sometimes you do get discouraged because you are at a public school. Kids at private schools get everything handed to them so you do have to work harder here. My grades will be good but I know that private schools are expected to be higher and have more intelligent kids. Some people do have a bad impression of our school but I usually say that it's not like that really. It's not a bad school. You still get the same education as any other school. Some of the private schools manage to cover up the problems that get media coverage in public schools (Interview with Abigail, New Vision Community College, 27th February 2012).

What is a westie?

Bubbling not far below the surface of many of the accounts from the young people we interviewed, were stereotypical classist comments referring to 'troubling images' (Cochran-Smith & Lytle, 2006) that ascribed disparaging identities to young people from a particular type of social background and the implications these had for education. The often used Australian shorthand, is of a 'westie', explained thus:

> A westie is like a bogan. It started in [the Western part of Federation City] but it's evolved to include people who steal and stuff. It's more about personality and lifestyle, not their conditions. There's not much of the westie element in this school now (Interview with Quentin, New Vision Community College, 28th February 2012).

> The new principal is pretty good. He's kicked the westies out. He just expels them. When they leave they do nothing but sit around at home (Interview with Bruce, New Vision Community College, 27th February 2012).

The Macquarie Dictionary [Urban Dictionary, 2013] says the term 'westie' in Australian English now refers to people from the outer suburbs that display a lower socioeconomic background, or to the stereotypes associated with such people. It also states that the term has spread throughout Australia and may be used to refer to people who may not live in the western part of their city. With reference to its use in Sydney, the Macquarie Slang Dictionary (Lambert, 2002) says 'the term is applied negatively to anyone that may live west of one's own suburb' (p. 261). The term 'westie' is often used to associate someone or something with a stereotype that depicts people from the outer suburbs as 'unsophisticated', unintelligent, undereducated, unmotivated, unrefined, 'uncouth', lacking in fashion sense, working-class or unemployed. Westie is also affiliated with wearing distinctive clothing such as 'flannelette shirts and Ugg boots' (p. 261), leopard-print fabric, Adidas outfits, and black t-shirts and ripped jeans are often regarded as the uniforms of the westies. In the Federation City context, the term 'westie' is often applied in a disparaging way to those living in a low income, housing commission neighborhood of the city [specifically, in the western part of the city]. However, from what the students told us it refers more generally to anyone whose behavior and demeanor does not fit with accepted norms. Students and families living in poor circumstances are often also referred to as 'feral', 'povs', 'bogans', or 'welfare bludgers'. At school they are regarded as unmotivated, trouble makers who don't comply with school rules.

A disparaging (and an accompanying unprintable) set of remarks about westies from the Urban Dictionary (www.urbandictionary.com/define.php?term=westie) portrays them as:

> A very under mannered person dealing in drugs and wearing raggy clothes eg: Dada!!!! Mainly found in [the west of Federation City]. (Untrustable People!) 'Get out of my garbage bin you fucking westie, it's not my fault you couldn't be fucked picking up your Centerlink payment'. A westie is a person that wears clothes such as dada, starts fights..., deals and uses drugs. The male version of a westie, can vary, having tattoos, piercings, is involved with more than one girl and is most likely a father to a child somewhere. The female version of a westie, tends to have more than one child to many different fathers, they may have tattoos and piercings and tend to mouth off at other females. Westies are generally found in [the west], but can also be found in other commission houses in the [Federation City] area. They have common unoriginal names such as Steph and Joe.

Note

1. We are most grateful to Reay (2004, p. 1011) for drawing our attention here to Schostak's most helpful work.

5. Celebrating space, place and neighborhoods

Introduction

In this chapter our starting point is one that is markedly at variance with the ways in which neighborhoods are usually portrayed or thought about in poor or disadvantaged areas. They are invariably regarded as 'problem' places that are dysfunctional and that need to be fixed. This is not to say that neighborhoods officially designated as being 'disadvantaged' do not have very considerable material and social issues in need of urgent attention. Our approach, however, departs significantly from official approaches that write off neighborhoods experiencing difficulties as 'basket cases' and that 'red-line' them so as to target them with 'solutions' to supposedly 'fix' the problem. We think this is a demeaning and wrong approach.

The chapter is organized into two parts. First we dissect and contest the negative construals of poor neighborhoods presented as unmitigated 'bundles of pathologies' (Warren, Thompson & Saegert, 2001) requiring resuscitation and in desperate need of being 'fixed up'. Second, we proceed in the direction of developing what Wacquant (2008) refers to as some new 'tools for rethinking...marginality' (p. 8) based on the view that neighborhoods possess 'rich cultural traditions and social resources that have much to offer the work of schools' (Warren, 2005, p. 135).

Contesting the deficit discourse

Our starting point here is theoretically anchored in Lefebvre's (1991) argument that spaces are not neutral in the sense that they are 'thing like' and able to be manipulated and fetishized. As Lefebvre (1991) cogently put it 'space…serves as a tool of thought and action [and] in addition to being a means of production it is also a means of control, and hence of domination, of power…' (p. 26). Wacquant (2008) adds that neighborhoods are not simply 'zones of regulation' or 'spatial containers' (p. 11) into which people's lives are poured. The logic seemingly behind the 'container' view is that neighborhoods of disadvantage, are places in which people who have had unfortunate life experiences need to be sequestered or hidden away, during which they are to be 'treated' programmatically. One of us summarized it as follows:

> Neighborhoods, are not simply benign dormitory spaces in which people reside, and from which they commute to and from if they have work, or points from which they access services if they are not part of the paid workforce. Nor are neighborhoods places to be homogenized, categorized, castigated, and used as compliant sites for government social experimentation. On the contrary, neighborhoods are places in which people live out their aspirations, where opportunities are constructed and contested, but also places in which peoples' worst fears and nightmares become realized and crystallized, and where neoliberalism has produced what Bauman (2011) calls 'collateral damage' through the ways in which distant forces of globalization, de-industrialization and economic re-structuring do their ugly deforming work. (Smyth & Wrigley, 2013, pp. 76–77)

There are a number of fundamental problems with the 'container' way of thinking about neighborhoods, or what Wacquant (2008) refers to as 'enclaves for marginais' (p. 11)—by which he means, those who experience 'group stigma and collective taint' (p. 11) in which they are represented as 'victims of regressive deindustrialization' and who, as a consequence, are 'foresaken to their fate in an informal street economy increasingly dominated by criminal activities and the entropic violence they generate' (p. 11).

When the view is allowed to prevail in ways that legitimate 'neighborhoods of relegation' (Wacquant, 2008, p. 11), which in essence is what occurs when labels like 'disadvantaged' are unproblematically promulgated, then there is a profound change in the nature of relationships. What gets to be enacted are 'rituals of marginality' that have the effect of binding people so labeled 'to the governing elite' (p. 11). In other words, when a hierarchical set of relationships are spoken into existence between inhabitants who are designated as 'clients', and 'public officials and agencies, schools and hospitals, housing and social welfare, fire fighting and transportation, the courts and police' (p. 11) who are positioned as the 'fixers', then the relationship becomes one in which the two are inextricably bound to one another in a dependent relationship. On the one hand, so-called 'clients' are deemed to be deficient and in need of recuperation, and on the other hand, officials and agencies become dependent on clients for their very existence to provide programs and 'solutions'. When the problem is naturalized in a way that makes it appear logical that the former have defects that can only be remediated by the latter, then the real nature of the dependency becomes obscured or laminated over. We want to trouble or worry this obscurity.

Whereas poverty in western countries was envisaged not that long ago as something that was 'largely residual or cyclical', which is to say temporary in nature, and to that extent 'embedded in working class communities' that would be corrected as a result of 'further market expansion', we seem to have moved a long way from that now in terms of something much more akin to what Wacquant (1999) calls long term 'advanced marginality' (p. 1640). Wacquant (1999) argues that what makes advanced marginality distinctive is the fact that it is characterized by 'rigid or rising spatial and social separation', largely on the basis of class, in a context in which 'social isolation and alienation feed upon each other as the chasm between those consigned there and the rest of society deepens' (p. 1640). Most importantly, Wacquant (1996) argues that 'the qualifier "advanced" is meant to indicate that those forms of marginality are not *behind* us and being progressively reabsorbed…by "free market" expansion…but rather that they still stand *ahead of us*' (p. 123 emphases in original).

Wacquant (1999) depicts what is occurring in this advanced stage of marginalization as being fuelled by four interacting and dynamic logics. First, there is a dynamic around 'the resurgence of social inequality' in which 'spectacular material betterment' during a period of 'sturdy growth' has been experienced by more privileged groups, at the same time as one of the greatest upswings ever witnessed among the 'homeless and destitute' (p. 1641). As Wacquant (1999) explains it, what appears to be occurring is a 'decoupl[ing] from cyclical fluctuations in the national economy' (p. 1642) with the accompanying danger, that:

> Unless this disconnection is somehow remedied, further economic growth promises to produce more…dislocation and depression among those thrust and trapped at the bottom of the emerging…order. (p. 1642)

Second, there is the 'economic dynamic', or 'the mutation of waged labor', that has both a 'quantitative' aspect—the rendering redundant of 'millions of low-skilled jobs' to automation and low cost foreign competition—at the same time as a 'qualitative' aspect, comprising the 'degradation' of 'basic conditions of work' for 'all but the most protected workers' (Wacquant, 1999, p. 1642).

Third, there is the 'political dynamic' around social policies that are not only seeking to ameliorate the worst excesses of inequality, but which perversely end up possibly worsening it by determining 'who gets relegated, how, where and for how long' (Wacquant, 1999, p. 1642). This becomes further exacerbated when responsibilities are shifted from governments dealing with such matters, to 'the incipient privatization of social policy' (Wacquant, 1999, p. 1643)—which is to say, private agencies competing with one another for market share while preying in a predatory way on the unfortunate situations of those already marginalized under rubrics such as allegedly 'serving their needs'.

Fourth, there is the 'spatial dynamic' in which the 'new marginality displays a distinct tendency to conglomerate in and coalesce around "hard core", "no go" areas that are clearly identified—by their own residents, no less outsiders—as…hellholes rife with deprivation, immorality and violence where only the outcasts of society would consider living' (Wacquant, 1999, pp. 1643–44). The effect is that these become places of 'territorial stigmatization' in which the inhabitants have 'discourses of demonization…firmly affixed' (Wacquant, 1999, p. 1644) to them. In the Australian context, for example, the discourse of derision deployed is to describe such people as 'westies' (most poor areas are in the western suburbs of Australian capital cities and larger towns), or 'bogans' (Nichols, 2011), or 'chavs' (Jones, 2011) as they are referred to in the UK. The spatial stigmatization that accompanies this kind of labeling is often accompanied, Wacquant (1999) argues, with a 'weakening of territoriality' based on strategies of 'distancing ("I am not one of them")' which further acts to 'undermine local solidarities and confirm deprecatory perceptions of the neighborhood' (p. 1644), even while being worn as a badge of honor in some instances by some inhabitants—but more about that later.

As Wittgenstein (1977, p. 55) perceptively noted, 'concepts may alleviate mischief or they may make it worse; foster it or check it' (cited in Wacquant, 1996, p. 123). One such notion that is pertinent here, and that in our view works to worsen the situation in poor areas, is to portray poor areas as being 'residual'—in the sense that they constitute 'remaining pockets of disadvantage in an otherwise functioning system' (Lupton, 2010, p. 122). This is one of the problems that comes with trying to label areas of 'comparative social disadvantage' that rank localities according to statistical indicators within postcode areas (see Vinson, 2007, p. xvii). Where we end up when we accept this 'areas of concentrated disadvantage' approach that 'assigns a single score to each locality' (p. ix), is with the misleading perception that social disadvantage is a phenomenon 'entrenched within a limited number of localities'

(Vinson, 2007, p. ix). This approach also opens the scope for programmatic area-based interventions, which we turn to now.

Speaking back to pathological views: area-based interventions as an exaggerated faith in a 'solution', or exacerbation of the 'problem'?

What we have been doing so far in this chapter is sketching out the background parameters that constitute the limitations as well as the possibilities for educational change in poor neighborhoods. We would argue that we need to understand something of the complexity of the broader social policy trajectory, and how it is positioned, if we are to understand the policy impact on young people and possible alternative policy options.

The social policy rationale, especially in countries like Britain and Australia, is that if geographical areas of poverty and disadvantage can be identified, then a key aspect that follows is the 'targeting [of] extra resources on those geographic areas that are experiencing the severest problems...[and thus] alleviating economic and social disadvantage and improving life chances more widely' (Power, Rees & Taylor, 2005, p. 101). Area-based initiatives (ABIs) is the code word used to describe government interventions that purport to have 'solutions' to what are designated 'problem' neighborhoods. This is the so-called 'territorial justice' (p. 103) argument that would see resources flow according to need—and at one level it seems sensible. However, it brings with it a number of 'deep-seated limitations' (Power, et al., 2005, p. 102), as we will explain.

The limited thinking behind this area-based approach and its associated strategies is several-fold. Firstly, it portrays disadvantage as multi-dimensional, which while not entirely inaccurate, argues that remediation needs to be on multiple fronts—'housing, physical environment, health care, crime prevention, as well as the improvement of educational provision' (Power, et al., 2005, p. 103). The flow-on from this has been so-called 'joined-up' approaches, but what often accompanies it are all kinds of bureaucratic dysfunctions, rivalries, and institutional jealousies that ultimately make such approaches extraordinarily wasteful and even unworkable (see Smyth & McInerney, 2013b). Within such approaches, as Power et al. (2005) note, education is portrayed as important, but never the primary objective.

Secondly, there is the further limitation that ABIs regard social and economic disadvantage as a 'residual category' (Power, et al., 2005, p. 104), as we mentioned earlier, in which 'pockets of disadvantage [exist] in a wider context of increasing affluence' (p. 104)—something that is demonstrably not the case since the GFC and its follow-on Euro implosion. Connell (1994) captured the closer reality some time ago when she talked of the notion of a social gradient of disadvantage:

> Regardless of which measures of class inequality and educational outcomes are used, gradients of advantage and disadvantage appear across the school population as a whole...We can identify an exceptionally advantaged minority as well as an exceptionally disadvantaged one, but focusing on either extreme is insufficient. The fundamental point is that class inequality is a problem that concerns the school system *as a whole*. (p. 130)

'Remaindering' the issue of disadvantage is highly problematic because of the way it disguises the real nature and extent of social, educational and economic disadvantage.

The third, and somewhat disturbing rationale underpinning the ABI approach, is the way it 'ascribes a major part of the responsibility for economic and social disadvantage to the disadvantaged themselves' (Power, et al., 2005, p. 104). The emphasis is placed upon portrayals of 'intergenerational transmission of deprivation through families, or even more contentiously, the "culture of poverty", thereby embedding poverty in particular areas over time' (p. 104).

Unless we challenge and confront what amount to such one-dimensional 'underclass' renditions constructed around notions of 'dysfunctional families' with 'domestic violence', absence of 'male role models', and supposed climates of 'indiscipline' (Power & Gewirtz, 2001, p. 46), then where we end up is in a very dangerous place:

> The dangers of discourse such as this is not just that inadequate diagnosis will lead to inappropriate treatment, but that when that treatment fails, it is these already disadvantaged communities that will pay the price of failure. (Power et al., 2005, p. 112)

What all of these limitations we have highlighted have in common is that they underestimate the role of 'structural factors' in the way poverty and disadvantage are socially constructed, and they purport instead to orchestrate attention around intervening at the level of 'internal' or 'inward looking' approaches that end up 'maintain[ing] or perpetuat[ing] socio-economic disadvantage' (Power, et al., 2005, p. 104). In short:

> ...they view the source of the 'problem' as internal to the neighborhood, and therefore are repeatedly characterized by their commitment to community development and empowerment to enhancing or improving the physical fabric of an area. (p. 104)

Even on those occasions in which they appear to be cognizant of 'structural economic shifts' they still collapse back to a singular human capital approach that resides 'in the need for individuals and communities to enhance their "employability" through participation in education and training' (Power, et al., 2005, p. 104; also see Smyth, 2010).

Power et al. (2005) ask the very pertinent question as to why despite these limitations and an inability to show significant positive lasting benefits, there continues to be a use of ABIs, and even a borrowing of them in places like Australia. There are three answers; first, whatever their shortcomings ABIs present as 'interventionist' and 'can do' approaches in the context of a requirement for urgent political delivery; second, they are evidence of an activist state 'with a social conscience' (p. 113); and third, they are a demonstration of the attempt to try and 'redress…the excesses of neo-liberal policies' through 'targeted investment…[in] those areas worst affected by the failures of the market' (p. 113).

Speaking of 'regeneration policies' Hall (1997) argues that they lead to the proliferation of ever more premature 'solutions' that are essentially ignorant of the complexity of the problem, while failing to embrace an iterative process of 'policy learning and change' (p. 873). In other words, we need to look closely at the deficiencies in current approaches, being honest about their limitations, and refocusing on the possibilities that might emerge from a deeper existential understanding of the lives of the people who are supposed to be assisted. What Hall (1997) is arguing for are 'outward-looking approaches' (p. 873) that seek to uncover and understand the social stresses and impediments in peoples' lives that contribute to them becoming 'peripheralized' (p. 877) in the first place, rather than blaming them and imposing 'bootstrap' approaches (p. 882) that are simplistic and ineffectual. This would mean, looking instead at the external factors that 'work on' people to make them the way they are. For example: what resources do people in contexts of disadvantage have?; how do they use these resources, and to what effect?; and, what might need to be provided to assist them to develop in a direction towards which they aspire?

If we were to start with thinking like this, then it moves us beyond the inherent limitations of the 'geography of inequality' that would have us believe that poverty and disadvantage are somehow 'framed spatially' (Power, et al., 2005, p. 109) and hermetically sealed awaiting some kind of benevolent targeted intervention. It also moves us out of the bind of having to regard areas as 'homogenous in terms of their social disadvantage' that envisages solutions as therefore having to restore some kind of 'imbalance' (p. 110). At the same time, we also move beyond notion of 'social exclusion' which have been heavily criticized by people like Shucksmith (2012) because 'it unduly emphasizes boundary formation and carries an implicit notion that all but a few are included in a cohesive society undifferentiated by class or social division' (p. 380). Most importantly, shifting outside of the area-based frame of reference allows us to jettison 'overly simplistic conceptions' (Power, et al., 2005, p. 111) and instead pursue approaches that are much more embedded in the lives and aspirations of people and they way *they* theorize about these.

This brings us back to Wacquant's (2008) claim about the urgent necessity for 'tools' with which to re-think advanced marginality. His argument and strategies are worth briefly rehearsing as a precursor to looking at some 'insider' instances from young people in our own research who were forging educational futures for themselves from within the margins.

For starters, we need to begin by breaking with the stigmatizing portrayals of neighborhoods positioned, through no fault of their own, at the 'bottom of the hierarchical system of places' (Wacquant, 2008, p. 1). Associated with this is the imperative to puncture and debunk the 'exoticizing' media discourses (p. 1) that unremittingly insist on demonizing them, and instead look 'inside these territories of relegation' (p. 1) so as to expose the fallacy that these are 'barren, chaotic and brutish' (p. 1). Much of what passes as poverty today, Wacquant (2008) argues, can be directly traced back to '*the collapse of public institutions*' (p. 3, emphasis in original) amounting to varying degrees of 'abandonment' (p. 3). This relates to what Lipman (2010) describes so graphically in the case of Chicago and its so-called Renaissance Plan, as 'privatization and displacement' (p. 66), which in the case of the neoliberalisation of schooling, for many bewildered people amounts to 'drowning in a sea' of choice and empowerment (Lipman, 2011, p. 134).

Wacquant's (2008) conceptual and ethnographic heuristic for analyzing marginality and his five areas or moments for action are helpful here:

First, we need to puncture the '*folk concepts* used by state decision-makers...to designate neighborhoods of exile', and to replace them with *analytical concepts* that have some hope of providing a 'critical examination of the categories and discourses' (p. 8, emphasis in original) within which we speak about disadvantage. The reason for doing this, he argues, is to puncture phony concepts like 'underclass' and 'ghettoes', which serve merely as evocative imagery that 'stop...inquiry just where it should get going' (p. 8).

Second, we need to go beyond the ahistorical treatment of neighborhoods, or at least derogatory versions of that history, and instead see neighborhoods of disadvantage as particular 'historical and political constructions' (p. 9), rather than as 'neighborhood effects' that are merely reflections of spatial social and economic differences.

Thirdly, and methodologically, we need *ethnographic observations* as a way of 'pierc[ing] the screen of discourses whirling around these territories' so as 'to capture the lived relations and meanings that are constitutive of the everyday reality' (p. 9) of the people concerned. Of necessity, this will encompass the integration of 'field observation, structural analysis and theoretical construction...[that will] advance in unison and mutually reinforce each other...' (p. 10).

Fourthly, we need to distinguish between several social *conditions* which characterize a neighborhood as 'a zone of relegation' and the culture that accompanies it; the *positioning* of a neighborhood within a hierarchy of places that have material and symbolic significance; and the function the neighborhood serves or performs—such as 'reservoirs of low-skill labor', 'warehouses for supernumerary populations that no longer have any identifiable political or economic utility in the new polarized capitalism', or 'spatial containers for the ostracization of undesirable social categories and activities' (p. 11). Wacquant (2008) says that neighborhoods can 'fulfill one or other of these functions in succession' (p. 11).

Finally, we need to examine the 'degree and form of state penetration' (p. 11) and the gap between government policies 'on paper' and the actions of 'street-level bureaucrats'. In particular, attention needs to be given to the activities of police as a 'frontline agency' directed towards 'precarious and marginal categories' (p. 12).

Bringing young people into the conversation

In the second part of this chapter we want to invoke the voices of young people who are the inhabitants of the kind of neighborhoods we have spoken about and that come across is such disparaging ways in the earlier part of the chapter. Listening to what these young people have to say, we get a very different sense to the portrayals of hopelessness, negativity and despair implicit in policies swirling around in neighborhoods and schools like the ones they inhabit and attend. Without overly romanticizing it because these young people in some instances faced some formidable problems, what strikes us is the surprisingly optimistic way these young people go about their everyday lives, about how they are forming purposeful educational identities for themselves, and the sociability with which they interact with their peers and adults around them—all a far cry from the debilitating policies being orchestrated at a distance and that are supposedly to benefit them. These two pictures seem like light years apart, and we can only surmise that the architects have not the faintest idea of what is going on in these young lives and have even less interest and inclination in finding out. It is almost as if, rather than getting up close to and understanding young lives, the policy experts seem content with putting out policies that are based on the spurious 'neighborhood effects' literature (see for example, van Ham, Manley, Bailey, Simpson & Maclennan, 2012) that says that living in a poor neighborhood has direct negative effects on a resident's life chances. We find this perspective to be far too deterministic and even self-serving in terms of the recuperative 'solutions' promulgated by agencies according to their definitions of the 'problems'.

In what follows we explore, through narrative portraits, the roles of families, neighborhoods, social networks and schools in shaping the educational identities, experiences and aspirations of young people in low socioeconomic circumstances. The portraits we have chosen are a relatively small sample from the 60 portraits crafted from transcripts of interviews with students attending New Vision Community College and City Campus of Federation High School. (Refer to Chapter 2 for details.) We begin with Emilia, a sixteen-year-old student from Federation City.

Emilia's story
There is plenty of evidence to suggest that access to higher education in Australia correlates closely with students' background including 'their socioeconomic status, race and Indigeneity' (Atweh & Bland, 2007, p. 1). The barriers include systemic factors, such as monetary costs, enrolment requirements and travel arrangements that take little account of the needs of disadvantaged students, and symbolic or cultural factors related to the gap between the habitus of marginalized students and the institutional habitus of the university (p. 2). Although solutions to the systemic barriers may be beyond individual schools and higher education institutions we contend that there is much that can be done by educators to contest prevailing myths about universities and to provide young people from working class backgrounds with opportunities to develop knowledge, skills and experiences necessary for participation in higher education. Elements of what this looks like in practice are revealed in Emilia's portrait. Currently studying year 11 at City Campus, Emilia has set her sights on becoming a kindergarten teacher, an occupational path she never envisaged in her early years of schooling. She credits her new school with opening her eyes to the possibility of higher education and acknowledges the importance of family support in following her aspiration.

> *'I never thought I'd ever want to be a teacher'*
>
> I lived in a small country town before moving to Federation City with mum and dad and my brother and sisters. I went to the West Campus in year 7 before coming here. My mum is a cook at a kinder centre and dad works at a hotel.

This year I am doing VET Community Services and several academic subjects—psychology, health and human development, English and maths. I am also studying black and white photography. I'm working towards becoming a kinder teacher. I have picked all the courses I need to and I will be going to Federation City University. Primary school wasn't so good for me, but this is an amazing place and there are heaps of opportunities. The learning environment is more comfortable and you get to be treated as a young adult. We are free to wear our own choice of clothing. This suits me. Here they want school to be more like a work place where you decide what you do and you can alter your timetables. I'm coping okay with the workload. Because I did a course in psychology one and two last year I can manage fairly well. I'm about average with my grades—like a B student. I work about seven to ten hours a week at McDonalds. In the work environment, I'm learning how to communicate better—the customer is always right. I'm the front of the counter dealing with the customers, although sometimes you have to get the manager to sort problems out. I like to swim, but it's only a hobby now. I'm also doing this thing with this other company where they help with journalism and writing.

I expect I will be moving from Federation City in the future. It doesn't worry me really. Federation City is not as limiting for a young person as my previous town but compared to a larger metropolitan city it is. I have an older sister living there who goes to childcare. I've always loved kids and I go down there to help with her little children, so that's helped me with kinder work. I have had a few teachers who have had a big effect on me. They were open-minded and they took the time to help me. I never thought I'd ever want to be a teacher. Besides school and work, your parents, family members and friends play a big part in your education. They didn't know that I was good with kids but they now support me in my plans to become a kinder teacher. I think I can stay focused on the pathway that I want to go (Extract from a portrait prepared from a transcript of an interview with Emilia on 29 February 2012).

Like most of her classmates, Emilia comes from a working class background. Neither of her parents attended university and she confesses she never imagined she would set out to become a kindergarten teacher. However, she says she has always loved kids and has gained practical experience caring for her sister's children. Importantly, her experience of an adult learning environment at the City Campus has raised her self-confidence and aspirations for higher education. She acknowledges the mentoring roles and efforts of open-minded teachers who went the extra yards to support her learning and raise her expectations of education. By providing students with a broad range of academic and vocational courses and pathways the counseling services of City Campus seems to have gone some way to overcoming the cultural barriers to participation in higher education encountered by young people like Emilia. Notwithstanding her close ties to her family, Emilia does not envisage a long-term connection to Federation City. Unlike some of her peers, she acknowledges the employment and social limitations of living in a regional city compared with a large metropolis. However, she will be able to undertake her education studies at a regional university campus close to her home—a major financial advantage not open to all students.

Jayden's story
Unlike Emilia who has moved from town to town in her early school years, sixteen-year-old Jayden has lived all his life in Broadacres, a rapidly growing residential and industrial suburb on the fringe of Federation City. Initially developed in the 1980s, the suburb has a population of 5000 and is predicted to reach 12000 by 2030. Despite the proliferation of new housing estates, Broadacres has a high level of socioeconomic disadvantage and welfare-dependent neighborhoods that experience what Wacquant (2007) calls 'territorial stigmatization'. Community facilities include two primary (elementary) schools, a recreation center, retirement village and reserves but the suburb is poorly served by public transport and lacks a major retail center and community hub. A median house price of $325000, as reported by realestate.com.au, makes this a relatively affordable suburb by metropolitan standards. Jayden attends New Vision Community College in the nearby suburb of Petersburg—a school which is within easy walking distance from his home. He is strongly connected to his neighborhood and projects an optimistic view of the employment and lifestyle opportunities in his community. In common with Emilia, he draws our attention to the crucial role of his school and family in shaping his educational identity.

> *'The things that help me the most to hold my education together are school and my family'*
>
> I live in Broadacres and I've been at New Vision College since year 7. Before that I went to the local primary school. I go to church every Sunday. I play badminton and I'm fairly good at it. It's pretty good in year 11 because you get time to do your studies during school. I enjoy school. I reckon it's a place to learn new things with people I know. I'm not going to somewhere where I don't know anyone. The good thing about this school is that there are heaps of subjects to choose from. I'm doing engineering and I'm in a music program. I play the cornet. I'm not sure where my education is heading but I'm interested in a career in sound recording. I know it's my decision as to what I want to do. My parents are happy with what I am doing but they hope that by the time I leave I will know what I want to do. My dad is a psychiatric nurse in a prison and mum used to be a nurse till she hurt her back. I'm not sure about going to university. Maybe I'll be doing the sound thing at TAFE. What's the attraction of living in Federation City? The weather! [Laughter] You can pretty much get what you want here and your friends are all here. There are heaps of jobs in the

city. I'd like to be doing something in the sound studio area. We don't have any of that equipment at school but there's a guy who has asked me to help him in the downtown studio. The things that help me the most to hold my education together are school and my family. My parents push me to do my homework. I probably get most support at school from the career teachers but all the teachers as well as my friends. They help you through hard times. Generally my friends don't distract me but there are some kids here who don't see any point in coming to school.

I have a bit to do with the community hub located on our school site. I'm into the music scene and it's got a gym as well. If they have any football here you can watch the game. Broadacres is an okay sort of place but it depends where you live. There's good and bad parts. I have friends everywhere but mostly around the new estate and a nearby suburb. The neighborhood is changing a lot with new houses and shops and it's easier to get around. When people want to wag school [truant] they usually go to [McDonalds] or [Kentucky Fried Chicken]. We don't have any big shopping centers yet—only Safeway—and there's not many parks around here. Some kids hang out at the skate park on the other side of the primary school and there's also a playground at the back of a housing estate. Our local footy club is Riverdale (a nearby suburb of Federation City). I play badminton with juniors in the local competition and with the schools. My older brothers are still at home so they drive me around to the different venues. I don't have a job at the moment but I have applied for casual work with KFC. I want to get paid work because I'm going to Malaysia at the end of the year with my family (Extract from a portrait developed from a transcript of an interview with Jayden on 27 February 2012).

Place and identity are powerfully connected. In their study of training and employment opportunities in three 'deprived' urban neighborhoods in England, White and Green (2011) describe the influential role of place attachment and social networks in informing how young people make decisions about education, employment and life choices. Where Jayden lives is an important part of his identity but his sense of attachment to the community is qualified. 'Broadacres is an okay sort of place', he says 'but it depends where you live'. Hinting at territorial stigmatization of neighborhoods (Wacquant, 2007), Jayden claims there are 'good and bad parts' of Broadacres. 'I have friends everywhere but mostly around the new estate and a nearby suburb', he says. One public housing estate in particular has been singled out as a 'no go zone' because of resident perceptions about the incidence of drug taking, vandalism and anti-social behavior in the neighborhood. Notwithstanding his criticism of the paucity of social and recreational amenities in Broadacres, Jayden is upbeat about what his community and Federation City have to offer young people. He participates in local sporting and recreational activities, finds space in the community to further his musical interests and is optimistic about employment prospects. 'You can pretty much get what you want here and your friends are all here', he suggests. However, as noted previously, his view that there are 'heaps of jobs in the city' is not necessarily shared by other students and he has yet to obtain employment himself. Though uncertain as to where his education will take him, he has in interest in the technical aspects of music and hankers after the prospect of finding work in a sound recording studio. Given his skills in the field, it may be that Jayden will get to play badminton at an elite competitive level.

Helen's story
Sixteen-year-old Helen lives on a small rural property near Clarence, some 16 kilometers from Federation City. The township of 3000 people has a rich mining heritage and is surrounded by plantations, making it a high bushfire risk in the scorching Australian summer. Helen attends City Campus and has aspirations to become a pastry chef.

> *'I think it's a good thing to help my community'*

> Well I've only been at City Campus for three weeks. Before that I was at the junior school campus of Federation High School. I live in Clarence, a small town outside Federation City. It takes about 40 minutes to get here from home. We have 22 acres of land and keep sheep, goats, chooks (chickens), a horse and dogs. Dad is a builder who does insurance assessing and mum's a teacher. I have one brother who is in the army now. You get a bit more independence in this campus. The subjects I'm studying are food and technology, English and maths, biology, health and human development. I wanted a broad range of subjects. I would like to be a pastry chef when I leave school because I like dessert and stuff like that. I don't know whether I can do the course at university or TAFE. I haven't looked into it. My other choice would be an occupational therapist but I haven't really decided yet. I was working in a kitchen in Clarence but they wouldn't let me cook. They wouldn't let me do anything. So I don't have any work at the moment. The transition from year 10 to year 11 has involved a little more work but the teachers don't hassle you. You have to take the responsibility. If you don't do it then it's your loss. But having a mother as a teacher is good because she will help me out if I don't understand things. She's a bit different when she is teaching to what she is at home. Both my parents are supportive and they're happy with what I want to do. I play netball and I am in the Country Fire Authority—the CFA. I've done my minimum skills and then there is the CFA competition side of it which is good fun. There were 88 teams from our state competing over the weekend. There are quite a lot of women in the juniors but they drop out when it gets to the seniors. In the CFA you learn more hands-on-skills than knowledge—like learning how to keep yourself safe I guess. I haven't been out in a fire yet and I'm a bit nervous about the idea. A lot of people my age think it's stupid getting volunteering with the CFA but I think it's a good thing to help my

community. I just don't pay attention to them. They wouldn't think it funny if their house was burning down. My dad and brother are in the CFA and that's how I got into the competition side. There are over 50 volunteers in our group. I enjoy living in a small town because you get to know everyone but the idea of traveling also appeals to me. I haven't been outside Australia. My family is here so I would come back (Extract from a portrait developed from a transcript of an interview with Helen 1 March 2012).

There are several fascinating aspects of Helen's narrative that give us an insight into her identity, aspirations and values. One concerns her views about the culture of learning at the City Campus of Federation City High School. Although she appreciates her new-found independence she says she prefers a more structured approach to schooling and is less enamored with the absence of uniform requirements and bells than many of her peers. The second relates to Helen's career aspirations. She has a passion for cooking and would like to be a pastry chef when she leaves school. Her parents are supportive of her decision and are probably well-placed to provide her with resources and opportunities to achieve her goal. Third, Helen's account reveals quite a lot about the importance of community and the ethic of volunteering that is part of her family tradition. Although she admits that joining the CFA may not be a fashionable thing for young people, she offers a spirited defense of the value of community work and the useful skills she has learnt from being part of a team. Overseas travel is on her agenda but she, like Jayden, expresses an intention to stay close to her family and community.

Russell's story

Russell is specializing in music performance at City Campus and hopes to become a professional musician or a guitar teacher but his dream is to be part of a big band and travel the world.

'Music is my biggest interest'

My name's Russell. I have four brothers and a sister and my parents work at a cafe near the university. The business is going from strength to strength. It's a 50s style café and they're still living in that sort of time. After primary school I went to the East campus of Federation City High School and finished year 10 before coming here this year. It's a lot less strict in this campus so it's better. I don't like the uniform and I used to get into a bit of trouble at my previous school. Here it is a bit more relaxed and they treat you more like adults. Music is my biggest interest. I'm doing a VET course in music performance and this is my second year. Music is something I want to get into. I study it here at City Campus where they have good facilities. My other subjects are English, maths, business management and studio arts. I want to be a musician or a guitar teacher. At 16 of course I'd prefer to be in the biggest band in the world but that's the big picture. I'm not in a band at the moment because my best mate is doing an apprenticeship in a trade. It's a real let-down. I taught him and he was a really good player. I'm into all sorts of music—heavy metal and blues. My older brothers all tried to play instruments but they have given up. My grandfather taught me and got me into it. The whole family were interested in music. Everyone asks me if I have a Plan B but I will make this one work. I'm staying at school for the sake of staying at school. I want to get my education as far as I can and I would like to go to university and continue with music. I could fall into this great band but going to university is something that I want to do. I'm not into sport at all. I'm not very coordinated. I don't have an outside job. My mum wants me to go into the café and sit in the corner and play but I don't know how that would go. I didn't really want to do business management but it might help me if I want to go into the music industry. As long as I am making a comfortable living I would go anywhere. I would love to travel. Getting into a music network is important (Extract from a portrait developed from a transcript of an interview with Russell on 1 March 2012).

According to Stokes and Wyn (2009) '[t]he performing arts play a key role in the construction of youth identities' (p.43). Indeed, for many of the young people we interviewed at City Campus, the school's vibrant performing arts curriculum was arguably one of the most important factors in keeping them connected to education. Conducted in a heritage-listed building by a team of instrumental teachers, including the campus head, the music program caters for students from public and private schools across Federation City. Students are able to join a school choir or band and have opportunities to perform at school, community and regional events. They can also tap into the artistic and cultural resources of the community. Federation City has a symphony orchestra, a vibrant live music scene and the university has a nationally acclaimed performing arts academy. Music is a very big part of Russell's life—something which he shares with other members of his family. At this stage, he plans to finish year 12 and go on to study music at university but his big ambition is to be in the biggest band in the world. At a time when a good deal of schooling is focused on vocational learning and economic advancement, Russell's narrative reveals the importance of the arts in young people's lives. It also highlights the influence of family in shaping young people's interests and aspirations—a factor which comes to the fore in our next portrait.

Claire's story
Fifteen-year-old Claire lives in the small town of Hay Springs about 12 kilometers west of Federation City. A year 10 student at New Vision Community College, she has participated in a course known as SCOPE which educates young people about issues and opportunities for people with disabilities. In the following portrait she reveals how a family member's experience of

disability has influenced her thinking about working with disabled people and she reflects on the dilemmas and uncertainties when it comes to making decisions about further education and training options.

'I just want to make a difference'

> I'm still struggling with what I want to do when I leave school. I'm torn between interior design and uni. I don't really like the idea of uni that much but I know that I'm going to have to do it. I also like the idea of helping the disabled. I have an uncle with Down Syndrome and the SCOPE course I did is helping me with the disabled side of things. The SCOPE teacher is awesome. I'm waiting to get a call today about work experience from a leisure centre where my uncle goes. I've also done a visual communication design class and that helped with interior design. But I have left that class for a while now. The careers manager set me up with the interior design course at a TAFE College in Federation City but I'm not sure what I want to do. I work about 6 days a week at Subway—mostly after school. I've been doing 20–25 hours a week lately and I've just had some time off because it was getting a bit much with school and everything. I guess I started working when I was 14 years old at the Plaster Fun House. I tried to get a job as early as possible so I could get lots of experience. It's been good experience but I know I don't want to work at a fast food place for the rest of my life. I will end up going to university but I just don't like the idea of it. I guess I won't be able to get a good job if I don't go. I don't like the thought of going there because I want to go out and travel and do stuff. Neither of my parents went to university but they encourage me to go. My mum works in retail and my dad operates machines all over Australia. He goes away for long periods of time and then comes back for four days—he operates big machines. My parents didn't go to uni and they are doing fine. I think maybe I don't need the hassle but I know that I should go.
>
> School is keeping me on track. New Vision College is so good like that, especially the career lady. She got one of the largest regional TAFE institutes to come to the careers expo here and has been helping me with work experience and classes I should be doing. But it's very difficult balancing all this stuff especially as my mum works and my dad is away a lot. Getting a ride in and out of school is also very hard. I want to stay around family but I also want to travel and do as much as I can. The reason I wanted to be an interior designer is because mum and I liked looking at the display homes and I loved seeing the way they set out the homes, but my uncle has Down Syndrome and I like helping him and I feel that I'm doing good. I just want to make a difference (Extract from a portrait developed from a transcript of an interview with Claire 22 August 2011).

Becoming educated, for Claire, is not just about getting a job and getting money, it's about being able to do things that make a difference for people. Claire has an uncle with Down Syndrome and following her participation in SCOPE is seriously contemplating a career in this field. However, she is still weighing up other options, including interior design. Claire is rather ambivalent about

going on to university. On the one hand, she accepts that she will probably have to go to university—something her parents never did—to gain qualifications in disability studies if she chooses this pathway. She has faith in her school's vocational counseling program and believes her school has resources to further her aspirations. However, she doesn't like the thought of being tied down to study when she could be doing other exciting things with her life. Balancing school and part-time work is a big challenge for Claire.

Jack's story
In his study of inequality, unemployment, and the new vocationalism in the United Kingdom, Phillip Brown (1987) identifies working class disposition to schooling as follows: (a) a minority who are prepared to knuckle down to school life in order to gain the necessary qualifications to advance their economic standing; (b) another minority who reject school as 'boring, irrelevant and frequently repressive' (p. 1); and (c) an 'invisible majority' of 'ordinary' kids who don't necessarily conform to the ethos of school but who are willing, nonetheless, to make an effort and hang-in with their studies. Though it may be a little too simplistic to categorize young people according to these typologies, fifteen-year-old Jack seems to fit Brown's second group of working class students—the ones that want to leave school. Now in year 10 at New Vision Community College Jack views school as largely irrelevant to his aspirations and interests. This is not to say that he lacks a sense of agency nor access to resources to further his employment intentions.

'School is not taking me anywhere'

School's not too bad. You just have to learn to stay out of trouble really. But it's not taking me anywhere. I just want to leave and get a job—something hands-on, like a builder or mechanic. My dad was a truck driver for 25 years and my brother is an apprentice builder. We have building construction here and VET auto course. I do that all day on Wednesday and it's pretty easy. I live in a small country town near Federation City. I went to primary school there and I came to New Vision Community College for my secondary schooling because my brother was here. So far as work goes, my parents say it's pretty much my choice. They know that I'm not really good at school so they want me to leave and get a job. My favorite subjects are probably auto and construction. I don't do maths and English. I'm not good at these subjects so there's no point in doing them. All our family is dyslexic and my dad's mum does all the paperwork and the faxes and sends all the bills and that so I don't really need English. School is an okay sort of place but I'm just sick of it. I expect I'll stick around here when I finish. We have a greyhound dog business at home. There's a few of these businesses in Federation City but we are the largest. We've got 80 or so greyhounds. We just break them in and then we give them back to the owners. It's not that hard really. It takes about four weeks to do each dog. We've broken in a lot of the good dogs, like Superman. I get up at 5 am every morning and clean out their pens and let them out into the yards and they get a run twice a week, I've been doing this for 15 years. I was over at the dog track when I was still in a cot. There's a big demand for this work and our family has been doing it about 80 odd years. My Pa started the business and my Dad took over when he died. My Pa was a big poultry farmer as well. He had about two million chooks and was the first person to put a chook in a bag. We don't have chooks (chickens) now, just greyhounds. I can't see myself taking over the business for a while yet. I would like to go out and work for 10 years or so and then might come back and do the greyhounds because I know that my dad won't do it forever. Federation City is a pretty good place to live, except for the weather. I like living in the country because it's pretty quiet and that (Portrait developed from a transcript of an interview with Jack on the 22nd of August 2011).

Becoming educated, from Jack's perspective, appears to require little more than the opportunity to study VET courses that will prepare him for possible employment in the building industry or mechanical trades. Whilst not entirely dismissive of hands-on learning that connects to his immediate interests, he claims that his schooling is taking him nowhere. In the circumstances he simply tries to stay out of trouble and not rock the boat. Jack expresses a pragmatic (perhaps naive) view about the relevance of maths and English to what he wants to make of himself. 'I'm not good at these subjects so there's no point in doing them', he remarks. Jack claims that all his family is dyslexic and his grandmother handles all the paperwork in their family business so there's no need for him to acquire written communication skills. Jack looks outside school for the resources he needs to achieve his goals. He has a strong sense of attachment to his family and local community and would like to manage the family greyhound business when his father retires. In the meantime, he wants to leave school as soon as possible and gain work experience. Jack's situation is somewhat unique because he has a fall-back employment position and access to economic and social resources that are not so readily available to many of his peers. For young people in these situations it seems that it's not what you know but who you know that counts most when it comes to getting a job.

From despair to hope: young peoples' narratives of place, identity and education

What Emilia, Jayden, Helen, Russell, Claire and Jack have to say about their aspirations and hopes for the future challenge the all too familiar deficit constructions and representations of young people in low socioeconomic communities. Contrary to popular rhetoric they come across as resilient, self-motivated and resourceful individuals who believe they can make something worthwhile of their lives. As we read their stories it also becomes abundantly clear that the households and neighborhoods in which they live are not unmitigated 'bundles of pathologies' in need of remediation, rather, they are places with unique histories, rich cultural traditions and funds of knowledge that play a vital role in nurturing the identities of young people. In the following diagram we have endeavored to pull together an emerging set of ideas around notions of space, place, identity and locally based resources which support the education of young people. These are summarized under four themes: (1) young people, (2) families and households, (3) communities and neighborhoods, and (4) schools.

FAMILIES AND HOUSEHOLDS
- Cultural knowledge
- Financial resources
- Social/emotional support
- Family networks
- Academic resources
- Affirming identity and aspirations

COMMUNITIES AND NEIGHBORHOODS
- Cultural amenities
- Performing arts/music
- Sport/recreation
- University/TAFE/Training institutes
- Workplaces
- Social welfare
- Churches
- Volunteer groups

Celebrating Space, Place and Neighborhood in Shaping Educational Identities
Accessing Resources for Learning

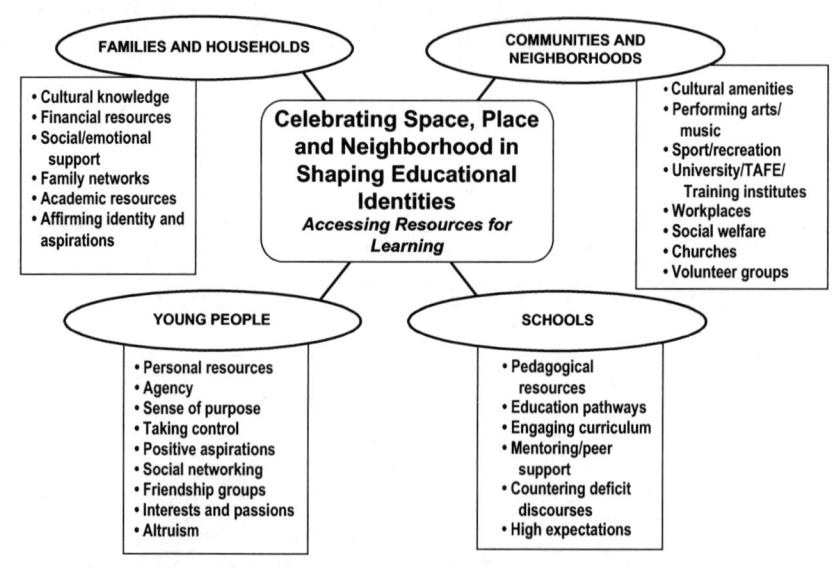

YOUNG PEOPLE
- Personal resources
- Agency
- Sense of purpose
- Taking control
- Positive aspirations
- Social networking
- Friendship groups
- Interests and passions
- Altruism

SCHOOLS
- Pedagogical resources
- Education pathways
- Engaging curriculum
- Mentoring/peer support
- Countering deficit discourses
- High expectations

Figure: 5.1 Space, place and neighborhood in educational identities

(1) ***Young people***: The individual and collective agency that young people possess is sometimes underrated. Green and White (2007) suggest that studies of social capital tend to view young people 'merely as consumers of social capital, as opposed to producers' (p. 36). Although the identities and aspirations of the participants in this study have been influenced by others we do get a strong sense that they are actively creating their own social worlds. In many instances, it appears they have acquired knowledge and skills from life experiences independent from adult lives and households—a point made by

Rios-Aguilar et al. (2011) in their study of funds of knowledge in poor Latino communities. In this context, we could cite the importance of resources personally acquired by young people through their engagement with social media, popular culture, the arts, and sporting and recreational activities. As evident in the portraits, several students had a passion for music and seemed to place a higher priority on pursuing this interest than vocationally oriented studies. Some were animated by a concern for the environment or the needs of people with disabilities. Almost without exception, they spoke optimistically about their goals for the future. We are not suggesting that they were free to pursue their aspirations in an unconstrained manner. Clearly the agency that young people possess exists within social structures which often limit their capacity for autonomous decision making. To illustrate the point, Heinz (2009) argues that '[i]ncreasing labor market volatility and declining coordination between education, training and employment have been making their transition [from school to work] not only extended but more precarious' (p. 392).

(2) *Families and households*: Working-class parents are often accused of not caring about school and showing little or no interest in their children's learning (Compton-Lilly, 2004; Gorski, 2008). However, we heard a vastly different story from the young people in this study. They told us that their parents do have high hopes of their education. At the very least, they want them to complete their formal schooling and gain a certificate of achievement. In general, they were overwhelmingly supportive of their aspirations and, in many instances, made enormous financial sacrifices to help them achieve their goals. It was also apparent that many young people had access to familial and household resources to advance their learning in areas such as farm management, gardening, photography, music, art, cooking, building construction and child care. Family networks had given some young people an added advantage in the labor market with families and friends providing valuable sources of support, and direct access to employment, as illustrated in Jack's story.

(3) *Communities and neighborhoods*: As explained previously, Federation City and the surrounding region contain an abundance of historical, environmental and cultural resources to enrich student learning. Many of the students we interviewed were actively involved in community sport and a surprisingly large number played in musical groups. A sizeable proportion had part-time jobs, chiefly in the fast food industries, and several acknowledge the value of skills they had learnt in communication and customer service. Students expressed varying degrees of

attachment to their neighborhoods and the wider community. Whilst family and friends were powerful connecting factors many (perhaps the majority) did not envisage a long-term future in Federation City, largely because of limited employment and further education opportunities. Blum and Ullman (2012) claim '[p]eople worldwide are being forced to negotiate their identities for survival in a globalized world' (p. 367). We suggest this is especially true for young people in regional communities where manufacturing jobs have largely disappeared from the economic landscape over the past two decades. For students it seems it's a case of 'getting on' by 'getting out'.

(4) *Schools*: As explained in Chapter 3, many of the students in this study experience degrees of 'educational disadvantage' as a consequence of their socioeconomic circumstances, and their cultural and linguistic backgrounds. Most expressed faith in their schooling and believed that success in the senior years would lead to worthwhile and engaging pathways in higher education, training and employment. The young people we interviewed told us that City Campus, in particular, was a place which gave them opportunities to further their academic and vocational interests in a more hospitable setting than a traditional high school. Students in both schools highlighted the range of courses available to them, the value of mentoring programs, after-school learning centers, and dedicated teachers. Not all students saw school in such a positive light. For those like Jack school offered little of relevance to their aspirations. However, public schools like New Vision Community College and City Campus do have pedagogical and cultural resources that can support and enhance the educational identities and aspirations of young people in low socioeconomic communities. Young people's experiences of schooling in these sites did encourage many of them to think more optimistically about future education pathways, including the option of going to university. Unfortunately, this does not always happen in secondary schools where a hierarchy of subjects and the increased emphasis on vocational education combines to exclude many low socioeconomic students from entering higher education (Tranter, 2012).

Concluding comments

When we titled this chapter, *Celebrating space, place and neighborhoods*, we were deeply conscious of the socio-spatial nature of stigmatization and its devastating impact on the identities of people living in neighborhoods categorized as 'disadvantaged'. It was apparent from the many conversations we have had with young people over the years that the deficit-ridden labels assigned to them by ill-informed media presenters, politicians, business leaders, policy makers and others, not only misrepresent in the most hurtful ways their lives and aspirations, but are cruelly implicated in perpetuating community prejudice and discrimination against them. In this chapter, we set out to describe and dissect the deceitful, demeaning and damaging nature of these portrayals and to offer a counter narrative based on young peoples' accounts of the traditions, assets and resources within their families, households and neighborhoods that contribute in a positive way to their educational identities. In celebrating space, place and neighborhoods we are mindful of the constraints to the realization of young people's aspirations arising from the social and economic circumstances of their lives and the failure of public policy to deliver more inclusive and equitable human services for the most marginalized youth. In the next chapter we focus more directly on how young people create learning identities for themselves in difficult times.

6. *Identity and capacity to aspire*

> Today we took a group of primary kids [from a disadvantaged school in a suburb in a capital city in a Southern Australian state] to the beach, and some kids expressed surprise that the water tasted salty! (Fieldnote from discussion with an Australian grade 1 teacher, sometime in 1994).

> We have fourteen year old students who have never been to our state capital (in Australia)…one hour away by train (Principal, City Campus, Federation City High School, Australia, nd).

Introduction and positioning

We start this chapter with two fairly shocking anecdotes to make the point about where we are writing from—all writing is positioned in some way, and in our case our positioning is one that seeks to challenge and undermine dominant or conventional positions.

It would not be an exaggeration to say that educational policy makers in western countries have gone into hyperdrive in recent times around the issue of 'aspirations'—especially the alleged absence among students from disadvantaged backgrounds. We want to trouble this viewpoint and supplant it with a more complex and nuanced view of what is involved in 'capacity to aspire' from the vantage point of the lives of young people, their families, schools, and the contexts in which they are located.

Some of the tendencies that have focused on the superficial and the misleading thinking around a topic like 'aspiration', have been most evident in the UK, but so too have been some of the most forceful endeavors to present another or alternative viewpoint. Chris Creegan (2008) pointed to 'the predicament identified by Joseph Rowntree a century ago…[when] he argued that "philanthropic effort was directed to remedying the more superficial manifestations of weaknesses or evil, while little thought or effort was directed to search out their underlying causes'" (p. 9). As Creegan (2008) summarized it:

> The reality is that, whether loss of opportunity is caused by something done to you, something that happens to you or something that you choose to do, if you are disadvantaged through poverty or inequality the limitations imposed are greater and the escape routes fewer. (p. 9)

What can easily be dismissed as lack of motivation or aspiration among young people—often argued to be intergenerational—*can* and *should* be presented more realistically as 'truncated opportunity' that is 'lost, limited or wasted through circumstances and events [which people] have varying degrees of control over' (Creegan, 2008, p. 1)—what Giroux (2012b) refers to as 'disposable youth'. This is akin to what Dickens (1999) calls 'network failure' (p. 410)—which refers to a breakdown in the structures of support that enable people to succeed educationally and vocationally. In other words, if 'opportunity and aspirations' are indeed 'two sides of the same coin', as Creegan (2008) argues in the title of his paper, then it is not ethically or morally possible to consider 'aspirations' without at the same time considering 'opportunities'. As Smyth has argued on numerous occasions (Smyth, 2006; 2010; 2011; 2012b; Smyth & Wrigley, 2013), 'disadvantage' is not a natural, given, or inevitable state—people are 'put at' a disadvantage through the operation of social, political and economic forces mostly beyond their control.

The essence of Creegan's (2008) argument is that we need to 'refram[e] the relationship between opportunity and aspiration' (p. 1), and the most crucial part in that reframing 'must include listening to those with experience of truncated opportunity' (p. 1), which is to say, 'eliciting the voices of people we do not usually hear' (p. 2).

Kintrea, St. Clair and Houston (2011) in a UK study of 'the influence of parents, place and poverty on educational attitudes and aspirations' by the Joseph Rowntree Foundation, sought to 'better understand the relationships between young people's aspirations and how they are formed' (p. 1). Their starting point was the proposition that policy initiatives were out-of-step with understandings and that as a topic, aspirations is 'under-theorized…despite its high profile in current policy' (p. 6). To correct this imbalance, Kintrea et al. (2011) sought 'to understand the contexts, structures and processes through which aspirations are formed beyond the view that aspirations are simply a matter of individual choice' (p. 6).

One of the myths dispelled by the study was the universal policy claim often propagated that among disadvantaged young people and their families, aspirations are too low and need to be raised. This is a claim not borne out by the evidence. If one were of a cynical persuasion it could be argued that positioning disadvantaged young people in this way is simply too convenient for policy makers. It amounts to blaming young people individually for their seeming failure to attain educationally or vocationally, while leaving open the scope for punitive and interventionist strategies that serve the interests of those other than the young people themselves.

What Kintrea et al. (2011) did find was a complex interaction between 'family, place and school' (p. 6) that 'seem to "push" in generally the same direction, either towards or away from high aspirations' (p. 65). Deficit perspectives were simply seen as unhelpful because 'family history, home culture and the local community world view can contribute to attitudes to education and careers that individuals simply cannot choose to change' (p. 63). While young people from contexts of disadvantage generally had aspirations for good jobs, they were also cognizant of labour market conditions in areas in which they lived, but this did not diminish their still 'aspiring to get a good job' (p. 66).

'Poverty of aspiration' or 'poverty of opportunity'?

The term 'poverty of aspiration' is a cruel phrase that has been invoked in the UK, but copied to varying degrees elsewhere, to position particular categories of people, who it is alleged need to 'lift their game'. In the words of one observer:

> It is a phrase that in three short words seeks to blame the victims of austerity, those left stranded by the abandonment of...manufacturing industry [in developed countries], trapped in over-crowded poor social housing or impossibly expensive private rental dumps and at under-resourced schools, people who through medical accident or unfortunate fate need the support of decent benefit payments being told to 'buck up', 'lift your sights', 'try harder' (Bennett, 2012).

As Bennett (2012) concludes, it is a phrase that 'would seem to fit better in the mouth of a frock-coated Victorian industrialist, urging the child chimney sweeps to climb faster', than an analysis in a sophisticated society trying to understand and come to grips with the ravages of rapidly restructuring global capitalism. St. Clair and Benjamin (2011) note that the current policy infatuation with a dearth of aspirations 'show no signs of abating' with the UK government setting out plans in 2009 'for public reform intending to lift the aspirations of 2.4 million children' (p. 501)—in a context where the overwhelming policy emphasis is one of 'bootstrapism' (p. 515). In other words, in the end people have to wear the responsibility for lifting themselves out of the desultory situations in which they exist.

What becomes conveniently concealed in this individualizing, psychologizing and pathologizing of 'problem' groups with allegedly low aspirations, is what McIntosh (1988) referred to as the 'invisible knapsack' of advantage and privilege. McIntosh's (1988) argument is that advantaging occurs when some people have an 'invisible package' of assets that are 'meant to remain oblivious' (p. 2). She says that 'privilege is like an invisible knapsack of special provisions, maps, passports, codebooks, visas, clothes, tools and blank checks' (p. 2). In effect, then, privilege is 'an elusive and fugitive "subject"' (p. 4) in which those who have it have been conditioned to 'think of their lives as morally neutral, normative and average' despite the fact that they draw daily from 'a base of unacknowledged privilege' (p. 2). To put it most forthrightly, Munro (2012) citing Zyngier, says that some 'children come to our classrooms with…their backpack full of privileges and others come with a backpack of disadvantage'.

Indicative of the kind of blindness to the complexity of how advantaging works, was former Australian Prime Minister, and Education Minister, Julia Gillard's (2009a) revealing comment that:

> I'm a stickler for standards. In fact, its my firm belief—which I share with people like Rupert Murdoch [and] Joel Klein [former Chancellor of the New York Public School system and now executive of News Corp]—that to expect anything but the highest standards for everyone is a cop out. Telling the disadvantaged that it's alright to be mediocre is to betray their future. George Bush was right to condemn the soft bigotry of low expectations. (p. 4)

Gillard's (2009b) response to 'overcoming a legacy of neglect' in the Australian educational context was to argue that 'disadvantage is not destiny', after which she proceeded to usher in 'a new era of transparency' (p. 3) with a 'new focus on accountability for outcomes, rather than control over inputs' and the creation of a new national monitoring agency the 'Australian Curriculum, Assessment and Reporting Authority' (p. 4). In what Lingard (2011) has labeled 'policy as numbers', Gillard (2009a) claimed 'that our aspiration is to have 40 per cent of all 25–34 year olds [with] a higher degree qualification by 2015', and 'by 2020 20 per cent of higher education enrolments at undergraduate level [to] be of people from low socio-economic backgrounds' (p. 4). So much for alleviating the poverty of expansive policy thinking!

Roberts (2009) is helpful to us in making sense of this when he invokes the heuristic of 'opportunity structures' which he defines as being 'formed by the inter-relationships between family origins, education, labour market processes and employers' recruitment practices' (p. 355). Roberts admits that opportunity structures have changed over time, but they are still 'maintained by the same processes, and by the same agents' (p. 355) as was always the case. What has changed is the contemporary emphasis on 'poverty of aspiration' as a way of purportedly explaining the seeming demise of many young people, but Roberts (2009) says young people making 'wrong choices' or having a dearth of aspiration 'cannot explain current imbalances in youth labour markets' (p. 355). Rather, he says, we have to look to:

> ...the root sources of the imbalances [that] lie in the opportunities within which different groups of young people are required to be reflexive and to make successive choices. (p. 355)

The way Roberts explains the changing context is that young people are making biographies for themselves from within wider social structures, and while there is an increasing emphasis on individualization this is not occurring outside the influence of social and economic structures. As Roberts says 'It is possible to overlook that Beck has never argued that individualization involves individuals freeing themselves from social structures' (p. 362). On the contrary, 'choice biographies' (du Bois-Reymond, 1995; 1998) and individualization as expressed by young people 'is a structural product, forced on individuals' (Roberts, 2009, p. 362). Reflecting on Ulrich Beck's (1992) *Risk Society*, Roberts argues that 'all the choices that individuals can make have uncertain outcomes...where risk can neither be off-loaded nor eliminated' (p. 362). As Roberts colorfully put it, in the risk society they find themselves in:

> ...young people from different social class backgrounds are no longer herded into metaphorical public transport vehicles which convey them all to certain destinations. Rather, they are dispatched into life in metaphorical private motor cars, albeit fitted with differently powered engines and with fuel supplies that will convey them over different ranges. Responsibility for outcomes is personalized (privatized), but outcomes are not simply personal choices. (p. 362)

In the swiftly moving current context of the post GFC and the economic implosion of parts of Europe, we need to be careful not to over-romanticize young peoples' ability to absorb the effects of massive structural shifts in global capitalism. While Roberts was writing during the early stages of the GFC, we need research that revisits and updates the view he was expressing, and the Beck (1992) 'reflexive biography' (p. 135) upon which it was based, that says 'Today's young people accept the features of the world into which they have grown...[and] are neither surprised nor alarmed that they cannot step right into jobs for life at age 16' (Roberts, 2009, p. 362). The evidence is beginning to mount that it may not be that straightforward (see Giroux, 2012c). It remains something of a moot point as to the extent to which 'Most [young people] are comfortable with uncertainty… [u]nlike adults whose careers have been shattered by economic restructuring' (p. 362). None of this is to deny the argument that even where young people come from 'deprived backgrounds', that there is still a strong desire to progress with their lives. It is a case of being confronted by 'risky steps' each of which 'involves investments…of time, money, social and emotional resources' (Roberts, 2009, p. 364), but in a context in which these are becoming increasingly unevenly distributed. As Smyth (2003) has demonstrated in relation to educational credentials, young people are no longer being 'propelled through schooling by the lure of a credential' (p. 127), but rather it is more of a case of them navigating individual pathways around various forms of 'accommodation and resistance' to policy credentials that are still besotted with versions of human capital skills formation, but which young people are coming to see as increasingly irrelevant despite claims 'to be inclusive of all' (p. 127).

Negotiating a learning identity in hard times

Even seemingly enlightened readings of what is happening in young lives conceal more than they reveal—they are far too tame, and in their domestication they fail at the most fundamental level to understand 'the conditions that enable young people to become either commodified, criminalized, or made disposable' (Giroux, 2010, p. xii).

What we want to do here is provide something of a correction to this limited view by providing a critical and political view of learning identity, and in doing that we want to invoke some of the polemical but devastatingly realistic writings of Henry Giroux on young people. For over 20 years Giroux has pursued an insightful and critical analysis of what is being done to young people around the world, but mostly in the U.S., by a malicious, dehumanizing and punishing ideology—and he has emerged at the other end with a clear and hopeful agenda of what young people are doing in reclaiming a more democratic future for themselves.

Our overall intent here, is to advance and explore a wider meaning of learning identity to that generally captured in the social and cultural identification of how young people make sense of what occurs around them in classrooms and schools (Wortham, 2006). We want to trouble the question—learning identity *within* and *against* what, and to *where*? Casting our net in this wider fashion enables us to see much more clearly the larger forces that young people are having to contend with and how they are going about responding to them.

Identity and capacity to aspire

In exploring the larger frames within which young people are constructing themselves as learners, we want to sketch out something of what Giroux (2012c) calls 'the politics of trickle-down cruelty' (p. 8) that constitutes the harsh reality of austerity cuts, that if they have not yet visited young people in your part of the world, then they are rapidly approaching. We want to posit this as something of a background to reframing the 'art of the possible' (Carnevale & Kelsey with Ranciere, 2007) around which young people are forming new and different learning identities for themselves.

Although Giroux draws his examples and illustrations predominantly from the United States, the efficacy of what he has to say varies only in the magnitude not the direction of its applicability to all other western countries—which have to varying degrees bought into the neoliberal project, with similar results for young people. In his *Youth in a Suspect Society*, Giroux (2010) argues that young people, as a result of 'free-market liberalism' in which 'social problems have become utterly privatized and removed from public consideration' (p. 2), have been rendered a 'disposable population' (p. 8). He says that the notion of 'citizen'—with a concern for the collective public good—has withered and been made redundant to that of the 'consumer' who is pushed so as to be relentlessly in search of the next 'bargain' (p. 2). Within a marketized context, consumers are as easily dispensed with as yesterday's have-to-have items. Disposable populations, Giroux (2010) says, are 'relegated...and removed from public view' and made 'redundant as a result of the collapse of the social state' (p. 9). The reason young people fit this disposable or 'expendable' category is that in all kinds of demonstrable ways, they are no longer seen as a social investment for the future, but rather as compliant and expendable consumers or troublesome threats to be demonized, controlled and policed. Little wonder, then, that Giroux (2010) labels young people as 'a generation of suspects in a society [at least in the US] destroyed by the merging of market fundamentalism, consumerism, and militarism' (p. 12). It would not be putting too fine a point on it to say that what we have here, to put it more accurately, is a highly 'suspect' (which is to say, distrustful) society.

Even a cursory glance at the prioritization of federal policies in the US makes it abundantly clear that the 'political culture rejects any ethical commitment to provide young people with the prospects of a decent and just future' (Giroux, 2010, p. 13), whether that be in respect of health, housing, education, or decent jobs. The 'evisceration [of] public services and reducing them to a network of farmed-out private providers' (Judt, 2010, p. 119) has produced an 'abandoned generation' (Giroux, 2003) of young people who are effectively cut loose to fend for themselves. The way Giroux (2010) describes it:

> ...youth in America increasingly constitute a series of disappearances, badly represented in the public domain and largely invisible in terms of their own needs and as a reminder of adult responsibility. All young people today are increasingly defined, if not assaulted, by market forces that commodify almost every aspect of their lives and lived relations, though different groups bear unequally the burden of a ruthless neoliberal order. Those young people on the margins of power who are viewed as flawed consumers or who resist the seduction of the commodity market increasingly fall prey to the dictates of a youth punishment-and-control complex that manages every aspect of their lives and increasingly governs their behavior through the modalities of surveillance and criminalization. (pp. 13–14)

In tracing what he calls the 'education and the youth crime complex', Giroux (2010) lays bare 'the voracious discourse and deformities of war as an organizer of collective experience [which] took on an ominous turn under the administration of George W. Bush' (p. 69), and that has subsequently been picked up in many other countries as well. In the US in particular, war has become the 'regulatory principle for organizing everyday life' (p. 69), and it was only ever going to be a very short step in translating the militaristic dialogue behind the invasion of Iraq and Afghanistan, into its reconfigured deployment on 'the domestic front' (p. 71) in a full frontal assault on public life. In this regard:

> ...what has been largely ignored is how the war at home [in the U.S.] both militarized public life and refashioned the criminal justice system, prisons and even schools, as pre-eminent spaces of...[legitimated] violence. (p. 71)

The tragic effect in the US has been that 'For many young people, the war at home has been transformed into a war against youth' (p. 71), which Giroux points out, has been perpetrated as a 'one-sided insidious view of young people as lazy, mindless, irresponsible and even dangerous' (p. 71). To reinforce the way in which young people are represented in different places over time, Giroux (2010) invokes Comaroff and Comaroff (2006) who conclude that 'the way young people are perceived, named and represented betrays a lot about the social and political constitution of a society' (p. 267). As Davis (2005) put it in this regard, the carceral state is what follows the collapse of the welfare state:

> [The prison in] U.S. society has evolved into that of a default solution to the major social problems of our times...[and] the logic of what has been called the imprisonment binge: instead of building housing, throw the homeless in prison. Instead of developing the education system, throw the illiterate in prison. Throw people in prison who lose jobs as the result of de-industrialization, globalization

of capital, and the dismantling of the welfare state. Get rid of all of them. Remove these dispensable populations from society. According to this logic the prison becomes a way of disappearing people in the false hope of disappearing the underlying social problems they represent. (cited in Giroux, 2010, p. 79)

As Giroux (2010) cryptically put it, 'Since the 1970s...building prisons has become America's housing policy for the poor...[with investment] in the prison-industrial complex as a way of managing large populations of people...who have been rendered disposable...' (p. 84). Furthermore, the school-to-prison pathway, according to Street (2005), is further solidified by a process in which 'half the nation's black male high school dropouts will be incarcerated—moving...from quasi-carceral lock-down high schools to the real "lock-down" thing—at some point in their lives' (p. 82). Zero-tolerance approaches and the increasingly militarization of US public schools (see Robbins, 2008; Saltman & Gabbard, 2003) reinforces a 'scapegoat' view of youth who are portrayed 'as an inferior class...responsible for society's ills and deserving of harsh penalties' (Koroknay-Palicz, 2001 cited in Giroux, 2010, p. 92).

Against such a devastatingly brutal and dismal assessment of the kind provided by Giroux, it is hard to see where the cracks and the crevices might be within the ruins, let alone the spaces for hope, but as Giroux (2013a) contends, reclamation lies with young people as they demand 'a more humane future...a new politics, a new set of values, and a renewed sense of the fragile nature of democracy' (p. 132).

'Young people as the new public intellectuals'[1]

Central in all kinds of ways to the reclamation being argued for by Giroux, is the notion of 'occupation'—which is to say of, physical place as well as the intellectual space of ideas. For him, the starting point is the fervent denial of disinterestedness, in which he argues that there is no such thing as being apolitical. The challenge lies in a preparedness to have the courage to confront and transcend the brutal and exploitative status quo, but there are distinct dangers too.

The Occupy Movement, in all of its chaotic colorfulness, provides us with some clues here, but the real issue is the message we take away from what occurred around what young people instigated in Wall Street in September 2011, and that has ricocheted around the world to literally hundreds of other countries since then.

Zizek (2012) has an interesting 'take' on this when he argues that we need to be extremely careful about what is defined as the 'enemy' in activities like the Occupy Movement, or we end up missing the point. He says that it is easy to get caught up in the 'collective carnivalesque experience' (Zizek, 2011, p. 2) of opposing the 'democratic institutional framework' (p. 11) of capitalism and its grotesque excesses. If we do that, he says, we are engaging in a 'general discontent with the global capitalist system' (p. 8), while at the same time implicitly endorsing the attempt to 'democratize' and 'extend' it (p. 10). Zizek wants to render problematic the very nature of the collective experience. Perverse as it might seem, and invoking Alain Badiou to make the point, Zizek (2011) says that the 'enemy…is not capitalism…[but] democracy' (pp. 11–12). According to Zizek (2011):

> The key to actual freedom rather resides in the apolitical, what appears to be apolitical. Networks of social relations. From the market to the family where the change needed if we want an actual improvement is not political reform but a change in apolitical social relations of production. (p. 11)

The danger in this 'overflow of critique of capitalism' and fighting against its 'excesses' comes in the form of a failure to think 'deeply about…democracy' and thereby simply extend its current form into a 'more interventionist one' (p. 10).

To round this out, Zizek's (2012) point is that there can be a 'fatal weakness [in] protests' like the Occupy Movement: 'they express an authentic rage which is not able to transform itself into a minimal positive program of sociopolitical change. They express a spirit of revolt without revolution' (p. 2). Notwithstanding, he argues that what should be resisted is 'a quick translation of the energy of the protest into a set of "concrete" pragmatic demands' (p. 2). What is needed is time 'to fill [the] vacuum in a proper way' (p. 3), and Zizek (2012) concludes with a humorous anecdote illustrating the importance of space in which to think and develop the 'language to articulate our unfreedom' (p. 3).

> In an old joke from the defunct German Democratic Republic, a German worker gets a job in Siberia. Aware of how all mail will be read by censors, he tells his friends:
>
> 'Let's establish a code: if a letter you will get from me is written in ordinary blue ink, it is true; if it is written in red ink, it is false'. After a month, his friends get the first letter written in blue ink:
>
> 'Everything is wonderful here: stores are full, food is abundant, apartments are large and properly heated, movie theaters show films from the west, there are many beautiful girls ready for an affair—the only thing unavailable is red ink'.…
>
> The task today is to give the protesters red ink. (p. 3)

The crucial question here really is: *in what sense are young people the 'new public intellectuals'* in the way Giroux has in mind?

In building upon and extending Giroux's idea, we want to make some connections to our own research with young people which provides some quite remarkable insights into both the social and economic deformities that confront young lives, but also it provides a commentary into the manner in which they encounter these obstacles and impediments and the way they work strategically to transform and alter them. This bring us back to the theme of this chapter which is an expanded view of what is meant by learning identity and how aspirations are formed and sustained, but also to the broader purpose of this book around what is meant by the term 'becoming educated'.

The backdrop to our starting point is Giroux's (2013a) argument that while young people 'might support a limited version of a market economy, they do not want to live in a market society—a society in which market values become the template for remedying all social ills' (pp. 132–133). Giroux argues that what marks these young people out, is the way they are prepared to robustly 'challeng[e] the toxic form of casino capitalism' (p. 133) in which financial systems are moving money around the globe with remarkable speed and indifference to economic destruction, all the while being propelled by a 'ruthless Social Darwinism' that is driven by 'an authoritarianism in which mindless self-gratification becomes the sanctioned norm' (Giroux, 2011, p. 2). Being an intellectual in this kind of context means having the courage to confront, speak up and speak back! For us, young people being intellectuals commences with and is embedded in the existential realities of their everyday lives in schools, communities and neighborhoods, and in their quest to pursue aspirations around getting a job. Across multiple fronts it inheres:

- in what they learn
- where they learn
- with whom and
- to what social ends

Aspirations and learning identity for 'ordinary kids'

It may seem like a huge leap from the worldwide activities of some young people who have become involved in the Occupy Movement and the daunting role Giroux assigns them as being the 'new public intellectuals', to the less politicized existential realities of what Brown (1987) labels 'ordinary kids', who are going about their lives of becoming educated and getting jobs within the constraints available to them. Our point in invoking Giroux is not to suggest that this is anything like the pathway being pursued by even the majority of ordinary kids, or that they are being politicized in the way Giroux is suggesting. Rather our point was well captured in the title of one of Giroux's (2013b) papers which referred to a coming into existence of 'Youth resistance in the age of predatory capitalism and crumbling authoritarianism'. So, what is important here is the growing realization in the psyche of young people that they no longer have to accept the harsh austerity measures being dished out and that there are 'counter public spheres and modes of resistance' (Giroux, 2013b, p. 1) that are important signifiers that young people have a right to speak back.

In the remainder of this chapter we want to look at the aspirations and associated learning identities of 'ordinary kids'. Jenkins (1983) was the first person, to our knowledge', to popularize the use of this kind of language in his ethnographic study of Ballytown estate on the outskirts of Belfast in the late 1970s, as the way many kids 'described themselves when...asked' (p. 47). For Jenkins (1983), ordinary kids presented differently to 'lads' (Willis, 1977) who were male-oriented in a world where women 'usually intruded as mothers or sex objects' (p. 47). Ordinary kids were also different from 'citizens' who held clear images of themselves, despite living on estates, as having a 'way of life, which they felt they must consciously defend and strive to maintain' (p. 52), for example, so as to distinguish themselves from their peers who had encountered the criminal justice system, those who 'came from a broken home', or 'a bad background' (p. 52—two decidedly quaint terms these days!).

For Brown (1987), ordinary kids in post-war Britain within the context of schooling, were the 'working class pupils who appeared to accept the school, usually because they believed that by arming themselves with enough qualifications to compete for middle-class jobs, they could get out of their class origin' (p. 1). Often the 'invisible majority' who distinguished themselves by virtue of their ordinariness, were the ones 'who neither left their names engraved on the school's honor boards, not gouged them into the top of classroom desks' (p. 1). While they may not always 'conform with the school ethos...[ordinary kids] were nevertheless willing to "make an effort"' (p. 1) and more or less passively go along with schooling. They were not revolutionary rebels! According to Brown (1987), it is because of their 'conformist' responses that ordinary kids 'have largely been ignored and misunderstood... [with their] apparent conformity [being] associated with female pupils' (p. 3). In other words, we have only a partial understanding of how these kids experience schooling, how it connects with the rest of their lives, where they see

Identity and capacity to aspire

school carrying them, and what other resources they deploy (or are missing) in 'becoming educated'.

We want to turn now to some of the narratives of these ordinary kids—paradoxically, from neighborhoods and schools officially designated as 'disadvantaged' as we described in earlier chapters—as we asked them questions about how they were going about making lives for themselves.

Before we hear some of the views of young people, we need to briefly revisit the notion of aspirations—as much as to dismiss what it is *not*, as to affirm what it might be. Our view is that aspiration is *not* an individual psychologistic quality that is present or absent in whatever degrees—which is the way the mainstream policy literature would have us believe. Positioned in this way, aspiration becomes a whip with which to assail individuals so that they can be blamed for not having it—they are slack, lazy, indolent, lacking in imagination and motivation, individually, collectively and even intergenerationally—and they need to be borne down upon! Appadurai (2004) argued that 'Aspirations are never simply individual (as the language of wants and choices inclines us to think). They are always formed in interaction and in the thick of social life' (p. 67).

We prefer to use Appadurai's (2004) concept of 'capacity to aspire' which he defines as 'the social and cultural capability to imagine alternative futures and find ways to shape them' (Appadurai, 2005, abstract). Capacity to aspire lends itself much more to unraveling the complexities that lie at the 'disjuncture…between economy, culture and politics' (p. 33) and has a much more relational inflection around the context in which people finds themselves interacting with. This more relational, and we would argue sociological, view of capacity to aspire, enables a focus on 'actually existing social forms' (p. 179) and the 'conjectures' and 'refutations' (p. 69) within which desires are formed and worked out.

From Appadurai (2004) we have developed four themes (see Smyth & McInerney, 2013b for an expanded discussion of these) which give us a useful discursive point of entry into the aspirational stories of some of the young people in our research, referred to in earlier chapters:

- Access to 'opportunity resources' and local immediacy
- Possessing and using navigational maps
- Opportunities to rehearse, share, and 'practice navigational capacity'
- 'Precedent setting and capacity to inspire'

We will discuss what we mean by each of these in the context of some portraits from some 'ordinary kids'.

(a) Access to 'opportunity resources' and local immediacy

Narrative portrait: Howard

What influence does a parent's occupation have on young peoples' choice of careers? How significant are parents in assisting them to secure jobs? Quite a few students do want to follow in their parent's footsteps, especially boys whose fathers are involved in the trades and engineering businesses. Equally, it appears that family and business connections give some students an edge in the employment stakes. Like many of his peers, sixteen-year-old Howard has a rather instrumental view of school—'it's important because it helps you get a job'—but he knows that he needs more than a school certificate to obtain an apprenticeship in the automotive business. He expects that his step father will use his influence to connect him to employment opportunities. This portrait was developed from a transcript of an interview with Howard conducted on the 22nd of August 2011.

> *'School is pretty important because it helps you get a job'*

I live in Hillview and went to the local primary school before coming to New Vision Community College. I'm in year 10 now. School's not too bad. It just depends on what class you're in. I'm not too good at maths and I have to study a bit more in that subject. School was a bit awkward in years 8 and 9 but over the last year I feel pretty comfortable. I want to get into engineering and stuff like that. The school finds you courses and things you can get yourself into. I'm pretty good at English but I don't like science too much. My favorite subject is engineering. My step dad drives trucks. I usually help him on the weekends and I enjoy that. I first wanted to be a builder and did work experience at joinery but didn't like it too much. I sort of know more about doing things on cars and trucks and stuff. My dad has his own trucking business. I wouldn't like to drive trucks but I would like to work on them, so I don't see myself taking over his business. I don't have a part-time job but I'm looking at getting an apprenticeship. My parents will be happy with whatever I get to do. I reckon I might move up to Bay City. I like it there with fishing and all that. I quite like living in Hillview. There are not many houses around and that I like the motor bikes and that stuff.

School is pretty important because it helps you get a job. My plan is to get year 10 and if I don't get an apprenticeship I would stay here or go to a TAFE college or something. My step dad has got a few connections and that. It's important who you know but I still have to have an education. Maths and English are pretty important. You need maths for measuring stuff and you need English for reading paperwork and engine numbers. I know my basic maths but I'm not too good with all the other stuff. Sometimes in class it's a bit hard to see how you are going to use maths. I like to have it explained a bit more to me so I actually get it. If they come and tell me I get it straight away. I reckon I could work out the circumference of a piston. I'm doing a building course now but since I did the work experience I've changed my mind. I'm not too bad with computers but not too advanced either. I'm more outdoorsy.

Howard makes it clear that for him school has a fairly *limited set of opportunity resources*, and he regards it in a fairly instrumental way. While he can see the value of education in a general way, he struggles to see how 'you are going to use maths'. The fact that he does not excel at maths and does not like science, and that school was a 'bit awkward in years 8 and 9', seems to have positioned Howard as a student who is not doing much better than getting by in school. His aspirational planning seems much more attuned to activities around his step father's work as a truck driver, and his own interests in motorbikes and fishing and his confessed predilection of being 'outdoorsy'. His plan to use his step father's connections to get him into an apprenticeship seems indicative of the *local immediacy of the source of resources* Howard deems to be important to him in forming and meeting his aspirations.

(b) Possessing and using navigational maps

Dialogic Portrait: Cooper and Jim

Appadurai (2004) regards the capacity to aspire as being *like a 'map' that people use* to explore and construct futures for themselves. In other words, 'a navigational capacity' (p. 69) that *is matured, honed and nurtured through the opportunity to use it* and learn from it in real world contexts. Where these opportunities are limited or do not exist, there is a 'less easy archiving of alternatives futures…[and] more brittle horizons of aspirations' (p. 69). As a teacher working with low SES students in Bok's (2010) study put it, 'It's like making them do a play without a script' (p. 175). Expecting students to map out a future for themselves when they have no examples to work off or appropriate cues to guide them, as well as no opportunity to rehearse and learn from their mistakes (and the experiences of others), is likely to be much more difficult and likely lead to a diminished result—but that is effectively what is occurring in the lives of many students.

The following dialogic portrait is a nice illustration of students working against the script provided by the school.

Cooper and Jim are in the middle years of schooling (both aged 14 and in year 8) at New Vision Community College and they have some rather pragmatic views about education. Jim, in particular, downplays the value of schooling over real life experiences. This condensed portrait was developed from a transcript of an interview with Cooper and Jim conducted on the 5th of April 2011 at New Vision College.

'It's better to have experience than knowledge. You need experience'

'Schools alright', says Jim, 'but it's the teacher's attitude that influences how much you are going to learn. If they just lay it out and not make it much fun then you're not going to learn much, but if the teacher is enthusiastic about the work then you are going to learn. Our game making teacher is pretty enthusiastic. He's my favorite one. He goes around to everyone and doesn't just sit at his desk on his laptop looking at the footy scores. The enthusiastic teachers talk to you about stuff. I had an enthusiastic teacher in maths last year and that's when I started to do my work. Now I don't really do much'. 'It's more or less the same for me', adds Cooper. 'Education is more about experience', states Cooper. 'Like some people can be educated and go in and do the accounting jobs and that but it's more social. Education is not all that important to get a job'. 'It's important but you don't need to be the best at it', says Jim. 'If you are social person there is no need to get an 'A' in all your subjects. If you are not that social, education is important, or else you will be working in Macca's. You need to be social even there to talk to the customers.'

'My dad thinks it's important to stay at school', says Cooper. 'He would like me to be an engineer because it pays the most. He's trying to get into the army and become an engineer but mum does nothing'. 'My dad's been working in joinery since he was sixteen', says Jim. He worked for 7 years with other people and now he has his own business. He builds kitchens. My mum works at a real estate agency. She got hired this year'. On the question of employment opportunities in the area, Jim remarks 'People do all different types of jobs in this neighborhood but there is one part of Broadacres [pseudonym] that some people don't work. It's kind of down that side where Cooper lives'. 'I live two blocks from the primary school', says Cooper. 'I'm not sure I will stay in this area in the future', says Jim. 'It depends on where I can get work and what type of work it will be. I think there are good accounting jobs in South Australia, or it might be in another place in Australia'. 'It's much too early to know where I'll be', Cooper remarks.

Jim has the final word: 'When it comes to education I think it's what you are best at. You can be good at footballer but you can be terrible at English. It's better to have experience than knowledge. You need experience'.

Both these young people hold fairly pragmatic views about education. Jim, in particular, downplays the value of schooling over real life experiences. As he sees it, being a 'social person', presumably one who can relate well to others, counts more than the knowledge acquired from school when it comes to getting a job. Both have aspirations to get well-paid employment but have not as yet attached much importance to schooling. Instead they believe that their work opportunities are likely to arise from the credibility gained from non-school experiences.

What we see here are two boys who, while they are compliant with their parents' view on the undifferentiated value of education and their desire that

Identity and capacity to aspire 121

the boys continue with school, are nevertheless working out quite different navigational maps for themselves that draw off being a 'social' person as one boy put it. Perhaps some of the enthusiasm of their game making teacher rubbed off in providing something of a role model. What Jim is saying is, that for him, he is prepared to trade off high grades and qualifications, and instead be a person who is good at relationships. Otherwise he says, you finish up in low paid insecure work in fast food outlets, albeit that even there you still need to be 'social'. Bok (2010) invoking Appadurai (2004), indicates that this is indicative that the simplistic 'high' versus 'low' aspirations is misleading: 'by exploring the notion that all people aspire, although socio-economic and cultural factors enable some to more powerfully pursue their aspirations than others' (p. 176).

(c) Opportunities to 'practice navigational capacity'

The following portrait of two young women reveals a reasonably well developed capacity to aspire and of how their school enables them to take advantage of and work through opportunities to rehearse how one piece of their biographies will help them move to the next stage. Although neither comes from a privileged background, they have worked out how hard work at school has the potential to reward them in careers they hope will take them beyond their immediate locale.

Dialogic Portrait: Teresa and Lexi

Teresa and Lexi present themselves as confident, well-spoken young women with a strong sense of direction in their education. Both are studying school subjects at a standard above their year 10 level and have aspirations to go to university. Teresa's main interest is in the performing arts whilst Lexi is keen to pursue a career in science. They are aware that private schools have a reputation for academic studies but believe that they can succeed with hard work and the support of teachers. This portrait was developed from a transcript of an interview on the 23rd of June 2011.

> *'I like to think that I'm doing really well and I try really hard'*
>
> Teresa and Lexi have well-formed thoughts about future education pathways and vocations. 'I want to get into acting for a career and picture myself living in England or America or somewhere, because of more opportunities', says Teresa. 'I've always been interested in acting. I was in the production of *Grease* and I'm doing year 11 theatre studies, one year above my level. Next year I'm going to do year 12 and after that I am planning on going to university and then go overseas. I would like to go to the Federation City University so I can stay close to my family. I won't see them much when I move overseas. My parents are supportive. They say that acting is good but if it doesn't work out then you need to have

something else to fall back on'. Lexi has a rather different career in mind. 'I'm really interested in animals and science and I want to be a vet', she explains. 'I like science and I am going on exchange to John Monash Science School next semester, for 5 weeks. I'm doing year 11 biology this year. It's a grade above my year level but I think it's easier. You really try harder to do your best. Science is a pretty broad area, and in science you can branch off in all directions'.

What motivates and encourages them to pursue these career interests? 'I enjoy animals and science and my inspiration has been my mum', says Lexi. 'She had a dream to be a midwife, but she never did because she married and had children. So she encourages all us girls. I'm the middle child. I have two younger and two older sisters'. 'Even though my parents didn't go to university they have got pretty good jobs', exclaims Teresa. 'But I want to be a little different to them. I want to see if at least I can get there. I've always wanted to go to university and do these different courses and all the things I have to learn'. Both girls claim that they are successful, hard working students although Teresa admits she has never been good at maths'. I need to try a little harder but I'm good at drama', she says. Lexi exclaims 'I like to think that I'm doing really well and I try really hard. I have my two older sisters who are very good. We help each other out a lot. One sister has been dux twice now and she is very supportive. We're both doing VCE biology. All the people I know are doing VCE but the people who don't want to do academic stuff are doing VCAL. I reckon about half and half at our school. Whether you choose VCE or VCAL depends on what you want to do and if you can do the work. The school just gives you the options to choose one path or the other. So we make up our own minds. With most things that I do I feel that this school gives me different opportunities', says Teresa. I take what I can. If you want to get somewhere you can without the costs of a private school.

Appadurai (2004) argues that while some people seem to mysteriously acquire the navigational capacity to envisage and enact coherent pathways, others do not. He says there is an inequitable distribution in the ability to formulate plans and realistically pull them off. In trying to make sense of this inequity, Du Bois-Reymond (1998) says that the difference is between 'normal biographies' and 'choice biographies', which Ball, Davies, David and Reay (2002) explain like this:

> Normal biographies are linear, anticipated and predictable, unreflexive transitions, often gender and class specific, rooted in well-established life-worlds. They are often driven by an absence of decisions.... [For example] going to university as 'automatic', 'taken for granted', 'always assumed'...'That was the family plan...' The decision to go to university it is a non-decision. (p. 57)

Ball et al., (2002) go on to say:

> ...middle-class young people 'move in their world as a fish in water' and 'need not engage in rational computation in order to reach goals that best suit their interests' (Bourdieu, 1990, p. 108)...[These] accounts...are rendered in

closed narrative forms' (Cohen & Hey, 2000) that are typically inscribed with transgenerational family scripts or 'inheritance codes'. They portray a 'continuous dramatic life historical thread'. (Ball et al., 2002, p. 57)

By contrast, young people from less advantaged (working class) backgrounds are characterized much more by 'doubts, ambivalences, and very deliberate decision making' (Ball, et al., 2002, p. 57) that lead them to biographies that require careful choice, which Du Bois-Reymond (1998) describes thus:

> 'Choice biographies' are by no means purely based on freedom and own choices... (young) people are forced to reflect on the available options and justify their decisions...it is the *tension between option/freedom and legitimation/coercion* which marks 'choice biographies'. (p. 65, emphases in original)

The latter is depicted by Ball, Davies, David and Reay (2002) as being 'rendered in open narrative forms and are more fragmentary and discontinuous...The future is unimagined or highly generic [such as getting] 'a good job' (p. 57).

Clearly, Teresa and Lexi do not fit comfortably into the 'normal biography' mould—they do not come from backgrounds that comfortably propel them along in a linear fashion. They display more of the features of the kind of unpredictability of the 'choice biography', albeit undertaken strategically through accessing the resources available through their school, that will likely lead them some way in the directions they have chosen for themselves. While nothing can be absolutely certain for young people like Teresa and Lexi, the fact that they are accessing the opportunities that will enable them to rehearse and practice their navigational capacity, bodes well for their futures, even if they have to refocus and perhaps develop some more realistically achievable options along the way.

(d) Precedent setting and 'capacity to aspire'

A crucial element in capacity to aspire are 'strategies for precedent setting' (Appadurai, 2004, p. 76) and this can take the form of entrepreneurial spirit and independence of thought. As Appadurai (2004) put it:

> ...strategies for precedent setting...constitute spaces for exploring the capacity to aspire and for testing the possibilities for changes...[involving] a map of a journey into the future.... (p. 76)

In a more philosophical tone, he saw precedent setting as:

> ...lending vision and horizon to immediate strategies and choices, lending immediacy and materiality to abstract wishes and desires, and struggling to reconcile the demands of the moment against the discipline of patience. (p. 76)

We can see some traces of each of these in the following portrait of a young person who has some big ideas as well as some practical strategies that she is drawing from.

Narrative portrait: Erin

Currently studying year 11 at New Vision Community College, sixteen-year-old Erin and her family live on a rural property about 15 kilometers from Federation City. Erin projects an image of an independent, entrepreneurial young person with a sense of agency and capacity for hard work. She is adamant that she does not want to follow in her mother's footsteps and go to university—rather her interests lie in the hospitality industry. She harbors the somewhat romantic notion of owning a country pub. Erin seems to enjoy school and is quick to acknowledge the support she has received from her teachers and parents in supporting her aspirations. Perhaps she will need to do more to realize her dream than 'sucking up' to her grandfather to obtain his bluestone cottage for her pub but there is no doubting her enthusiasm and determination. This portrait was developed from transcripts of interviews with Erin on the 22nd of August 2011 and the 28th of February 2012.

'I know it's strange but I want to get my pub'

We have a 20 acre property and a few horses. My dad's a builder and mum's a dentist. Although she studied to be a nurse she decided to become a dentist. Mum doesn't necessarily want me to go down the university route. As long as I finish school she will be happy and she is supportive of my future plans. This year I'm doing VCE maths and English and the rest are VCAL subjects, including a school-based apprenticeship in Business Administration at the Royal Hotel in Federation City. I'm doing reception work in the hotel now but when I'm 18 I want to work in the pub because I'd like to own a pub. I've even got a money box and started saving for it. Mum and dad don't even go to pubs and they think that it's very weird me wanting to own a pub. I would like to run a country pub but then I don't know about how many customers I would get.

I play netball and coach three netball teams and I'm getting paid for the hours that I do at the hotel and I can work on Sundays. The work has helped me heaps because I never knew how to use computer programs. I got an offer to do the certificate here but I thought I would get much more experience doing it in person. They offered me a full time apprenticeship but I wanted to finish year 12 first. I'm looking forward to 'schoolies week' and the debutante ball and all that. The small business class and the hospitality course I'm doing at school are helping me and it's all leading me in that direction. I'd really like to own a pub in Smith's Creek [pseudonym]. There's a blue-stone building my granddad owns—it's just an old house—and my father is a builder so it could be done. I've been sucking up to my granddad big time. The people in the hotel help me a lot and my parents are supporting me. I know it's strange but I want to get my pub.

Appadurai (2004) claims that precedents are crucial, as we have seen so far in these young people's narratives around 'becoming educated'. Sometimes 'ordinary kids' make some extraordinary progress towards mapping a journey of their future, even when they don't have much in the way of 'precedent setting' to help them. This point was made clearly in Kahl's (1953) seminal study on the place of parental support in shaping and enabling young people's ambitions:

> An intelligent common man boy was not college oriented in high school unless he had a special reason for so being. Behind all the reasons stood one pre-eminent force: parental pressure. (p. 201)

There is no actual evidence that this kind of pressure existed in the case of Erin, although we can surmise that Kahl is likely correct. Notwithstanding, while Erin might have only limited exemplars from her immediate family background, she looks like she is working at coming up with a strategy to suture together what she can muster within her family support structures, together with what she can garner from other (educational) sources—to produce a credible plan. This is quite contrary to the view of aspirations behind programs like AimHigher (DfES, 2003) which commenced in the UK in 2004 with the intent of widening the participation in higher education among students from 'non-traditional' (read non-middle-class) backgrounds.

It seems that Erin, in the absence of any direct precedent setting by her parents (even in spite of it in the case of her mother), is relying on what Ball and Vincent (1998) refer to as 'grapevine' or 'hot knowledge' which is 'based on affective responses ['I know its strange, but I want to get my pub…Mum and Dad don't even go to pubs, they think it is very weird'] or direct experience ['I'm doing reception work in a hotel now']' (p. 380). This Contrasts sharply with 'cold knowledge' or 'official' knowledge that is 'constructed specifically for public dissemination' (p. 380) through career guidance counseling in places like schools. The kind of intuitive knowledge Erin is drawing from is of a kind that she regards as being 'more reliable' than 'official' knowledge, that is most unlikely to exist for her unusual project.

In this chapter what we have canvassed is a set of views that rather than see aspiration as residing in some aggregation or 'bundles of idiosyncratic' (even psychologistic) qualities (Appadurai, 2004, p. 68), we have argued instead that when viewed culturally, capacity to aspire presents as an uneven distribution of a resource that can have quite profound effects on how young people go about the project of developing a learning identity around becoming 'somebody'.

Note

1. Giroux, 2013a, p. 132.

7. Re-framing what it means to be educated

Why are we having 'boring, meaningless shit'[1]?

Elsewhere in our writing we have explored extensively and intensively why it is that so many young people in affluent western countries are giving up on school (see: Smyth, et al., 2000; Smyth & Hattam, 2004; Smyth & McInerney, 2007; 2012), and with such damaging and devastating consequences on young lives. If we strip it back to its essentials, the short answer to the mythical student behind Novinger and O'Brien's question is because what passes as schooling for many of these young people is a curriculum and forms of pedagogy that are 'irrelevant, fragmented [and] meaningless' (Novinger & O'Brien, 2003, p. 3). Despite seemingly monumental efforts to reform schooling around the world, for a disproportionately large number of young people what is on offer in school collapses down to being no more than 'boring, meaningless shit' (p. 3).

In some respects in this book we have stepped sideways a little from the theme of our earlier work—the standardized, regulated, controlled, surveilled and contrived nature of contemporary schooling—to examine some topics that have a different inflection. What we have done is bring our socially critical lens to bear on a number of other protracted social attributes that present as significant additional impediments and obstacles to young people 'becoming somebody' (Wexler, 1992) as they engage in identity formation within the contexts of their schooling.

One of the things we have strenuously attempted to do in this book is to engage in what amounts to a form of resistance to the way educational systems and so-called reforms have dumbed-down schools and made them inhospitable places for the already most marginalized students.

For almost three decades now we have vigorously and tenaciously held to the view that the most powerful form of resistance with which to 'speak back' to forms of educational policy idiocy, is through crafting and conveying the experiences of young people in respect of their schooling. After all, there are not many other credible alternatives—as adults we seem to have completely lost it! Young people are the ones who should be listened to because they are the most informed and profound witnesses of what is being *done to* them educationally.

Both in terms of its substance as well as the method by which we have gone about our craft of researching young lives in this book, our work falls within what C. Wright Mills ([1959]1971) referred to as a 'sociological imagination'—that is to say the 'ability to create possible reconstructions of larger social forces which affect our lives', as Shannon (1999, p. 396) put it. The storied and narrative way we have gone about this—we call them 'portraits' (see Smyth & McInerney, 2013a)—is so as to make visible what is normally hidden, concealed, shrouded or silenced. What we are referring to, of course, are the lives, experiences, desires and aspirations of young people, which have been totally invisibled in the official educational policy discourses of schooling. As Shannon (1999), a long time activist and advocate for the power of story telling, put it, 'things aren't what they appear to be' and what are in reality 'public issues' are mischievously packaged and presented as if they are 'personal troubles', alluding to C.W. Mills ([1959]1971, p. 397). The way Shannon (1999) sees it, stories are important to people because they are political, in a context where people are supposed to be apolitical:

> Stories are how people make sense of themselves and their worlds. In a real sense, stories make people. For these reasons, stories are political. Whose stories get told? What can these stories mean? Who benefits from their telling? These are political questions because they address the ways in which people's identities—their beliefs, attitudes, and values—are created and maintained. (p. 397)

For us, as well as the young people we had conversations with in our research, there was something quite remarkable and profound occurring as they talked with us, and as we (and they) made sense of what it was they were saying. From our vantage point, and in this regard, Shannon (1999) argues that:

> Stories set the parameters for our thinking as we blend the stories we've read, heard, and seen with the events in our lives that also seem to come to us as stories. That is, we read our lives as if they were texts and we negotiate meaning from and with those texts. (p. 397)

For the young people in our research, what was important was the act of creation that they were engaged in as they talked to us—in all likelihood, the first such conversations they had experienced with adults who were not either their parents or teachers. Most of what they had to say was outside of and beyond what was contained in or conveyed to them in classrooms, through teachers, or in government documents that are coming to increasingly manacle the kinds of teaching they are experiencing. The process of trying to make sense of their lives and convey it to us, is in no small measure indicative of their use of various forms of literacy. Again as Shannon (1999) points out:

> Despite what governments want us to believe, texts are more than written [or proclaimed forms of] language...Texts are the symbols that surround us in our daily lives that we must interpret for the meaning in our lives. Our abilities to interpret and negotiate meaning from texts makes us literate. (p. 397)

There is something else going on here that is even more important than the functional decoding of symbols in order to make sense of them, and it has to do with how literacy enables an assertion of power and control over action:

> Our abilities to use that literacy in order to make sense of our lives and those of others, and to take action upon what we learn about ourselves and the world gives us some power and enables us to have some control over our lives. (p. 397)

Being able to interrupt and penetrate the complexities, paradoxes and political nonsense increasingly put around us, by tying 'private problems' to 'public issues' is indicative of what it means to be an 'educated' person. With that challenge in mind, let us reach back a little into our own text.

As we look across the portraits in Chapter 3 we cannot help but be struck by the way in which at least some of these young people were standing up to and puncturing deficit notions of 'disadvantage' being assigned to them.

A good example is seventeen-year-old, year 12 Derek from New Vision College, who produced the 'jaw dropping' response from his parents, neither of who had been to university, when he declared he intended to try and get a high enough entry score to study physiotherapy at university. His story is a far cry from the popular and media representation of students in his school who are widely regarded as only really being suited and qualified to perform 'hands-on', menial, manual-type work.

Fifteen-year-old Fatima who migrated from the Sudan (possibly as a refugee?) with her mother and siblings and who at the age of 6 could speak no English, even at year 10 has a very clear view of the importance of education to her future, and is working to leverage what she can from education to pursue a career in hairdressing and the ambition to own a salon. Her friend Tanya has ambitions to be a forensic scientist even though she has some as yet unresolved issues about how she will transgress the gap between liking study but being lukewarm about school. Both are quite sanguine that, unlike some of their peers who plan to drop out of school, they see this as a one-way path to a bleak future in insecure, poorly paid, casual work at fast food outlets. In this sense, whatever the limitations they might have in bringing their plans to fruition, both Fatima and Tanya are operating strategically against the orthodoxy that young people like them can only ever be fodder for the fast-food industry.

Sixteen-year-old, year 11 Tony from another school in Federation City, who was brought up by his single mother, wants to build on his interests in computer games to pursue a career in multi-media design and graphics animation. Because of his family situation he had to learn responsibility at an early age, and this has given him maturity beyond his years to work out complex things like time management and school/home/leisure balance. He can see how these skills will be important to him in pursuing university studies beyond Federation City and possible work overseas. These are important tangible indicators that young people like Tony who might not have an abundance of family networks and capital to draw upon, have nevertheless acquired the most important attribute of all—a faith instilled by his mother of the importance of education. In some quarters, aspiring to be educated is supposedly the preserve of the more affluent and advantaged classes. People like Ruby Payne (2002; 2005), entrepreneur and sometime proselytizer of a 'culture of poverty', argue that young working class people like Tony are essentially ineducable because of their deficits of middle-class values.

Sixteen-year-old independent living Shirley even at year 10 level is aware that she has been shunted into a track that will not enable her to access the kind of university program necessary for her to gain the management skills to pursue her passion in events management. While we don't have access to all of the details, it is not hard to surmise that she may be a case of an institutional decision that young people like Shirley, who have become estranged from home, are probably cases of where it is simply easier to just allow her to follow the seemingly natural course of morphing into continuing with casual work at the 'curry shack', rather than invest the substantial resources involved in trying to get her to succeed in a university track. She has become what scholars like Booher-Jennings (2005) and Youdell (2004) call a case of 'educational triage'—a part of the collateral damage that is necessary in order that some of her more advantaged peers might receive the educational assistance necessary to succeed.

Fifteen-year-old, year 11 Abigail has worked out that the decks are severely stacked against her in the way her public school is unfairly and inaccurately portrayed publicly in the media—a fact that she is unclear as to how it will work against her in getting into a highly coveted university veterinary science program, which she aspires to. What is interesting about Abigail's case is that she has worked out how the stereotyping of her school is propagated, and that to counter this, she will have to study even harder—with possibly unknown dire consequences, against students from wealthy elite private schools.

Unlike some of their peers who, on the basis of encountering the 'boring, meaningless shit' often served up by schools, had rejected school as being 'not for them', the young informants we spoke with seemed to have been able to summon up the internal resources with which to go beyond that kind of seemingly short-sighted response. That is not to say that life was therefore a breeze for them—far from it. They found that opportunities available to them were far from equitably distributed. They encountered strong forces that sought to naturalize the way things were by constructing 'at risk' categories into which they could be conveniently placed. It was as if this placement then excused the kind of diminished or ameliorative treatment they were subsequently given—a kind of self-reinforcing prophecy. It seemed that the rationale behind these kinds of stratifying policy maneuverings was something that *had to be* accepted within a competitive market-driven system. By definition, there *had to be* casualties or collateral damage. What our stories revealed, is that it is not possible to simply pathologize young people like these based only upon the demographics of who they are, their kind of family upbringing, or where they live. Smart young people have ways of puncturing those false renditions, and in the process, learning something powerful about what it means to 'become educated'—no testing regimes, league tables, or achievement scores anywhere in sight here!

Looking for the 'print of class' in the process of becoming educated

The theme we pursued in Chapter 4 was around Reay's (2005) notion of the affective nature of class, which is to say, 'how social class is actually lived' (p. 913) and how it pulses through the veins of working class young people in the ways they think and act out what they believe it means to go about becoming educated. To that extent, we were very much taken by what Savage (2003) described as looking for the traces of the 'print of class' (p. 536) in places where it might hitherto been thought to be invisible or only faintly present. Here we confronted the difficult reality mentioned by Reay (2005), that young people rarely ever mention or name social class—but it is palpable and visceral beneath their skin.

Where our sociological 'detective work' (Savage, 2003, p. 536) took us was into the kind of 'hanging on while letting go' struggles evident in young people like fifteen-year-old Lydia (pp. 74–75)—who wanted to simultaneously leave school midway though year 11 to join her departed friends, while also trying to live her mother's reality of her finishing school, by becoming a vet. These are two seemingly completely irreconcilable realities.

Seventeen-year-old, year 12 student Elisha (p. 75) was also living the struggle, in a different way, as she battled with how to continue with her passion for horse riding, while at the same time realizing that without a lot of hard work and careful strategyzing this would not result in her getting into university. Interestingly, Elisha was able to see clearly the way in which her school was deeply implicated in sorting and sifting people like her, while mouthing the rhetoric of 'becoming anything you want'. She could see how what the school labeled as the 'less able' students were being shunted into 'hands-on' vocational directions, reinforcing the class divide in which the more 'academic' students 'looked down' on their supposedly less able peers—to reinforce a socially constructed divide.

Without wishing to become unduly sidetracked, there is an important piece of history we need to insert here that is not irrelevant, albeit that some of the language might be a little more muted and circumspect these days. In the early part of the twentieth century, education in Victoria, Australia, had the dubious reputation of leading the world, for all the wrong reasons. Medical anthropologist Ross Jones (2007), in his *Humanity's Mirrors: 150 years of Anatomy in Melbourne* documents in detail the ideas and research activities of Professor Richard Berry, a professor of anatomy at The Melbourne University and a leading protagonist and advocate in the eugenics movement. Berry's research was based on craniometry (the measurement of head size) which he claimed was demonstrably linked to intelligence, which he strenuously argued was crucial in promoting 'national efficiency' or 'social efficiency' (in modern day language 'economic rationalism') (p. 107). The larger argument that this set of views was feeding was the worldwide 'battle for evolutionary supremacy' known more commonly as 'social Darwinism' (p. 107). Berry's claim was that 'the mentally deficient' placed an unsustainable burden 'on the community through the cost to social welfare, lost productivity, social unrest and institutionalization was severely detrimental to Australia's development' (p. 108). In what was a blatantly racist position, Berry used the tools of anatomy 'to convince Australian governments to implement policies to improve the race and thus increase national efficiency' (p. 110). Australia at the time 'had one of the best standards of living in the world' (p. 112) and this had to be preserved through 'social efficiency' by ensuring 'the best possible population [to] fill the empty continent' (p. 114). What transpired was that Berry advocated for 'a radical reordering of social merit based on intelligence as expressed by head size' (p. 123). As if conflating ideas of 'inferior races and inferior individuals' with 'smaller brain sizes' and 'intelligence' were not bad enough, Berry's ideas were to deeply infect policies at the time, most notably 'the White Australia policy' (p. 126).

Educationally Berry had a profound influence, with Jones (2007) summarizing it thus:

> There was no point, according to Berry, in offering a wide range of opportunities to all students as the hierarchy of intelligence was established at birth, and became obvious by, at the latest, the twelfth year. Berry's conclusion supported by a graduated and multistreamed system of secondary education providing education for each citizen to the age of sixteen, at which stage, according to Berry, the brain would constitute eighty-two per cent of its final adult size. Brighter children (classified as members of Berry's superior class), would receive an education from the age of twelve that would lead to university and the professions. The lower classes would receive a technical education that would include training to be a good citizen. (p. 124)

Confronting and puncturing the 'hands-on' myth

While Australia may no longer have such an overt system of educational apartheid in public education (it certainly has one between public and private schools), framed as it was by the early 1900s eugenics movement in the form of distinct high schools (academically oriented) and technical schools (vocationally oriented), at least in Victoria—the residue is nevertheless still very much in existence. The eugenics binary gets to be sustained and maintained in much more polite ways these days that do not involve measuring and promoting the size of anatomy parts.

One of the most common refrains we have heard from the several thousand young people we have interviewed over the years, including in the research in this book, is that 'we are hands-on people'. It is no coincidence that all of our research has occurred in what are officially designated 'disadvantaged' schools—whether that is an accurate label or not might be a matter of dispute.

What we take 'hands-on' to mean—at least from the way young people put it to us—is that this is a term they have internalized or absorbed from being told so repeatedly by their teachers, schools, the media, society and through exposure to limited familial role models, that they are only suited to manual pursuits that don't require abstract thinking, reasoning, reading, or sustained writing. Schools, education systems and a substantial industry (see for example http://handsonlearning.org.au) feed this misperception through euphemistic labels like 'applied learning' or 'vocational education' that leads young people to believe that whoever is so labeling them must be right, that they are 'at risk', because they are struggling with what they see as academic pursuits, and besides, there are alternative 'options' provided for people just like them. The whole thing becomes a circular self-fulfilling prophecy. A more accurate reality might be that they have been *made into* 'casualties' by a system of educational triage that is so stressed or under-resourced that they have to be sacrificed. The already advantaged are thus able to continue to maintain a boundary of difference between themselves and the remainder, who have been 'othered'.

Seventeen-year-old Crystal (p. 76) has seemingly worked out how to handle the social class divide and sees herself as being on the right side of the divide to put her on a path to a university forensic science course. She is mindful of the obstacles, such as 'kids that don't want to learn', and she regards the safety net for these kids of 'applied learning certificates' as being 'really good' for the half of her year level who are not switched on to school in the way she is. She expressed concern at the way her school finds it hard to escape from its 'tech school' past and the recent reputation it has gained as a result of a stabbing incident. Despite these impediments she is very optimistic and 'doesn't feel at all hopeless [and] wants to prove people wrong'—by which she means collectively and individually.

Of all the young people we interviewed in this research, sixteen-year-old, year 11 Brett (pp. 77–78) presented one of the most sophisticated analyses of what was going on. He had developed a capacity to see that the reforms being implemented at his school in pursuit of a marketized neo-liberal agenda by the new principal (discipline, attendance, uniforms) as having benefited individuals, but the school as a collective had taken on the hue of a 'penitentiary'. He expressed concern about the welfare and futures of those of his peers who had been excluded and shunted out, and for whom school had become a difficult place to deal with because of extraneous factors in their lives outside of school, mostly because he saw their working classed backgrounds as not fitting with the middle-class ethos of the school.

Seventeen-year-old Riley (pp. 78–79) on the other hand, who was on track to pursue a career in psychology could see the problem confronting his school in terms of some of his peers who 'are mucking around [and] are getting kicked out...[and] not show[ing] up any more'. He makes an astute observation about the origins and effects: 'Most of the kids mucking up in primary school end up doing applied learning studies. The smarter ones do the academic course'.

What we see here is a young person echoing the policy mantra of what Roberts and Evans (2012) refer to as young people acting as an 'active rational individual agent' (p. 72) in which there is little space for an understanding of the place of 'class background and position' (p. 72). While Riley can see the incubation of the problem early on in the lives of some of his peers, like many other people he seems to find it hard to move beyond the individualizing of responsibility. This is indicative of the more general point we have been making throughout Chapter 4, and the book, that it is much easier to individualize the problem (i.e., privatize it) rather than accept that there has to be a more complex and collectivist (i.e., public) way of approaching the solution.

What we do see in this chapter through the commentary of Abigail, Quentin and Bruce is something of the way the individualizing takes on a more worrying and collectivist hue in the pathological ascribing of the term 'westie' to separate off the differentiation of themselves as followers of middle-class norms, from 'others' with less desirable lifestyles and attributes.

Are these really broken communities?

What we robustly challenge in Chapter 5 in 'celebrating space, place and neighborhoods' is the kind of intellectual laziness that comes with deficit forms of thinking and labeling, and that allow 'solutions' to supposed 'problems' to be collapsed down to pathologies which are deemed to have simple technical answers—rather than attaching to or emerging out of any local strengths or merits residing in these communities. In other words, what is constructed is the perception of a 'crisis' around the notion that these are 'broken communities' (Savage, 2012) which can only be fixed using the resources and expertise that resides in outsiders. This is a demeaning, derogatory and dependent model. We see this most recently being given expression in the so-called 'Big Society' (Norman, 2010) agenda being pursued by the conservative political parties in Britain. As Savage (2012) summarized it, the allegation is that the:

> Big Society is about helping people come together to improve their own lives, It's about putting more power in people's hands—a massive transfer of power… to local communities. (p. 145)

As Savage (2012) goes on to point out, the problem with approaches that preach a 'fusion of apocalyptic pessimism and banal policy prescription' is that they invariably:

> …misunderstand communal social relations in two ways. First, there is no simple moral breakdown or loss of social support in poor deprived working-class

areas. Rather, a range of powerful and pervasive support mechanisms are in evidence…(p. 146). Second, if we are concerned with moral breakdown, it is to the practices of the very wealthy that we should turn…To seek to 'foist' communal attachments which they would not personally adopt on poorer communities is therefore a form of calculated hypocrisy,…or 'symbolic violence'. (pp. 146–147)

These are precisely the kind of problems that accompany the area-based interventions we describe in this chapter as being inflicted on the communities served by New Visions College and Federation City Senior Secondary School Campus.

What we have done by getting up close to the voices of the young people in both these research schools is develop a sense of the sophistication of the relational resources they have drawn upon in their project of Becoming Educated, as they go about speaking back to negative and deterministic policy portrayals.

Sixteen-year-old year 11 Emilia (p. 91) is surprised, given her background, that she would ever have envisaged herself as entertaining the possibility of going to university to become a kindergarten teacher. She argues that this has only been possible because of the supportive attitude and help extended towards her by this 'amazing place [that gave her] heaps of opportunities' and 'teachers who have had a big effect on me' and who 'were open-minded and took the time to help me'.

Jayden's story (pp. 92–93), from New Vision Community College, is that of a sixteen-year-old who comes from Broadacres and knows only too well what it means to have to live with the stigmatizing that comes with being in one of the most struggling communities in the town, region and the state. Notwithstanding, what we hear from Jayden is a remarkably optimistic and up-beat story about how he hopes to pursue his interests in sound recording building on existing contacts he has in the industry, and using contacts at school, among friends and family. He left us in no doubt that it is his school and his family that he turns to in 'hard times', and it is these who are helping him to hold his education together.

Far from young people in communities like the ones we studied suffering from 'detachment and isolation' (Savage, 2012, p. 152), which is often touted as symptomatic of what is dysfunctional about them, we encountered some quite different accounts. Sixteen-year-old aspiring pastry chef Helen (pp. 94–95) from the small community of Clarence, as well as her school-related story, gave us a remarkable account of her community volunteering for the Country Fire Authority. Not only has she learnt a lot of relational skills that will be with her for life, but most importantly she has learned what it means to put back something of immense value into her local community. It seems this is something of a family tradition.

Finally, fifteen-year-old Jack (pp. 98–99) at New Vision Community College presented as something of a unique case. He had acquired some remarkable inter-generation relational learning that will likely prove more valuable to him than formal knowledge he may acquire from school. In all likelihood, he will inherit the greyhound breaking-in business, established by his grandfather and carried on by his father, with school leaving him with some residue of practical mechanical skills that will help him along the way.

In considering these various cases, we take the point made by Savage (2012) of the need to be careful 'not to over-generalize from specific cases' (p. 153), nor to over-romanticize. However, the conclusion we reached was that the young people we interviewed did not present or constitute part of 'a large group of disengaged and atomized individuals at the lower reaches of the social structure' (p. 153), nor were they necessarily indicative as a group of displaying 'wide ranging communal attachments' (p. 153). Probably the best we can say is that in many cases they exhibited more positive features than the deficits we might otherwise have believed resided in such contexts, if we had been inclined to have listened to the pejorative policy discourses.

Aspirations or imagined futures: are they the same thing, and does it really matter?

The notion of aspirations has become the new contemporary battleground on which social policy relating to social class is being waged in a number of western countries. In a sense, aspirations are the new wedge that is being used in the application of the neoliberal agenda of exporting responsibility onto individuals for improving their personal educational performance in ways that will lift collective national economic wellbeing. In policy terms, the 'politics of aspiration' (Holloway & Pimlott-Wilson, 2011) is seen as a neat way of both diagnosing the alleged 'problem' as well as articulating preferred 'solutions'. The metaphor is one of leveraging, with the argument being that if we can 'raise' the aspirations of young people from backgrounds where work is disappearing, or in immanent threat of doing so, then national economic performance will improve as a result. Roberts and Evans (2012) put it like this:

> ...individual's aspirations are a central priority for policymakers being at once the potential Achilles' heel and the potential savior of national economies. 'Low aspirations', policymakers feel, are in part the cause of contemporary social and economic ills; the remedy, according to the broad political consensus...is to raise these aspirations. (pp. 70–71)

The default positions seem to be those of middle-class norms and ideals of delayed sexual gratification and parenthood, commitment to education leading to gainful employment, and an ethic of hard work leading to success—qualities that are regarded as missing from lazy, unmotivated, feckless and indolent lower social class young people.

The salience of the problem as Roberts and Evans (2012) note is that what are considered to be 'legitimate' or 'appropriate' aspirations as developed by policy makers at a distance, are not easily 'disentangled from *class backgrounds and positions*' (p. 72, emphases in original). The reason this is a problem is that the 'symbolic and material attacks (in rhetoric and social policy)' (p. 72) may bear no relationship whatsoever to the 'fantasy work' of hopes and future desires being formulated by young people accessing whatever resources they can in their everyday lives. Furthermore, not only does the 'rhetoric of aspiration not take the *realities of social inequality* into account' (p. 73, emphases in original), but the blame is directed at those who are the victims of the inequality in the first place. This failure to pay adequate attention to inequality, and we see this regularly with exhortations to young people to proceed with further and higher education while governments raise the fees they are required to pay, produces a situation in which 'the government is selling a dream but young people end up living a nightmare' (p. 77).

In our research in this book we have by and large distanced ourselves from this kind of social engineering, preferring instead to explore the 'emotional geographies' (Brown, 2011; Kenway & Youdell, 2011; Nairn & Higgins, 2011; Smyth & McInerney, 2013c; Zembylas, 2011) of how some working class young people are going about crafting some imagined futures for themselves in the context of their existential realities and 'geographies of educational opportunity' (Smyth & McInerney, 2013b, p. 1).

Pursuing 'geographies of education' (Holloway, et al., 2010), or 'emotional geographies' (Brown, 2011) of young people, requires as Holloway et al. (2010) put it 'foregrounding young people as the subjects rather than the objects of education' and paying serious attention to 'their current and future lifeworlds' (p. 583)—something we have been at pains to do in this book.

Brown (2011) offers us four helpful ways of understanding the 'effective and emotional geographies of young people's aspirations' (p. 9) and which we intend using to revisit what the young people in our study had to say in Chapter 6:

> First…[there is] an affective orientation to the future (aspiring to become something). Second…an emotional disposition (being aspirational). Third…an emotional state (…through widening participation activities specifically designed to act on the emotions). Fourth…an emotional state that affects other emotions (…for example, the excitement of deciding on a personally fulfilling career, or the fear of actually leaving friends and family behind to go to university). (p. 9)

All four of these actually operate within 'particular spatial imaginaries' (p. 9) that young people live their lives in, and now we want to re-focus on the experiences of our young people in Chapter 6.

Young sixteen-year-old Howard (pp. 118–119) in year 10, admitted that for him years 8 and 9 were 'a bit awkward' but okay now. He had started out with the ambition of pursuing a career in the building trades, but after work experience in a joinery had decided that his real passion was to work with 'cars and trucks and stuff'. While he declares he 'could work out the circumference of a piston', he can no longer see the relevance of the building course he had embarked upon. He is not too stressed about this as he can see himself finding work in or through his step father's trucking business, or an apprenticeship if he can secure one. Howard seems to display Brown's (2011) *emotional disposition* in wanting to pursue what he calls 'outdoorsy' type of work, even though he has done some re-focusing from what he originally intended. There seems to be some strong traces here of a bringing together of what Brown (2011) refers to as 'an assemblage of attributes that together offer...the possibility of an alternative future, rather than being fixed on a single ambition' (p. 13).

Jim and Cooper (p. 120) both fourteen-year-olds in year 8, had an interesting conversation with us around what they saw as the importance of 'experience' which they went on to depict as having 'social' qualities, over the possession of academic credentials. It seemed that they were placing an emphasis on Brown's (2011) *affective orientation to the future* that was taking the form of a set of relational or experiential skills that they saw as carrying them further than bookish knowledge.

We encountered the case of Teresa and Lexi (pp. 121–122) who were both fifteen-year-old, year 10 self-confessed earnest students with well-formulated directions they wanted to take in their lives. For Teresa, it was an acting career built out of university study that would then take her overseas to England or America. In Lexi's case, her interest in animals and science had her with sights firmly set on university, and she was excitedly looking forward to a five-week exchange with a highly regarded science academy in Melbourne at the time of the interview. Both girls are illustrative of young people who had developed a strong work ethic that was paying off in terms of grade results, and they were clearly very excited in terms of what Brown (2011) calls *entanglements with other emotions* as to where their decisions would carry them. Although neither had parents who had pursued university studies, albeit they had good jobs, neither girl seemed to be at all fazed about the impending prospects.

Brown (2011) speaks of what often lies behind government policies around notions of aspiration as typically being about producing 'self-reliant, entrepreneurial citizen(s) with an aspiration to the future' (p. 14).

Sixteen-year-old, year 11 Erin (p. 124) is a classic illustration of this particular emotional state of Brown's (2011) *raising aspirations*. She has a highly developed emotional connection to her desire to finish school, build on her work experience in a hotel, in order to open and own a pub in the country community in which she lives. While Erin does not fit the stereotypical case of someone who might be regarded as following a 'perceived hierarchy of acceptable future careers' (Brown, 2011, p. 14) in the sense of wanting to go to university, she more than fits the warrant of someone imbued with a strongly developed individualized entrepreneurial spirit, that is an implicit part of the aspirational policy agenda. The 'wow moment' which Brown (2011, p. 14) mentions that often comes in such cases, came for Erin in her discovery that her grandfather owned an old house ripe for conversion into a pub, along with the fact that her father is a builder. The fact that her parents 'don't even go to pubs' and that they 'think it is all a bit weird', seems to be more than compensated for in their support for what is clearly a strongly felt emotion on the part of Erin.

While these young people are certainly not indicative of all young people from similar circumstances, one thing that becomes glaringly apparent from their stories is that they dispel the dual popular myths that 'working class teenagers are [only] motivated by dreams of glamour, wealth and celebrity' (Brown, 2011, p. 20), or on the other hand, they are totally lacking in aspirations. We concur with Brown (2011), that the young people in our research were not fixated 'solely...on achieving success in their exams and progressing to university' nor were they in most cases caught up in a zone of 'abstract dreams for an unspecified future' (p. 16). Like Brown's informants, these young people seemed to be quite focused on 'particular careers or other goals and had a sound understanding of what they might need to achieve in order to realize them, and clear plans towards this end' (p. 16). In this regard, they had ambition that 'develops through a spatial, as well as a temporal imagination' (p. 16).

Some last words...at least for the moment!

Becoming Educated, our signature words in this book, is never finished—it is always in a process of being advanced. In this book we have tackled what is a seemingly pedestrian or everyday topic—something that everyone is compelled to endure or experience, as the case may be, for a certain period of time and in a particular space and location. Rarely do we stop and ask the question 'what does it mean to become educated? What we have done in this book is to interrupt the normally taken-for-granted process of young people picking up their knapsacks (or backpacks) of books and lunch packs, engaging in the social hustle and bustle in corridors and school grounds, and responding to days punctuated by bells and public address announcements, all the while dealing with tasks set for them by their teachers. At one level there is a certain degree of ordinariness to all of this as documented in classic ethnographies like *Life in Classrooms* (Jackson, 1968), *Inside High School* (Cusick, 1973) and *Life in Schools* (McLaren, 1989). However, as we have shown in this book, there is another complex but largely invisible game being played out as young people draw in different ways and to varying degrees on resources available to them including their families and neighborhoods, to make a life for themselves.

As we draw what we have been able to understand for the moment to some kind of provisional conclusion, we are reminded of Raymond Williams' (1989) comment in his *Resources of Hope*, about a 'structure of feeling' (p. 7)—something that changes in the light of new experiences—which seems to nicely capture the way the young people we spoke to envisaged what it meant to be engaged in *Becoming Educated*.

Note

1. Novinger & O'Brien, 2003.

References

Anderson, G., & Scott, J. (2012). Toward an intersectional understanding of process causality and social context. *Qualitative Inquiry, 18*(8), 674–685.
Angus, L. (1993). The sociology of school effectiveness. *British Journal of Sociology of Education, 14*(3), 333–345.
Angus, L. (2012a). Preparing teachers as informed professionals: working with a critical ethnographic disposition and socially democratic imaginary. In B. Down & J. Smyth (Eds.), *Critical voices in teacher education: teaching for social justice in conservative times* (pp. 45–61). Dordrecht: Springer.
Angus, L. (2012b). Teaching with and against the circle of privilege: reforming teachers, reforming schools. *Journal of Education Policy, 27*(2), 231–251.
Angus, L., Snyder, I., & Sutherland-Smith, W. (2003). Families, cultural resources and the digital divide: ICTS and educational (dis)advantage. *Australian Journal of Education, 47*(1), 18–39.
Anyon, J. (2005). What 'counts' as educational research? Notes towards a new paradigm. *Harvard Educational Review, 75*(1), 65–82.
Appadurai, A. (2004). The capacity to aspire: culture and the terms of recognition. In V. Rao & M. Walton (Eds.), *Culture and public action* (pp. 59–84). Stanford, CA: Stanford University Press with the World Bank.
Appadurai, A. (2005, 12–13 December). *Grassroots research and the capacity to aspire: lessons from Europe, lessons for Europe (Abstract)*. Paper presented at the Citizens and Governance in a Knowledge-Based Society Conference, Brussels.
Apple, M. (2010). Putting "critical" back into education research. *Educational Researcher, 39*(2), 152–162.
Apple, M. (2012). Some lessons in educational equality. *Educational Researcher, 41*(6), 230–232.
Argy, F. (2007). Education inequalities in Australia. *Institute of Advanced Studies.* http://www.ias.uwa.edu.au Accessed on October 18 2012, Issue 5.

Aronowitz, S., & DiFazio, W. (2010). *The jobless future*. Minneapolis: University of Minnesota Press.

Aronowitz, S., & Giroux, H. (1987). *Education under siege*. London: Routledge and Kegan Paul Ltd.

Atweh, B., & Bland, D. (2007). *Social disadvantage and access to higher education: what potential students don't know and how to address their needs*. Paper presented at the Australian Association for Research in Education Annual Conference, Fremantle.

Australian Council of Social Services. (2012). *Poverty in Australia. Paper 194*. Strawberry Hills, NSW: ACOSS.

Australian Government [Gonski Report]. (2011). *Review of Funding for Schooling: Final Report*. Canberra: Department of Education, Employment and Workplace Relations.

Australian Productivity Commission. (2010). Report of government services 2010. Retrieved on 9 May 2010 from: http://www.pc.gov.au.gsp/reports/rogs/2010

Australian Social Inclusion Board. (2012). *Social inclusion in Australia: how Australia is faring* (2nd edition). Canberra: Department of Primary Minister and Cabinet.

Ball, S., Davies, J., David, M., & Reay, D. (2002). 'Classification' and 'judgement': social class and the 'cognitive structures' of choice in higher education. *British Journal of Sociology of Education, 23*(1), 51–72.

Ball, S., Maguire, M., & Macrae, S. (2000). *Choice, pathways and transitions post-16: new youth, new economies in the global city*. London & New York: Routledge/Falmer.

Ball, S., & Vincent, C. (1998). 'I heard it on the grapevine': 'hot' knowledge and school choice. *British Journal of Sociology of Education, 19*(3), 377–400.

Bardsley, D. (2007). Education for all in a global era? The social justice of Australian secondary school education in a risk society. *Journal of Education Policy, 22*(5), 493–508.

Bauman, Z. (2011). *Collateral damage: social inequalities in a global age*. Cambridge: Polity Press.

Beck, U. (1992). *Risk society: towards a new modernity*. London: Sage.

Bennett, N. (2012, 9 August). 'Poverty of aspiration'—a phrase that should have gone out with Victorian frock coats. *Newstatesman*. http://www.newstatesman.com/blogs/politics/2012/08/poverty-aspiration-phrase-should-have-gone-out-victorian-frock-coats. Accessed 27th August 2013.

Bernstein, B. (1996). *Pedagogy, symbolic control and identity: theory, research, critique*. Bristol, PA: Taylor and Francis.

Bernstein, R. (1992). *The new constellation: the ethical-political horizons of modernity/post-modernity*. Cambridge: Polity Press.

Bickerstaff, S. (2010). "I felt untraditional": high school leavers negotiating dominant discourses on "dropout". *Journal of Education, 190*(3), 37–45.

Black, R. (2011). Student participation and disadvantage: limitations in policy and practice. *Journal of Youth Studies, 14*(4), 463–474.

Blum, D., & Ullman, C. (2012). The globalization and corporatization of education: the limits and liminality of the market mantra. *International Journal of Qualitative Studies in Education, 25*(4), 367–373.

References

Bodenham, S., & Appleton, P. (2010). *Submission by [Federation City] to the Parliament of Victorial (Rural and Regional Committee) "Inquiry into the extent and nature of disadvantage and inequity in rural and regional Victoria"*: [Federation City].

Bok, J. (2010). The capacity to aspire to higher education: 'It's like making them do a play without a script'. *Critical Studies in Education, 51*(2), 163–178.

Bonnor, C. (2012). Teachers in the frontline—again. *Dissent, 40*(Summer), 39–44.

Booher-Jennings, J. (2005). Below the bubble: 'educational triage' and the Texas accountability system. *American Educational Research Journal, 42*(2), 231–268.

Bourdieu, P. (1990). *The logic of practice*. Cambridge: Polity Press.

Bourdieu, P., & Passeron, J. (1979). *The inheritors: french students and their relations to culture*. Chicago: University of Chicago Press.

Bowles, S., & Gintis, H. (1976). *Schooling in capitalist America: educational reform and the contradictions of economic life*. London and Henley: Routledge & Kegan Paul.

Bradley, D. (2008). *Review of Australian Higher Education*. Canberra, ACT: Department of Education, Employment and Workplace Relations.

Brodkey, L. (1987). Writing ethnographic narratives. *Written Communication, 4*(1), 25–50.

Brown, G. (2011). Emotional geographies of young people's aspirations for adult life. *Children's Geographies, 9*(1), 7–22.

Brown, P. (1987). *Schooling ordinary kids: unemployment and new vocationalism*. London: Tavistock.

Burawoy, M. (1998). The extended case method. *Sociological Theory, 16*(1), 4–33.

Burawoy, M., Blum, J., George, S., Gille, Z., Gowan, T., Hanly, L., et al. (2000). *Global ethnography: forces, connections and imagination in a postmodern world*. New York: Rowman & Littleford.

Byrne, D. (2005). Class, culture and identity: a reflection on absences against presences. *Sociology, 39*(5), 807–816.

Carnevale, F., & Kelsey, J., with Ranciere, J. (2007). Art of the possible; an interview with Jacques Ranciere. *Artforum, March*, 257–269.

Ceglowski, D., Bacigalupa, C., & Peck, E. (2011). Aced out: censorship of qualitative research in an age of 'scientifically based research'. *Qualitative Inquiry, 17*(8), 679–686.

Clandinin, D., & Rosiek, J. (2007). Mapping a landscape of narrative inquiry: borderland spaces and tensions. In D. Clandinin (Ed.), *Handbook of narrative inquiry* (pp. 35–75). Thousand Oaks: Sage.

Cochran-Smith, M., & Lytle, S. (2006). Troubling images of teaching in No Child Left Behind. *Harvard Educational Review, 76*(4), 668–697.

Cohen, P., & Hey, V. (2000). *Studies in learning regeneration: consultation document*. London: University of East London & Brunel University.

Collins Australian Concise Dictionary. (2001). *Australian Concise Dictionary Fifth Edition*. Glasgow: HarperCollins.

Comaroff, J., & Comaroff, J. (2006). Reflections of youth, from the past to the postcolony. In M. Fisher & G. Downey (Eds.), *Frontiers of capital: ethnographic reflections on the new economy* (pp. 267–281). Durham, NC: Duke University Press.

Compton-Lilly, C. (2004). *Confronting racism, poverty, and power: classroom strategies to change the world*. Portsmouth, New Hampshire: Heinemann.
Connell, B. (1994). Poverty and education. *Harvard Educational Review, 64*(2), 125–149.
Connell, R. (1998). Schools, markets, justice: education in a fractured world. In A. Reid (Ed.), *Going public: education policy and public education in Australia* (pp. 88–96). West Deakin: Curriculum Studies Association.
Connell, R. (2006). Northern theory: the political geography of general social theory. *Theory and Society, 35*(2), 237–264.
Connell, R. (2007). *Southern theory: the global dynamics of knowledge in social science*. Cambridge: Polity Press.
Connell, R. (2011). *Confronting equality: gender, knowledge and global change*. Cambridge: Polity Press.
Connell, R., White, V., & Johnston, K. (Eds.). (1991). *'Running twice as hard': the disadvantaged schools program in Australia*. Geelong, Victoria: Deakin University.
Considine, G., & Zappala, G. (2002). The influence of social and economic disadvantage in the academic performance of school students in Australia. *Journal of Sociology, 38*(2), 129–148.
Coram, S. (2008). 'Mainstreaming' indigenous inequality as disadvantage and the silencing of 'race' in Australian social, educational and vocational training policy. *ACRAWSA e-journal, 4*(1), 1–13.
Creegan, C. (2008). *Opportunity and aspiration: two sides of the same coin (Summary)*. York: Joseph Rowntree Foundation.
Cusick, P. (1973). *Inside high school*. New York: Holt, Rinehart & Winston.
Davis, A. (2005). *Abolition democracy: beyond empire, prisons and torture*. New York: Seven Stories Press.
Denzin, N. (2008). The new paradigm dialogs and qualitative inquiry. *International Journal of Qualitative Studies in Education, 21*(4), 315–325.
Denzin, N., Lincoln, Y., & Giardina, M. (2006). Disciplining qualitative research. *International Journal of Qualitative Studies in Education, 19*(6), 769–782.
Department for Education and Skills (UK). (2003). *Aim high: raising the achievement of minority ethnic pupils*. London: DfES.
Department of Education Employment and Workplace Relations. (2012). *Interim evaluation of the National Partnership in Youth Attainment and Transitions*. Retrieved August 16, 2012 from http://www.deewr.gov.au/Youth/YouthAttainmentandTransitions/Documents/InterimEvaluationReport-Accessible.pdf.
Department of Immigration and Citizenship. (2007). *Sudanese community profile*. Canberra: Commonwealth of Australia.
Department of Planning and Community Development. (2011). *Change and disadvantage in the Grampians region*. Melbourne: State Government of Victoria.
Dickens, W. (1999). Rebuilding urban labour markets: what community development can accomplish. In R. Ferguson & W. Dickens (Eds.), *Urban problems and community development* (pp. 381–435). Washington, DC: Brookings Institute Press.

References

Donnelly, K. (2009). Universities should not pander to disadvantaged students. *The Sydney Morning Herald.* http://www.smh.com.au/federal-politics/political-opinion/universities-should-not-pander-to-disadvantaged-students. Accessed 27 August 2013.

Down, B. (2009). Schooling, productivity and the enterprising self: beyond market values. *Critical Studies in Education, 50*(1), 51–64.

Du Bois-Reymond, M. (1995). Future orientations of Dutch youth; the emergence of a choice biography. In A. Caralli & Gallard (Eds.), *Youth in Europe* (pp. 201–222). London: Pinter.

Du Bois-Reymond, M. (1998). 'I don't want to commit myself yet': young people's life concepts. *Journal of Youth Studies, 1*(1), 63–79.

Eade, J. (Ed.). (1997). *Living the global city: globalisation as local process.* London: Routledge.

Fearnley, K. (24 January, 2013). Australia Day address Sydney Conservatorium of Music. www.abc.net.au/rampup/articles/2013/01/24/3675605.htm. Accessed February 20th 2013.

Ferrari, J. (2012a, 12 December). Bell tolls for classroom reform. *The Australian.*

Ferrari, J. (2012b, 12 December). Improve the teachers, help the kids. *The Australian.*

Foley, D. (2010). The rise of class culture theory in educational anthropology. *Anthropology and Education Quarterly, 41*(3), 215–227.

Fordham, S., & Ogbu, J. (1986). Black students' school success: coping with the 'Burden of "Acting White"'. *The Urban Review, 18*(3), 176–206.

Foucault, M. (1977). *Discipline and punish: the birth of the prison* (A. Sheridan, Trans.). Harmondsworth: Penguin.

Foucault, M. (1988). The ethic of care for self as a practice of freedom: an interview (J. Gaithier, Trans.). In J. Bernauer & D. Rasmussen (Eds.), *The final Foucault* pp. 1–20. Cambridge, MA: MIT Press.

Foundation for Young Australians. (2010). *How young people are faring 2010: a national report on the learning and work situation of young Australians.* Melbourne: The Foundation for Young Australians.

Foundation for Young Australians. (2011). *How young people are faring 2011: a national report on the learning and work situation of young Australians.* Melbourne: The Foundation for Young Australians.

Fraser, N. (1997). *Justice interruptus: critical reflections on the 'postsocialist' condition.* New York: Routledge.

Freire, P. (1996). *Pedagogy of the oppressed.* London: Penguin Books.

Gale, T. (2012). Towards a southern theory of student equity in Australian higher education: enlarging the rational for expansion. *RISE-International Journal of Sociology of Education, 1*(3), 238–262.

Gale, T., & Densmore, K. (2000). *Just schooling: explorations in the cultural politics of teaching.* Buckingham, Philadelphia: Open University Press.

Giddens, A. (1984). *The constitution of society: outline of the theory of structuration.* Cambridge: Polity Press.

Gillard, J. (2009a, 4 March). Speech to the 'Australian Financial Review' Higher Education conference—Media Release. Canberra, Australia.

Gillard, J. (2009b, 27 March). *National public education forum speech.* media@deewr.gov.au. Canberra.

Gille, Z. (2001). Critical ethnography in the time of globalization: towards a new concept of site. *Cultural Studies <=> Critical Methodologies, 1*(3), 319–334.

Gilloch, G. (2002). *Walter Benjamin: critical constellations.* Cambridge: Polity Press.

Giroux, H. (1988). *Teachers as intellectuals: towards a critical pedagogy of learning.* Westport, Connecticut: Bergin & Garvey.

Giroux, H. (2003). *The abandoned generation: democracy beyond the culture of fear.* London: Palgrave Macmillan.

Giroux, H. (2010). *Youth in a suspect society. Democracy or disposability?* New York: Palgrave Macmillan.

Giroux, H. (2011). *Zombie politics and culture in the age of casino capitalism.* New York: Peter Lang.

Giroux, H. (2012a). *Education and the crisis of public values: challenging the assault on teachers, students and public education.* New York: Peter Lang.

Giroux, H. (2012b). *Disposable youth: racialized memories, and the culture of cruelty.* New York: Routledge.

Giroux, H. (2012c). *Twilight of the social: resurgent publics in the age of disposability.* Boulder, CO: Paradigm Publishers.

Giroux, H. (2013a). *Youth in revolt: reclaiming a democratic future.* Boulder, CO: Paradigm Publishers.

Giroux, H. (2013b). Youth resistance in the age of predatory capitalism and crumbling authoritarianism. *Unilinks.org—Academic Publication Series.* Accessed 5 July 2013.

Glass, G. (2008). *Fertilizers, pills and magnetic strips: the fate of public education in America.* Charlotte, NC: Information Age Publishers.

Gluckman, M. (1958). *Analysis of a social situation in modern Zululand.* Manchester: Manchester University Press.

Goffman, I. (1963). *Stigma: notes on the management of spoiled identity.* New York: Simon & Schuster.

Gordon, S., Smyth, J., & Diehl, J. (2008). The Iraq war, "sound science" and "science-based" educational reform: how the Bush Administration uses deception, manipulation and subterfuge to advance its chosen ideology. *Journal for Critical Education Policy Studies 6*(1), pp. 173–203.

Gorski, P. (2008). Peddling poverty for profit: elements of oppression in Ruby Payne's framework. *Equity and Excellence in Education, 41*(1), 130–148.

Green, A., & White, R. (2007). *Attachment to place: social networks, mobility and prospects of young people.* New York: Joseph Rowntree Foundation.

Green, B., & Letts, W. (2007). Space, equity, and rural education: a 'trialectical' account. In K. Gulson & C. Symes (Eds.), *Spatial theories of education* (pp. 57–76). New York: Routledge.

Greig, A., Lewins, F., & White, K. (2003). *Inequality in Australia.* Cambridge, UK: Cambridge University Press.

References

Gulson, K., & Symes, C. (Eds.). (2007). *Spatial theories of education: policy and geography matters*. New York: Taylor & Francis.

Haberman, M. (1991). The pedagogy of poverty versus good teaching. *Phi Delta Kappan, 23*(4), 290–294.

Hall, P. (1997). Regeneration policies for peripheral housing estates: inward-and outward-looking approaches. *Urban Studies, 34*(5–6), 873–890.

Heinz, W. (2009). Structure and agency in transition research. *Journal of Education and Work, 22*(5), 391–404.

Henderson, R., Harcourt, A., & Harper, R. (1970). *People in poverty: a Melbourne survey*. Melbourne: Cheshire.

Hirst, J. (2013, 2 January). Guns debate has parallels on our shores. *The Age*. http://www.theage.com.au/federal-politics/society-and-culture/guns-debate-has-parallels-on-our-shores. Accessed 27 August 2013.

Holloway, S., Hubbard, P., Jons, H., & Pimlott-Wilson, H. (2010). Geographies of education and the significance of children, youth and families. *Progress in Human Geography, 34*(5), 583–600.

Holloway, S., & Pimlott-Wilson, H. (2011). The politics of aspiration: neo-liberal education policy, 'low' parental aspirations, and primary school Extended Services in disadvantaged communities. *Children's Geographies, 9*(1), 79–94.

hooks, b. (2000). *Where we stand: class matters*. New York: Routledge.

Horkheimer, M. (1972). *Critical theory: selected essays*. New York: Seabury Press.

Imber, D. (2010). *Inclusive education: opportunities for every Victorian child to reach their full potential*. Melbourne: Inclusive Education Working Group Victoria.

Interim Committee for the Australian Schools Commission. (1973). *School in Australia*. Canberra: AGPS.

Jackson, P. (1968). *Life in classrooms*. New York: Holt, Rinehart & Winston.

Jay, M. (1984). *Adorno*. Cambridge, MA: Harvard University Press.

Jenkins, R. (1983). *Lads, citizens and ordinary kids*. London: Routledge & Kegan Paul.

Johnston, K. (1993). Inequality and educational reform: lessons from the Disadvantaged Schools Program. In B. Lingard, J. Knight & P. Porter (Eds.), *Schooling reform in hard times* (pp. 106–119). London: Falmer Press.

Jones, B. (2007, 30 May). Our education failures. *The Age*, p. 15.

Jones, O. (2011). *Chavs: the demonization of the working class*. London & New York: Verso.

Jones, R. (2007). *Humanity's mirror: 150 years of anatomy in Melbourne*. Melbourne: Haddington Press.

Judt, T. (2010). *Ill fares the land*. London: Allen & Lane.

Kahl, J. (1953). Educational and occupational aspirations of "common man" boys. *Harvard Educational Review, 23*, 186–203.

Kellner, D. (1989). *Critical theory, Marxism and modernity*. Baltimore: The Johns Hopkins University Press.

Kenway, J., & Youdell, D. (2011). The emotional geographies of education: beginning a conversation. *Emotion, Space and Society, 4*(3), 131–136.

Kim, J., & Latta, M. (2010). Narrative inquiry: seeking relations as modes of interactions. *Journal of Educational Research, 103*, 69–71.
Kincheloe, J. (2010). *Knowledge and critical pedagogy: an introduction.* Dordrecht: Springer.
Kincheloe, J., & McLaren, P. (1994). Rethinking critical theory and qualitative research. In K. Denzin & Y. Lincoln (Eds.), *Handbook of qualitative research* (pp. 138–157). Thousand Oaks: Sage.
Kincheloe, J., & Tobin, K. (2009). The much exaggerated death of positivism. *Cultural Studies of Science Education, 4*(3), 513–528.
Kintrea, K., St. Clair, R., & Houston, M. (2011). *The influence of parents, places and poverty on educational attitudes and aspirations (Summary and Full Report).* York: Josephy Rowntree Foundation.
Kirk, J. (2007). *Class, culture and social change: on the trail of the working class.* Basingstoke: Palgrave Macmillan.
Koroknay-Palicz, A. (2001 December). Scapegoating of youth. *National Youth Rights Association.* http://www.youthrights.org/scapegoat.php.
Kress, T. (2011). Inside the 'thick wrapper' of critical pedagogy and research. *International Journal of Qualitative Studies in Education, 24*(3), 261–266.
Krumer-Nevo, M., & Sidi, M. (2012). Writing against othering. *Qualitative Inquiry, 18*(4), 200–309.
Kuhn, A. (2002). *Family secrets: acts of memory and imagination.* London: Verso.
Lambert, J. (2002). *Macquarie slang dictionary.* Sydney, NSW: Macquarie Library, Macquarie University.
Lawler, S. (2005). Introduction: class, culture and identity. *Sociology, 39*(5), 797–806.
Lawrence-Lightfoot, S., & Davis, J. (1997). *The art and science of portraiture.* San Francisco: Jossey-Bass.
Lefebvre, H. (1991). *The production of space.* Oxford: Blackwell.
Leonardo, Z. (2004). Critical social theory and transfromative knowledge: the functions of criticism in quality education. *Educational Researcher, 33*(6), 11–18.
Levinson, B., Foley, D., & Holland, D. (Eds.). (1996). *The cultural production of the educated person: critical ethnographies of schooling and local practice.* Albany, NY: State University of New York Press.
Lincoln, Y. (2010). 'What a long, strange trip it's been…': twenty-five years of qualitative and new paradigm research. *Qualitative Inquiry, 16*(1), 3–9.
Lingard, B. (2011). Policy as numbers: accounting for educational research. *Australian Educational Researcher, 38*(4), 355–383.
Lipman, P. (2010). Neo-liberal urban education policy: Chicago, a paradigmatic case of the production of inequality, and racial exclusion. In C. Raffo, A. Dyson, H. Gunter, D. Hall, L. Jones & A. Kalambouka (Eds.), *Education and poverty in affluent countries* (pp. 59–71). Abingdon, Oxon & New York: Routledge.
Lipman, P. (2011). *The new political economy of urban education: neoliberalism, race and the right to the city.* New York: Routledge.

References

Lucey, H., & Reay, D. (2000). Social class and psyche. *Soundings: a Journal of Politics and Culture, 15*, 139–154.

Lupton, R. (2003). *'Neighbourhood effects': can we measure them and does it matter?* London: London School of Economics Centre for Analysis of Social Exclusion.

Lupton, R. (2010). Area-based initiatives in English education: what place for place and space? In C. Raffo, A. Dyson, H. Gunter, D. Hall, L. Jones & A. Kalambouka (Eds.), *Education and poverty in affluent countries* (pp. 111–123). New York & London: Routledge.

Marginson, S. (1997). *Educating Australia: government, economy and citizen since 1960.* Cambridge, UK: Cambridge University Press.

Mason, J., & Danby, S. (2011). Children as experts in their own lives: child inclusive research. *Child Indicators Research, 4*(2), 185–189.

Massey, D. (1994). *Space, place and gender.* Cambridge: Polity Press.

Massola, J. (2012, 3 September). PM announces education 'crusade'. *Australian Financial Review*. http://afr.com/p/national/pm_announces_education_crusade_pXioTlwEoHQcoPMsugGEqL. Retrieved 20 November, 2013.

Maxwell, J. (2012). The importance of qualitative research for causal explanation in education. *Qualitative Inquiry, 18*(8), 655–661.

McCarty, T. (2012). Enduring inequities, imagined futures—circulating policy discourses and dilemmas in the anthropology of education. *Anthropology and Education Quarterly, 43*(1), 1–12.

McGregor, G. (2009). Educating for (whose) success? schooling in an age of neo-liberalism. *British Journal of Sociology of Education, 30*(3), 345–358.

McInerney, P. (2004). *Making hope practical: school reform for social justice.* Flaxton, Queensland: Post Pressed.

McInerney, P. (2007). The ethics of problem representation in public education: from educational disadvantage to individual deficits. *Policy and Society, 26*(3), 83–96.

McInerney, P., Smyth, J., & Down, B. (2011). 'Coming to a place near you?' The politics and possibilities of a critical pedagogy of place-based education. *Asia-Pacific Journal of Teacher Education, 39*(1), 3–16.

McIntosh, P. (1988). White privilege: unpacking the invisible knapsack. http://kasamaproject.org/2012/03/25/white-privilege-unpacking-the-invisible-knapsack 1988. Accessed 3 July 2013.

McLaren, P. (1989). *Life in schools: an introduction to critical pedagogy in the foundations of education.* New York: Longman.

Mehan, H. (2008). Engaging the sociological imagination: my journey into design research and public sociology. *Anthropology and Education Quarterly, 39*(1), 77–91.

Mehan, H. (2012). Reducing inequities by linking basic research and political action. *Anthropology and Education Quarterly, 43*(1), 20–23.

Mills, C. ([1959]1971). *The sociological imagination.* Harmondsworth: Penguin.

Mills, C., & Gale, T. (2010). *Schooling in disadvantaged communities: playing the game from the back of the field.* Dordrecht, The Netherlands: Springer.

Mills, C., & Gale, T. (2011). Re-asserting the place of context in explaining student (under-)achievement. *British Journal of Sociology of Education, 32*(2), 239–256.

Moen, T. (2006). Reflections on the narrative research process. *International Journal of Qualitative Methods, 5*(4), 1–11.

Morrow, R., & Brown, D. (1994). *Critical theory and methodology.* Thousand Oaks: SAGE Publications.

Moss, G. (2004). Provisions of trustworthiness in critical narrative research: bridging intersubjectivity and fidelity. *The Qualitative Report, 9*(2), 359–374.

Munro, P. (2012, 9 September). The invisible backpack and why it makes the education gap hard to close. *Sunday Age.* http://www.theage.com.au/national/education/the-invisible-backpac...-why-it-makes-the-education-gap-hard-to-close-20120908-25lcv.html. Retrieved 20 November, 2013.

Nairn, K., & Higgins, J. (2011). The emotional geographies of neoliberal school reforms: spaces of refuge and containment. *Emotion, Space and Society, 4*(3), 180–186.

Nichols, D. (2011). *The bogan delusion.* Mulgrave, Vic: Affirm Press.

Norman, J. (2010). *The big society: the anatomy of the new politics.* Buckingham: University of Buckingham Press.

Novinger, S., & O'Brien, L. (2003). Beyond 'boring, meaningless shit' in the academy: early childhood teachers educators under the regulatory gaze. *Contemporary Issues in Early Childhood 4*(1), 3–31.

Ogbu, J. (2003). *Black American students in an affluent suburb: a study of academic disengagement.* Mahwah, NJ: Lawrence Erlbaum.

Pakulski, J., & Waters, M. (1996). *The death of class.* London & Thousand Oaks, CA: SAGE.

Payne, R. (2002). *Hidden rules of class and work.* Highlands, TX: Aha Process Inc.

Payne, R. (2005). *A framework for understanding poverty: the how, the why, the what.* Highlands, TX: Aha Process Inc.

Pierides, D. (2010). Multi-sited ethnography and the field of educational research. *Critical Studies in Education, 51*(2), 179–195.

Polesel, J. (2010). Vocational education and training (VET) and young people: the pathway of the poor. *Education and Training, 52*(5), 415–426.

Power, S., & Gewirtz, S. (2001). Reading education action zones. *Journal of Education Policy, 16*(1), 39–51.

Power, S., Rees, G., & Taylor, C. (2005). New labour and educational disadvantage: the limits of area-based initiatives. *London Review of Education, 3*(2), 101–116.

Price-Robertson, R. (2011). *What is community disadvantage? Understanding the issues, overcoming the problem.* Melbourne, Australia: Australian Institute of Family Studies.

Prosser, B. (2007, 28 November). *Weaving a cloth: metaphor as a response to representational challenges in critical narrative research.* Paper presented at the Australian Association for Research in Education Conference, Fremantle, WA.

Quality of Education Review Committee. (1985). *Quality of education in Australia.* Canberra: Commonwealth of Australia.

Quinlan, D. (2011, 11 June). [Federation City] residents call on welfare help for winter. *[source anonymised]*.

Reay, D. (1996). Contextualising choice: social power and parental involvement. *British Educational Research Journal, 22*(5), 581–596.

Reay, D. (2004). Mostly roughs and toughs: social class, race and representation in inner city schooling. *Sociology, 38*(5), 1005–1023.

Reay, D. (2005). Beyond consciousness? The psychic landscape of social class. *Sociology, 39*(5), 911–928.

Rios-Aguilar, C., Kiyama, J., Gravitt, M., & Moll, L. (2011). Funds of knowledge for the poor and forms of capital for the rich? A capital approach to examining funds of knowledge. *Theory and Research in Education, 92*(2), 163–184.

Robbins, C. (2008). *Expelling hope: the assault on youth and the militarization of schooling*. Albany: SUNY Press.

Roberts, K. (2009). Opportunity structures then and now. *Journal of Education and Work, 22*(5), 355–368.

Roberts, S., & Evans, S. (2012). 'Aspirations' and imagined futures: the impossibilities for Britain's young working class. In W. Atkinson, S. Roberts & M. Savage (Eds.), *Class inequality in austerity Britain: power, difference and suffering* (pp. 70–89). Basingstoke: Palgrave Macmillan.

Roper, T. (1970). *The myth of equality*. North Melbourne: The National Union of University Students.

Rose, M. (2005). *Lives on the boundary*. New York: Penguin Books.

Sahlberg, P. (2011). *Finnish lessons: what can the world learn from educational change in Finland?* New York: Teachers College Press.

Saltman, K., & Gabbard, D. (Eds.). (2003). *Education as enforcement: the militarization and corporation of schools*. London: Routledge/Falmer.

Saunders, P. (2011). *Down and out: poverty and exclusion in Australia*. Bristol: Policy Press.

Savage, G. (2012). Broken communities. In W. Atkinson, S. Roberts & M. Savage (Eds.), *Class inequality in austerity Britain: power, difference and suffering* (pp. 145–162). Basingstoke: Palgrave Macmillan.

Savage, M. (2003). Review essay: a new class paradigm? *British Journal of Sociology of Education, 24*(4), 535–541.

Sayer, A. (2005a). *The moral significance of social class*. Cambridge: Cambridge University Press.

Sayer, A. (2005b). Class, moral worth and recognition. *Sociology, 39*(5), 947–963.

Schneekloth, L., & Shibley, R. (1995). *Placemaking: the art and practice of building communities*. New York: John Wiley.

Schostak, J. (2000). Developing under developing circumstances: the personal and social development of students in the process of schooling In H. Altrichter & J. Elliott (Eds.), *Images of educational change* (pp. 37–52). Buckingham: Open University Press.

Sen, A. (1992). *Inequality Re-examined.* Cambridge, MA: Harvard University Press.

Sen, A. (2001). Global doubts as global solutions. The Alfred Deakin Lectures ABC Radio National. Melbourne Town Hall, 15 May http://realvoice.blogspot.com.au/2004/11/global-doubts-as-global-solutions.html. Retrieved 20 November, 2013

Sennett, R., & Cobb, J. (1977). *The hidden injuries of class.* Cambridge: Cambridge University Press.

Shannon, P. (1999). Sociological imagination, stories and learning to be literate. *Theories and Research in Social Education, 27*(3), 396–407.

Shucksmith, M. (2012). Class, power and inequality in rural areas: beyond social exclusion? *Sociologia Ruralis, 52*(4), 377–397.

Sibley, D. (1995). *Geographies of exclusion.* London and New York: Routledge.

Skattebol, J., Saunders, P., Redmond, G., Bedford, M., & Cass, B. (2012). *Making a difference: building on young peoples' experience of economic adversity Final Report.* Sydney, University of New South Wales: Social Policy Research Centre.

Smit, R. (2012). Towards a clearer understanding of student disadvantage in higher education: problematising deficit thinking. *Higher Education Research and Development, 31*(3), 369–380.

Smithers, R. (2000, 4 August). Exam regime harms pupils. *The Guardian.* http://www.guardian.co.uk/uk/2000/aug/04/education.schools. Retrieved 20 November, 2013

Smrekar, C., & Bentley, L. (2011, December). Social context of education. *Education.* http:www.oxfordbibliographies.com. Accessed 6 December 2012.

Smyth, J. (2003). The making of young lives with/against the school credential. *Journal of Education and Work, 16*(2), 127–146.

Smyth, J. (2006). Schools and communities put at a disadvantage: relational power, resistance, boundary work and capacity building in educational identity formation. *Learning Communities: International Journal of Learning in Social Contexts, 3,* 7–39.

Smyth, J. (2010). Speaking back to educational policy: why social inclusion will not work for *disadvantaged* Australian schools. *Critical Studies in Education, 51*(2), 113–128.

Smyth, J. (2011). *Critical pedagogy for social justice.* London & New York: Continuum.

Smyth, J. (2012a). Teachers as *classed* cultural workers *speaking bac*k through critical reflection. In B. Down & J. Smyth (Eds.), *Critical voices on teacher education: teaching for social justice in conservative times* (pp. 81–95). Dordrecht, The Netherlands: Springer Publishing.

Smyth, J. (2012b). The socially just school and critical pedagogies in communities put at a disadvantage. *Critical Studies in Education, 53*(1), 9–18.

Smyth, J., Angus, L., Down, B., & McInerney, P. (2008). *Critically engaged learning: connecting to young lives.* New York: Peter Lang.

Smyth, J., Down, B., & McInerney, P. (2010). *Hanging in with kids in tough times: engagement in contexts of educational disadvantage in the relational school.* New York: Peter Lang.

Smyth, J., & Fasoli, L. (2007). Climbing over the rocks in the road to student engagement and learning in a challenging high school in Australia. *Educational Researcher, 49*(3), 273–295.

References

Smyth, J., Hattam, R., Cannon, J., Edwards, J., Wilson, N., & Wurst, S. (2000). *Listen to me, I'm leaving: early school leaving in south Australian secondary schools*. Adelaide: Flinders Institute for the Study of Teaching; Department of Employment, Education and Training; and Senior Secondary Assessment Board of South Australia.

Smyth, J., Hattam, R., & Lawson, M. (Eds.). (1998). *Schooling for a fair go*. Sydney: Federation Press.

Smyth, J., Hattam, R., with Cannon, J., Edwards, J., Wilson, N., & Wurst, S. (2004). *'Dropping out', drifting off, being excluded: becoming somebody without school*. New York: Peter Lang.

Smyth, J., & McInerney, P. (2007). *Teachers in the middle: reclaiming the wasteland of the adolescent years of schooling*. New York: Peter Lang.

Smyth, J., & McInerney, P. (2012). *From silent witnesses to active agents: student voice in reengaging with learning*. New York: Peter Lang.

Smyth, J., & McInerney, P. (2013a). Whose side are you on? Advocacy ethnography: some methodological aspects of narrative portraits of disadvantaged young people, in socially critical research. *International Journal of Qualitative Studies in Education 26*(1), 1–20.

Smyth, J., & McInerney, P. (2013b). 'Ordinary kids' navigating geographies of educational opportunity in the context of an Australian 'place-based intervention'. *Journal of Education Policy, iFirst*, pp. 1–18.

Smyth, J., & McInerney, P. (2013c). Making 'space': young people put at a disadvantage re-engaging with learning. *British Journal of Sociology of Education, 34*(1), 39–55.

Smyth, J., & Shacklock, G. (1998). *Re-making teaching: ideology, policy and practice*. London & New York: Routledge.

Smyth, J., & Wrigley, T. (2013). *Living on the edge: re-thinking poverty, class and schooling*. New York: Peter Lang.

St. Clair, R., & Benjamin, A. (2011). Performing desires: the dilemma of aspirations and educational attainment. *British Educational Research Journal, 37*(3), 501–517.

Stokes, H., & Wyn, J. (2009). Learning identities for living. In K. te Riele (Ed.), *Making schools different: alternative approaches to educating young people*. Los Angeles: SAGE.

Street, P. (2005). *Segregated schools: educational apartheid in post-civil rights America*. New York: Routledge.

Sydney Morning Herald, Editorial (2012, 13 February). Equal educational opportunity? Soon we hope. *The Age*. http://www.smh.com.au/federal-politics/editorial/equal-education-al-opportunity-soon-we-hope-20120212-1szn2.html Retrieved 19 November, 2013

Taylor, S., Rizvi, F., Lingard, B., & Henry, M. (1997). *Educational policy and the politics of change*. London: Routledge.

te Riele, K. (2006). Youth 'at risk': further marginalizing the marginalized? *Journal of Education Policy, 21*(2), 128–145.

te Riele, K. (2011). Raising educational attainment: how young peoples' experiences speak back to the *Compact with young Australians*. *Critical Studies in Education, 52*(1), 93–107.

Teese, R. (2011). *From opportunity to outcomes. The changing role of public schooling in Australia and national funding arrangements.* Melbourne, Victoria: Centre for Research on Education Systems, University of Melbourne.

Teese, R., & Polesel, J. (2003). *Undemocratic schooling: equity and quality in mass secondary education in Australia.* Carlton, Victoria: Melbourne University Press.

Thomson, P. (2002). *Schooling the rust belt kids: making the difference in changing times.* Crows Nest, NSW: Allen & Unwin.

Thomson, P. (2007). Working the invisible geographies of school exclusion. In K. Gulson & C. Symes (Eds.), *Spatial theories of education* (pp. 111–130). New York: Routledge.

Thomson, P., & Comber, B. (2003). Deficient "disadvantaged students" or media-savy meaning makers? Engaging new metaphors for redesigning classrooms and pedagogies. *McGill Journal of Education, 38*(2), 305–328.

Thomson, S., Hillman, K., Wernert, N., Schmid, M., Buckley, S., & Munene, A. (2012). *Highlights from TIMSS and PIRLS 2011.* Hawthorn, Victoria: Australian Council for Educational Research.

Topsfield, J. (2012, 12 December). Australia's disaster in education. *The Age.* http://www.theage.com.au/national/education/australias-disaster-in-education-20121211-2b7y8.html. Retrieved 20 November, 2013

Topsfield, J., & Butt, C. (2012, 20 December). Lauriston girls leads the state in VCE results. *The Age.* http://www/theage/com.au/national/tertiary-education/lauriston-girls-leads-the-state-in-vce-results-2012121/.

Tranter, D. (2012). Unequal schooling: how the school curriculum keeps students from low socio-economic backgrounds out of university. *International Journal of Inclusive Education, 16*(9), 901–916.

Urban Dictionary. (2013). Westie. www.urbandictionary.com/define.php?term=westie. Retrieved 22 January 2013

Usher, R. (2002). Putting space back on the map: globalisation, place and identity. *Educational Philosophy and Theory, 34*(1), 41–55.

Valencia, R. (2010). *Dismantling contemporary deficit thinking: educational thought and practice.* New York: Routledge.

Van Galen, J. (2004). Seeing classes: towards a broadened research agenda for critical qualitative researchers. *International Journal of Qualitative Studies in Education, 17*(5), 663–684.

van Ham, M., Manley, D., Bailey, N., Simpson, L., & Maclennan, D. (Eds.). (2012). *Neighbourhood effects research: new perspectives.* Dordredcht, Netherlands: Springer.

Van Velsen, J. (1967). The extended case method and situational analysis. In A Epstein (Ed.), *The craft of urban anthropology* (pp. 29-53). London: Tavistock.

Varenne, H., & McDermott, R. (1999). *Successful failure: the school America builds.* Boulder, CO: Westview Press.

Vinson, T. (2004). *Community adversity and resilience: the distribution of social disadvantage in Victoria and New South Wales and the mediating role of social cohesion.* Sydney: The Ignatius Centre for Social Policy and Research.

References

Vinson, T. (2007). *Dropping off the edge: the distribution of disadvantage in Australia*. Richmond, Victoria: Jesuit Social Services & Catholic Social Services Australia.
Wacquant, L. (1996). The rise of advanced marginality: notes on its nature and implications. *Acta Sociologica, 39*, 121–139.
Wacquant, L. (1999). Urban marginality in the coming millennium. *Urban Studies, 36*(10), 1639–1647.
Wacquant, L. (2007). Territorial stigmatization in the age of advanced marginality. *Thesis Eleven, 9*, 66–77.
Wacquant, L. (2008). *Urban outcasts: a comparative sociology of advanced marginality*. Cambridge: Polity.
Warren, M. (2005). Communities and schools: a new view of urban school reform. *Harvard Educational Review, 75*(2), 133–173.
Warren, M., Thompson, J., & Saegert, S. (2001). The role of social capital in combating poverty. In S. Saegert, J. Thompson & M. Warren (Eds.), *Social capital and poor communities* (pp. 1–28). New York: Russell Sage Foundation.
Weis, L. (1996). Foreword. In B. Levinson, D. Foley & D. Holland (Eds.), *The cultural production of the educated person: critical ethnographies of schooling and local practice* (pp. ix–xiv). Albany, NY: State University of New York Press.
Western, M., & Baxter, J. (2007). Class and inequality in Australia. In J. Germov & M. Poole (Eds.), *Public sociology: an introduction to Australian society* (pp. 214–236). Crows Nest, NSW: Allen & Unwin.
Wexler, P. (1992). *Becoming somebody: toward a social psychology of school*. London: Falmer Press.
White, R., & Green, A. (2011). Opening up or closing down opportunities?: the role of social networks and attachment to place in informing young peoples' attitudes and access to training and employment. *Urban Studies, 48*(1), 41–60.
Williams, R. (1989). *Resources of hope: culture, democracy, socialism*. London: Verso.
Willis, P. (1977). *Learning to labor: how working class kids get working class jobs*. Westmead, England: Gower.
Wittgenstein, L. (1977). *Vermischte Bemerkungen*. Frankfurt: Syndicat Verlag.
Wortham, S. (2006). *Learning identity*. New York: Cambridge University Press.
Wyse, D., Nikolajeva, M., Charlton, E., Cliff Hodges, G., Pointon, P., & Taylor, L. (2012). Place-related identity, texts and transcultural meanings. *British Educational Research Journal, 38*(6), 1019–1039.
Youdell, D. (2004). Engineering school markets, constituting schools and subjectivating students: the bureaucratic, institutional and classroom dimensions of educational triage. *Journal of Education Policy, 19*(4), 407–431.
Zembylas, M. (2011). Investigating the emotional geographies of exclusion at a multicultural school. *Emotion, Space and Society, 4*(3), 151–159.
Zizek, S. (2011, 26 October). *Speech on the Occupy Movement to the St. Marks Bookshop, New York (transcript)*. http://www.imposemagazine.com/bytes/transcript-slavoj-zizek-at-st-marks. Accessed 4 July 2013.

Zizek, S. (2012, 30 April). How the Occupy Movement can confront a capitalist system that defies reform. *The Guardian*. http://www.alternet.org/print/story/155206/zizek%3A_how_the_occupy_movement_can_confront_a_capitalist_system_that_defies_reform. Retrieved 20 November, 2013

Zweig, M. (Ed.). (2004). *What's class got to do with it? American society in the twenty-first century*. Ithaca, NY: Cornell University Press.

Author Index

A

Anderson, G., 6, 7, 16, 20
Angus, L., 6, 22, 39, 43, 47, 57
Anyon, J., 17
Appadurai, A., 117, 119, 121–123, 125
Apple, M., 17, 19
Appleton, P., 38
Argy, F., 21, 22
Aronowitz, S., 37, 44
Atweh, B., 90
Australian Council of Social Services, 21, 23
Australian Government, 21, 22, 36
Australian Productivity Commission, 37
Australian Social Inclusion Board, 66

B

Bacigalupa, D., 15
Bailey, N., 90
Ball, S., 71, 122, 123, 125
Bardsley, D., 47, 48
Bauman, Z., 82
Baxter, J., 67
Beck, U., 109
Bedford, M., 21
Benjamin, A., 107
Bennett, N., 107
Bentley, I., 7
Berstein, B., 10, 43
Bickerstaff, S., 30

Black, R., 50
Bland, D., 90
Blum, D., 102
Bodenham, S., 38
Bok, J., 119, 121
Bonnor, C., 66, 67
Booher-Jennings, J., 130
Bourdieu, P., 43, 122
Bowles, S., 43
Bradley, D., 21
Brodkey, L., 31
Brown, D., 18
Brown, G., 138–140
Brown, P., 11, 71, 98, 115, 116
Burawoy, M., 28
Butt, C., 67
Byrne, D., 64, 65

C

Carnevale, F., 111
Cass, B., 21
Ceglowski, D., 15
Charlton, E., 20
Clandinin, D., 31
Cliff Hodges, G., 20
Cobb, J., 70
Cochran-Smith, M., 79
Cohen, P., 123
Collins Australian Concise Dictionary, 42
Comaroff, J., 112

Compton-Lilly, C., 101
Connell, R., 1, 2, 6, 9, 12, 46, 86
Considine, G., 37
Coram, S., 37, 48
Creegan, C., 105, 106
Cusick, P., 141

D

Danby, S., 13
David, M., 122, 123
Davies, J., 122, 123
Davis, A., 112
Davis, J., 32
Densmore, K., 36, 42
Denzin, N., 15
Department for Education and Skills, 125
Department of Education Employment and Workplace Relations, 23
Department of Immigration and Citizenship, 54
Department of Planning and Community Development, 25
Dickens, W., 106
Diehl, J., 16
DiFazio, W., 37
Donnelly, K., 41
Down, B., 14, 22, 23, 39, 43, 50
Du Bois-Reymond, M., 109, 122, 123

E

Eade, J., 28
Evans, S., 135, 137

F

Fasoli, L., 48
Fearnley, K., 52
Ferrari, J., 9
Foley, D., 7, 19
Fordham, S., 72
Foucault, M., 3, 19
Foundation for Young Australians, 21, 22

Fraser, N., 19
Freire, P., 17, 18

G

Gabbard, D., 113
Gale, T., 4, 8, 9, 36, 42
Gewirtz, S., 86
Giardina, M., 15
Giddens, A., 4
Gillard, J., 6, 41, 108
Gille, Z., 10, 15
Gilloch, G., 10
Gintis, H., 43
Giroux, H., 41, 43, 44, 106, 109, 110–113, 115, 116,125
Glass, G., 68
Gluckman, M., 27
Goffman, I., 70
Gordon, S., 16
Gorski, P., 36, 101
Green, A., 93, 100
Green, B., 23
Greig, A., 40
Gulson, K., 23, 24

H

Haberman, M., 48
Hall, P., 87
Harcourt, A., 44
Harper, R., 44
Hattam, R., 8, 9, 64, 127
Heinz, W., 101
Henderson, R., 44
Henry, M., 44
Hey, V., 123
Higgins, J., 138
Hirst, J., 67
Holland, D., 7
Holloway, S., 137, 138
hooks, b., 72
Horkheimer, M., 18
Houston, M., 106, 107
Hubbard, P., 138

Author Index

I

Imber, D., 52
Interim Committee for the Australian Schools Commission, 45

J

Jackson, P., 141
Jay, M., 10
Jenkins, R., 116
Johnston, K., 46, 47
Jones, B., 67
Jones, O., 84
Jones, R., 132, 133
Jons, H., 138
Judt, T., 111

K

Kahl, J., 125
Kellner, D., 18, 19
Kelsey, J., 111
Kenway, J., 138
Kim, J., 30
Kincheloe, J., 15–19
Kintrea, K., 106, 107
Kirk, J., 4
Koroknay-Palicz, A., 113
Kress, T., 19
Krumer-Nevo, M., 31
Kuhn, A., 69

L

Lambert, J., 80
Latta, M., 30
Lawler, S., 65
Lawrence-Lightfoot, S., 32
Lawson, M., 64
Lefebvre, H., 81
Leonardo, Z., 18
Letts, W., 23
Levinson, B., 7, 8, 11
Lewins, F., 40

Lincoln, Y., 15
Lingard, B., 44, 108
Lipman, P., 88
Lucey, H., 70
Lupton, R., 11, 24, 25, 84
Lytle, S., 79

M

Maclennan, D., 90
Macrae, S., 71
Maguire, M., 71
Manley, D., 90
Marginson, S., 46
Mason, J., 13
Massey, D., 24
Massola, J., 6
Maxwell, J., 20
McCarty, T., 20
McDermott, R., 63
McGregor, G., 19
McInerney, P., 14, 23, 32, 39, 43, 47–50, 54, 64, 85, 117, 127, 128, 138
McIntosh, P., 108
McLaren, P., 18, 19, 43, 48, 141
Mehan, H., 19
Mills, C., 8, 9, 42, 128
Moen, T., 30
Morrow, R., 18
Moss, G., 14, 30
Munro, P., 106

N

Nairn, K., 138
Nichols, D., 84
Nikolajeva, M., 20
Norman, J., 135
Novinger, S., 127, 141

O

O'Brien, L., 141
Ogbu, J., 72

P

Pakulski, J., 64
Passeron, J., 43
Payne, R., 36, 43, 46, 130
Peck, E., 15
Pierides, D., 20
Pimlott-Wilson, H., 137
Pointon, P., 20
Polesel, J., 37, 49, 60
Power, S., 85, 86, 87, 88
Price-Robertson, R., 36
Prosser, B., 30, 31

Q

Quality of Education Review Committee, 47
Quinlan, D., 39

R

Ranciere, J., 111
Reay, D., 65, 68–70, 72, 73, 80, 122, 123, 131
Redmond, G., 21
Rees, G., 85–88
Rios-Agular, C., 101
Rizvi, F., 44
Robbins, C., 113
Roberts, K., 108–110
Roberts, S., 135, 137
Roper, T., 44
Rose, M., 41
Rosiek, J., 31

S

Saegert, S., 81
Sahlberg, P., 4, 5
Saltman, K., 113
Saunders, P., 21, 38
Savage, G., 135–137
Savage, M., 68, 132

Sayer, A., 69, 70
Schneekloth, L., 28
Schostak, J., 73, 74
Scott, J., 6, 7, 16, 20
Sen, A., 11, 37
Sennett, R., 70
Shacklock, G., 4
Shannon, P., 128, 129
Shibley, R., 28
Shucksmith, M., 88
Sibley, D., 49
Sidi, M., 31
Simpson, L., 90
Skattebol, J., 21
Smit, R., 47
Smithers, R., 71
Smrekar, C., 7
Smyth, J., 4, 8, 9, 14, 16, 23, 32, 39, 43, 48–50, 64, 71, 82, 85, 87, 106, 110, 117, 127, 128, 138
St. Clair, R., 106, 107
Stokes, H., 96
Street, P., 113
Sydney Morning Herald, 61
Symes, C., 23, 24

T

Taylor, C., 85–88
Taylor, L., 20
Taylor, S., 44
te Riele, K., 14, 23
Teese, R., 37, 47, 60
Thompson, J., 81
Thomson, P., 24, 46, 48
Thomson, S., 6
Tobin, K., 15
Topsfield, J., 6, 67
Tranter, D., 102

U

Ullman, C., 102
Urban Dictionary, 80
Usher, R., 23

Author Index

V

Valencia, R., 14, 42
Van Galen, J., 14
van Ham, M., 90
Van Velsen, J., 27, 28
Varenne, H., 63
Vincent, C., 125
Vinson, T., 21, 25, 36, 38, 84, 85

W

Wacquant, L., 81–84, 88, 89, 92, 93
Warren, M., 81
Waters, M., 64
Weis, L., 7
Western, M., 67
Wexler, P., 127
White, K., 40
White, R., 93, 100
White, V., 46
Williams, R., 65
Willis, P., 7, 44, 116
Wittgenstein, L., 84
Wortham, S., 110
Wrigley, T., 82, 106
Wyn, J., 96
Wyse, D., 20

Y

Youdell, D., 130, 138

Z

Zappala, G., 37
Zembylas, M., 138
Zizek, S., 113, 114
Zweig, M., 65

Subject Index

A

abandoned generation, 111
abandonment, 88, 107
Aboriginal and Torres Strait Islander, 47
academic vocational divide, 78
accessing resources, 123
accommodation and resistance, 10, 15, 110
accountability, 3, 25, 40, 48, 108
active agents, 14, 135
active informed participants, 50
adult learning environment, 56, 91
advanced marginality, 83, 88
advantaging and disadvantaging, 37
affective nature of class, 131
affective orientation to future, 139
agency, 6, 7, 14, 36, 44, 45, 57, 58, 60, 61, 89, 98, 100, 101, 108, 120, 124
ahistorical treatment of neighborhoods, 88
ambivalent defensiveness, 72
ameliorative, 11
anthropology, 18, 27, 30
anti-democratic agenda, 26
apparent conformity, 116
applied learning, 26, 49, 54, 57, 58, 75, 76, 78, 79, 134
area-based initiatives (ABIs), 85
areas of concentrated disadvantage, 84
art of the possible, 111
aspirations, 13, 23, 24, 34, 28, 49, 53, 58, 64, 70, 76, 79, 82, 88, 90, 91, 94–96, 98, 99, 100–103, 105–108, 115–117, 119, 120, 121, 124, 125, 128, 137, 138, 140
asymmetric power, 18
at-risk, 47, 48, 60
Australia Day, 35, 52
Australian government, 22, 36
Australian Tertiary Admission Rank (ATAR), 60
authoritarianism, 115

B

Badiou, A., 114
banal policy prescription, 135
barriers to school participation, 39
Beazley, K., 67
becoming somebody, 125
becoming white, 72
benchmarking, 6, 9, 23
beneath the skin, 131
Benjamin, W., 10
Berry, R., 132
Big Society, 135
big sociological idea, 2
blaming victims, 107
blindness to complexity, 108
bogans, 80, 84
bootstrap approaches, 87, 107
boundary formation, 88
broken communities, 135
bundles of pathologies, 81, 100

Bush, G., 108, 112
Business Council of Australia, 49

C

callous indifference, 41
can-do approaches, 87
capacities, 70
capacity for hard work, 124
capacity to aspire, 11, 105, 117, 119, 121, 123, 125
capitalism, 2, 4, 10, 18, 19, 36, 38, 42–44, 69, 89, 107, 109, 114, 115, 116
carceral state, 112
career intentions, 58
casino capitalism, 115
causal explanation, 15, 16, 20
causes of disadvantage, 47
Centrelink, 23
Certificate of Applied Learning (VCAL), 49, 75, 122, 124
chavs, 84
choice biographies, 109, 122, 123
claims for entitlement, 65
class, 6–10, 13, 14, 17, 19, 25–27, 29, 32, 33, 39, 42–44, 46, 49, 50–52, 54–57, 59, 61, 63–65, 67–80, 83, 86, 88, 90, 91, 97, 98, 101, 108–110, 113, 116, 118, 122–125, 129–135, 137, 138, 140, 141
class divide, 132
class location, 65
class positioning, 67, 72
class relations, 46, 68
class size, 56
class suicide, 72
classed identities, 76
clients, 82, 83
cold knowledge, 125
collateral damage, 82, 130, 131
collective agency, 64, 100
common educational good, 41
community hub, 92, 93
community solidarity, 25
compensatory programs, 48
competition, 66

competitive academic curriculum, 19
compliance measures, 26
conjectures and refutations, 117
constellation, 9, 10, 11
constraints and limitations, 61
constraints and opportunities, 14
constructed categories, 10, 36
consumer-attractive, 74
consumerism, 111
container way of thinking, 82
context, 1, 2, 6–8, 10, 14, 16, 19, 20, 27, 28, 30, 42, 44, 47, 50, 64–66, 67, 71, 72, 83–85, 87, 101, 105–111, 115–117, 119, 127, 128, 137, 138
corporate federalism, 25
corporatized image, 74
counter narrative, 103
counter public spheres, 116
crafting educational identities, 2
craniometry, 132
credentialing, 8
criminalization, 112
crisis, 19, 38, 66, 135
critical ethnographic approach, 13, 33
critical ethnography, 10, 15, 29
critical perspective, 20
critical placemaking, 28
critical race theory, 17
critical research agenda, 19
critical researchers, 14, 15, 18, 19
critical social theory, 17, 31, 150
critical sociological framework, 20
critical theory, 17, 18, 19, 20
criticalist tradition, 20
critique of domination, 18
crumbling authoritarianism, 116
cultural capital, 43, 46, 57
cultural production, 7, 8, 19
cultural turn to class, 64
culture, 3, 7, 15, 19, 20, 22, 24, 26, 31, 32, 35, 36, 41–44, 46, 49, 57, 70, 73, 86, 89, 95, 101, 107, 111, 117, 130
culture of humiliation, 41
culture of managerialism, 22
culture of materialism, 41
culture of poverty, 36, 46, 86, 130
cycle of poverty, 44, 45

D

dangerous places, 29
de-industrialization, 4, 68, 82, 112
decontextualized, 16
deficit discourses, 31, 48, 100, 107
deficit thinking, 14, 36, 37, 42, 49, 60, 103
deficits, 35, 36, 41, 42, 45, 57, 61, 99, 130, 137
degradation of working conditions, 83
dehumanizing, 16
democracy, 114
demonizing, 84, 88
deprecatory perceptions, 84
detachment and isolation, 136
deterministic policy portrayals, 136
devolution, 26
Dewey, J., 23
dialectical, 64
dialogic portrait, 53, 54, 119, 121
digital divide, 39
disabilities, 38, 47, 52, 58, 61, 96, 101
disadvantage, 10, 11, 13, 20–22, 28, 30, 35–50, 52, 54, 56, 57, 60, 61, 64, 66, 82, 84–88, 92, 102, 106, 107, 108, 129
Disadvantaged School Programme (DSP), 45, 46
disadvantaged schools, 46, 48
disciplinary technologies, 76
discourse of disadvantage, 36, 37, 46, 61
discourse of entitlement, 73
discourse of possibility, 18
disinterested enquiry, 18
disposable, 110, 111, 113
distribution of social disadvantage, 38
distrustful, 111
domestication, 110
dominant representations, 72
dominant society, 44
dress code regulations, 76

E

early school leavers, 8, 55
eased out, 76
economic and social degradation, 60
economic capital, 25
economic rationalism, 132
education and training, 87
educational apartheid, 133
educational chances, 41
educational disadvantage, 20, 21, 36, 37, 39, 42, 44, 45, 46, 48, 54, 56, 57, 60, 102
educational identity, 24, 54, 92
educational inequalities, 16, 17, 36, 43
educational opportunities, 28, 30, 37, 53
educational outcomes, 8, 86
educational revolution, 46
educational testing, 6
educational triage, 130, 134
egalitarian, 66
egalitarian sensibility, 64
egalitarian society, 21, 35, 67
eliciting the voices, 106
embedded interviews, 29
emotional and affective dimensions, 65
emotional aspects of classed identities, 70
emotional costs, 72
emotional disposition, 139
emotional geographies, 138
emotions, 70
entrepreneurial spirit, 140
equality of opportunity, 37, 44, 61, 66
ethic of volunteering, 95
ethnographic observations, 89
ethnographic themes, 11
ethnography, 10, 15, 28, 31
eugenics, 132, 133
euro implosion, 86
everyday lives, 89
evidence-based approach, 16
evolving criticality, 17
excellence, 26, 66
expected educational trajectory, 73
extended case method, 10, 13, 14, 27–29, 34
extended learning hubs, 28

F

failure, 63, 71, 107
fair go, 35, 66

family backgrounds, 53
family support, 23, 30, 37, 55, 76, 90, 125
family support structures, 101, 125
fantasies, fears, hopes, desires, 70
fashioning of self, 69
fast-food industry fodder, 130
fear anxiety and unease, 71, 73
featureless cleared space, 3
Federation City, 24–27, 29, 32–34, 37–41, 50–53, 55, 56, 59, 61, 77, 79, 80, 90–99, 101, 102, 105, 121, 124, 130, 136
Federation City Secondary School, 27
feelings and emotions, 65
feelings of loss, 72
feminist theories, 17
ferals, povs, bogans, 80
FIDUROD, 16
Finland, 4–6
fish in water, 122
fix the problem, 81, 82
folk concepts, 88
framed spatially, 87
Frankfurt Institute of Social Research, 18
free-market, 42, 61, 111
frontline agency, 89
funds of knowledge, 100, 101

G

gender, 7, 8, 14, 49, 122
geographies of educational opportunity, 138
geography of inequality, 87
gestures of exclusion, 2, 3
getting a job, 30, 40, 58, 97, 99, 115, 120
getting on by getting out, 102
ghettoes, 88
Gillard, J., 6, 41, 108
giving up on school, 127
global capitalism, 19, 28, 36–38, 107, 109
Global Educational Reform Movement (GERM), 4, 5, 6
global ethnography, 28
global financial crisis (GFC), 38, 66, 86, 109
global forces, 65
globalization, 22, 28, 82, 112

Gonski Report, 21, 22, 36
government social experimentation, 82
grand erasure, 1, 2, 3
group inequality, 48
Group of Eight universities, 21
group stigma, 82

H

hands-on, 48, 54, 75, 94, 99, 129, 132, 133
hard work at school, 121
harsh penalties, 113
hegemonic curriculum, 44, 48, 75
hermetically sealed, 87
hidden curriculum, 43
hierarchy of subjects, 102
high stakes testing, 5, 33
higher education, 21, 22, 30, 47, 54, 55, 57, 60, 76, 90, 91, 102, 108, 138
homeless, 39, 66, 83, 112
Hong Kong, 6
honor the voices, 31
hot knowledge, 125
Howard, J., 67
human capital, 87, 110
humane and inclusive, 56

I

identity, 4, 8, 11, 13, 20, 23–25, 27, 54, 61, 64, 65, 69, 74, 92, 93, 95, 99, 100, 105, 107, 109, 110, 111, 113, 115, 117, 119, 121, 123, 125, 127
ill-informed media, 103
imagined alternative futures, 117
in situ observations, 29
indigenous, 1, 3, 8, 9, 39
indigenous knowledges, 3
indigenous students, 39
indigenous voices, 9
individual disadvantage, 48
individual effort, 67
individual subjectivities, 47
individualizing, psychologizing and pathologizing, 108
individualizing responsibility, 135

Subject Index

inequality, 66
inequality of opportunity, 45
inequitably structured, 70
inferior class, 113
informed consent, 29
inoculation against disease, 47
insecure work, 49
insider instances, 88
insider perspectives, 14
insider understanding, 76
institutional habitus, 90
institutional practices, 20
institutional pressures, 75
institutional resources, 76
institutions, 4, 14, 19, 20–22, 31, 48, 49, 88, 90
instrumental view of school, 118
intergenerational transmission of deprivation, 86
International Association for the Evaluation of Educational Achievement (IEA), 6
international comparisons, 9
International Monetary Fund (IMF), 4
international predator organizations, 4
interpreting and negotiating meaning, 129
interpretive scheme, 63
interrupt and puncture, 64
interview transcripts, 32
invisible game, 141
invisible knapsack, 108
invisible majority, 98
invisible package of assets, 108
inward looking approaches, 86

J

Japan, 5
job-ready, 49
joined-up approaches, 85
just world, 18

K

Karmel Report, 45
Klein, J., 108

knowledgeable agents, 4
Korea, 5, 6

L

labor market, 22, 28, 37, 49, 101
larger frames, 111
league tables, 8, 67, 131
learn or earn policy, 23
learning identities, 11, 23, 34, 61, 103, 110, 111, 115, 116, 125
learning intention, 78
least powerful members, 20
liberalisation of schooling, 88
lift their game, 107
limited employment and further education opportunities, 102
limited opportunity resources, 119
listening, 89, 106, 128
literacy, 6, 15, 33, 47, 129
lived experience, 31
living the global, 10, 15, 28, 34
local immediacy, 117–119
local solidarities, 84
locally based resources, 100
locus for change, 45
"long revolution," 65

M

mainstreaming, 52
making biographies, 109
managerialism, 22, 40
marginalized students, 90
market-driven approaches, 16
market-driven paradigm, 5
market economy, 115
market forces, 112
market fundamentalism, 111
market place, 47, 48
market society, 115
marketized neo-liberal agenda, 134
markets, 5, 16, 22, 26, 28, 36, 37, 42, 47–49, 73, 83, 84, 87, 101, 107, 108, 111, 112, 114, 115, 131
Marxist, 17, 19, 65

material and social conditions, 24
media coverage, 79
mentally deficient, 132
meritocracy, 10, 44, 64
metropole, 1, 2, 3
middle class, 25, 44, 50, 57, 68, 71–73, 76, 116, 122, 125, 130, 134, 135, 137
middle-class standpoint, 68
militarism, 111–113
misrecognition and discrimination, 69
multi-level analyses, 20
Murdoch, R., 108
muscular behavior management, 74
muscular policy rhetoric, 6

N

narrative portraits, 30–33, 90, 118, 124
narrative research, 15, 30, 34
narratives, 13, 23, 30–32, 37, 50, 54, 61, 99, 117, 125
narratives of disadvantage, 13, 37, 50
National Assessment Program—Literacy and Numeracy (NAPLAN), 15
national curriculum, 26
national efficiency, 132
navigating individual pathways, 110
navigational capacity, 11, 117, 119, 121, 122, 123
navigational maps, 117, 119
needs-based funding, 22, 45
negative media, 26, 60, 76
negative stereotyping, 37
negotiate identities, 102
neighborhood effects, 24, 88, 90
neighborhood poverty, 17
neighborhood renewal programs, 25
neighborhoods, 3, 11, 14, 19, 20, 24, 25, 28, 29, 37, 39, 50, 61, 64, 74, 81–83, 85, 87–93, 95, 97, 99, 100–103, 115, 117, 135, 141
neo-Marxist, 17
neo-Weberian, 19

neoliberal, 5, 6, 15, 19, 20, 21–23, 36, 42, 47, 48, 66, 73, 111, 112, 137
neoliberal education policies, 22, 73
neoliberal order, 112
neoliberal policies, 23, 36
neoliberal project, 111
neoliberal reforms, 21
neoliberal state, 15, 20
network failure, 106
neutrality, 18
new class paradigm, 68
new education policy paradigm, 17
new educational orthodoxy, 4
new public intellectuals, 113, 115
new sociology of class, 68
New Vision Community College, 26, 29, 35, 37, 39, 40, 49, 53, 57, 59, 73–76, 78, 79, 90, 92, 96, 98, 102, 118, 119, 124, 136, 137
new vocationalism, 98
Newstart Allowance, 23, 40
No Child Left Behind, 15
no go areas, 84, 93
non-government schools, 22, 67
normal biographies, 122
northern sociology, 2, 3

O

objectivity, 18, 31
Occupy Movement, 113–115
official zealotry, 17
one dimensional, 16
opportunity and aspirations, 106
opportunity resources, 117–119
opportunity structures, 108, 109
opposing shames, 73
oppression, 17–20
ordinary kids, 11, 70, 71, 98, 115–117
ordinary lives, 65
Organization for Economic Co-operation and Development (OECD), 4, 22, 37, 52, 67
othering, 31, 134
outsourcing child rearing, 67
outward-looking approaches, 87

Subject Index

P

parental support, 125
part-time casual employment, 40, 54, 55, 58, 59, 74, 98, 101, 118
participant's story, 32
partisanship, 18
pathological views, 36, 85
pathologizing discourse, 47, 131
pedagogy of poverty, 48
pejorative policy discourses, 137
penetrate the complexities, 129
penitentiary, 78, 134
performers of class, 69
peripheralized, 87
personal troubles, 128
place, 11, 13, 19–24, 27–29, 33, 34, 37, 47, 48, 51, 56, 58, 59, 63–69, 73–77, 79, 81, 83, 85–87, 89, 91–93, 95, 97–103, 106, 107, 113, 120, 125, 131, 134–136, 138
place-based interventions, 11, 20, 28, 34
placemaking, 10, 15
play without a script, 119
playing the game, 9
pockets of disadvantage, 84, 85
pockets of poverty, 38
policy as numbers, 108
policy credentials, 110
policy experts, 90
policy mantra, 135
policy solution, 48
policy texts, 13
political act, 17
political authors, 13, 14, 31, 34
political economy, 14, 19, 20, 64
political landscape, 21
political view of learning identity, 110
politics of aspiration, 137
politics of hope, 19
politics of trickle down cruelty, 111
portraits, 29, 30, 32, 37, 50, 90, 101, 128, 129
positivism, 15, 16, 18, 31
positivist research, 15
post codes, 46
post-structuralist, 17
postcolonialist approaches, 17
postmodernist, 17
poverty, 10, 11, 17, 20, 21, 23, 25, 36–48, 50, 52, 66, 83, 85–88, 106–109, 130
poverty of aspiration, 109
poverty of expansive policy thinking, 108
poverty of opportunity, 107
power, 8, 9, 15, 17, 18, 38, 43, 44, 45, 70, 71, 82, 85–88, 112, 128, 129, 135
practice navigational capacity, 117
practices of freedom, 19
praxis, 18
precedent setting, 117, 123, 125
predatory capitalism, 116
prescribed curriculum, 5
print of class, 131
private providers, 111
private schools, 46, 47, 60, 61, 76, 79, 96, 121, 131, 133
privatization and displacement, 88
privatization of social policy, 84
privileged, 4, 41, 43, 46, 67, 83, 108
privileged enclosure, 67
privileged theory, 4
problem neighborhoods, 85
Progress in International Reading Literacy Study (PIRLS), 6
psychic damage, 69, 71
psychic economy, 68, 71
psychic landscape of social class, 70
public issues, 128
puncturing deficit notions, 88, 129, 131
punishing ideology, 110
punitive discipline regimes, 50
punitive practices, 3
purification, 73
purposeful conversation, 29
purposeful educational identities, 89
pushed out, 76
put at a disadvantage, 64, 106

Q

quasi-market mechanism, 26
quick fix solutions, 3, 9

R

race, 7, 8, 17,19, 90, 132
racist, 132
radical research agenda, 17
raising aspirations, 140
randomized controlled experiments, 15, 16
ranked ability groups, 45
re-inventing a school around removing waste, 73
re-positioning of relations, 68
reading from the center, 2
recuperation, 83
red-line, 81
redistributive and recognitive justice, 19
reductionist, 16, 71
reflexive biography, 109
reflexivity, 28, 31
regeneration policies, 87
relational, 45, 64, 117, 136, 137, 139
relational learning, 137
relational or experiential skills, 136, 139
relational power, 45
relationships, 21, 23, 47, 50, 58, 82, 106, 108, 121
remaindering, 86
representational and ethical issues, 31
reproduction theorists, 44
residual, 74, 84, 85
resistance, 3, 10, 15, 44, 77, 110, 116, 127, 128
restructuring global capitalism, 107
resurgence of social inequality, 83
retrieval of subjectivity, 31
rhetoric of aspiration, 138
rich cultural traditions, 100
risk factors, 11
rituals of everyday life, 19
rituals of marginality, 82
Rowntree, J., 105
rubbish school, 72
rural and regional communities, 55
Russia, 6
rust belt, 46

S

safety nets, 73
school certificate, 118
school choice, 47, 66
school culture, 43, 44, 73
school dropouts, 113
school effectiveness, 3, 15, 42
school ethnographies, 19
school funding, 36
school improvement, 76
school leadership, 26, 57
school reform movement, 17
school retention, 22, 39, 47
schooling and industry, 47
scientific-based research (SBR), 15, 16
scripts, 11, 123
semi-structured interviews, 29
sense of entitlement, 78
sense of shame, 69
sets of resources, 11
sets of social networks, 25
Singapore, 6
sites of liberation, 48
skilling the workforce, 22
slights of social class, 71
social and economic deformities, 115
social and economic inequality, 75
social background, 79
social capital, 74, 75, 100
social constructions, 7, 86
social context, 6, 7, 44
Social Darwinism, 115, 132
social democratic approach, 46
social divide, 75
social efficiency, 132
social exclusion, 20, 21, 25, 36, 37, 87
social gradient of disadvantage, 86
social hierarchy, 74
social investment, 111
social justice, 22, 48
social merit, 133
social mobility, 10, 19
social person, 120, 121
social policy rationale, 85
social relations, 8, 19, 24, 28, 70, 114, 135
social reproduction, 42–44, 50

Subject Index

social stresses and impediments, 87
socially critical lens, 127
socially democratic approach, 45
socio-economic, cultural and linguistic factors, 54
socio-political fog, 15
socio-spatial, 37, 49, 102
socio-spatial stigmatization, 102
sociological detective work, 132
sociological imagination, 128
sociology, 2, 3, 18, 30, 43, 68
soft bigotry of low expectations, 108
sorting streaming practices, 75
South Korea, 6
southern theory, 2
space, 3, 7, 8, 11, 13, 14, 19, 23–25, 27, 29, 30, 51, 64, 68, 71, 81, 82, 83, 85, 87, 89, 91, 93, 95, 97, 99, 100–103, 112–114, 123, 135, 140
spatial dimensions of poverty, 39
spatial landscape, 21, 23
speaking back, 14, 72, 85, 115, 116, 128, 136
spoiled identities, 70
standardization, 5
standardized testing, 26, 48
standards, 8, 9, 22, 37, 46, 73, 108, 132
status quo, 16, 19, 113
stereotypical portrayals, 36
stereotyping, 24, 49, 78, 79, 131
stigmatization, 24, 37, 84, 92, 93, 102, 136
stigmatizing neighborhoods, 88
stories, 11, 23, 24, 30, 31, 36, 49, 53, 65, 76, 100, 117, 128, 131, 140
streaming practices, 48
strengths and capabilities, 35, 61
structural analyses of class, 68
structural changes, 37
structural economic shifts, 87
structural favors, 86
structure, 7, 8, 11, 15, 17, 20, 26, 27, 29, 34, 43, 44, 47, 55, 63, 65, 70, 76, 77, 95, 101, 106, 108, 109, 125, 137, 141
structure and agency, 7
structure of feeling, 141
structures and practices, 34

student engagement, 39, 40
student teacher interactions, 56
student voice, 3
students at risk, 47
students' background, 90
studied from below, 10, 15, 28
subaltern, 2, 9
Sudanese, 54
symbolic and material attacks, 138
systemic disadvantage, 36, 90

T

taken-for-granted, 140
targeted intervention, 87
targeted investment, 87
targeting, 85
targeting populations, 10, 36
targets, 26, 27, 73, 76
teachers as classed actors, 71
teachers going the extra yards, 91
Technical and Further Education (TAFE), 32, 59, 92, 94, 100, 118, 133
techno-capitalism, 19
temporal imagination, 140
territorial justice, 85
territorial stigmatization, 84, 92, 93
territories of relegation, 88
test performance, 71
testing regimes, 131
textual representation, 14, 31, 34
theories of resistance, 44
theories of space, 24
tool for economic growth, 22
tools for rethinking marginality, 81
tracking and streaming, 58
transformation of society, 17, 19
transformative knowledge, 18
treated as young adult, 91
treated programmatically, 82
Trends in International Mathematics and Science Study (TIMSS), 6
trouble makers, 27, 40, 78, 80
troubling images, 79
truncated opportunity, 106
two speed economy, 38

U

uncertainty, 110
under your skin, 69
underclass, 86, 88
underlying causes, 106
unique histories, 100
universality, 2, 16
unjust social structures, 44
urban schooling, 17
utilitarian goals, 22

V

victims, 41, 48, 54, 82, 107, 138
Victorian Certificate of Education (VCE), 49
vocational education, 26, 27, 48, 49, 53, 54, 75, 101, 102, 134
Vocational Education and Training (VET), 27, 32, 47, 49, 55, 59, 60, 74, 75, 77, 79, 91, 95, 98, 99, 122, 132
voiceless objects, 8
volunteering, 136

W

warehousing effect of poverty, 11
warehousing of supernumerary populations, 89
waste products, 74
welfare bludgers, 80
welfare policies, 55
welfare state, 112, 113
westies, 78–80, 84
White Australia Policy, 133
Whitlam, G., 45
witnesses, 128
work, disappearing of, 137
work-oriented curriculum, 49
working class, 14, 29, 44, 50, 57, 65, 70, 76, 80, 101, 130, 131, 138, 135, 140
working class background, 26, 54, 90, 91, 123
working class communities, 83
working class disposition, 98
working class neighborhood, 70
working class students, 49, 50, 71, 72, 75, 79, 116
working of class power, 71
World Bank, 4
World Trade Organisation (WTO), 4
wrong choices, 109

Y

young people as intellectuals, 115
young people's perspective, 15
youth resistance, 116
youth unemployment, 37

Z

zero-tolerance, 113
zone of relegation, 82, 89

AC/SS — Adolescent Cultures, School & Society

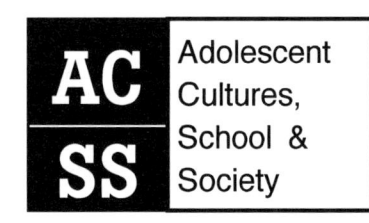

Joseph L. DeVitis & Linda Irwin-DeVitis

GENERAL EDITORS

As schools struggle to redefine and restructure themselves, they need to be aware of the new realities of adolescents. Thus, this series of monographs and texts is committed to depicting the variety of adolescent cultures that exist in today's troubled world. It is primarily a qualitative research, practice, and policy series devoted to contextual interpretation and analysis that encompasses a broad range of interdisciplinary critique. In addition, this series seeks to address issues of curriculum theory and practice; multicultural education; aggression, bullying, and violence; the media and arts; school dropouts; homeless and runaway youth; gangs and other alienated youth; at-risk adolescent populations; family structures and parental involvement; and race, ethnicity, class, and gender/LGBTQ studies.

Send proposals and manuscripts to the general editors at:
>   Joseph L. DeVitis & Linda Irwin-DeVitis
>   Darden College of Education
>   Old Dominion University
>   Norfolk, VA 23503

To order other books in this series, please contact our Customer Service Department at:
>   (800) 770-LANG (within the U.S.)
>   (212) 647-7706 (outside the U.S.)
>   (212) 647-7707 FAX

or browse online by series at:
>   WWW.PETERLANG.COM